The Intersection of Cultures

The Intersection of Cultures

Multicultural Education in the United States and the Global Economy

THIRD EDITION

Joel Spring
New School University

Boston   Burr Ridge, IL   Dubuque, IA   Madison, WI   New York
San Francisco   St. Louis   Bangkok   Bogotá   Caracas   Kuala Lumpur
Lisbon   London   Madrid   Mexico City   Milan   Montreal   New Delhi
Santiago   Seoul   Singapore   Sydney   Taipei   Toronto

McGraw-Hill Higher Education

*A Division of The **McGraw-Hill** Companies*

THE INTERSECTION OF CULTURES
Published by McGraw-Hill, a business unit of The McGraw-Hill Companies, Inc., 1221 Avenue of the Americas, New York, NY, 10020. Copyright © 2004, 2000, 1995, by The McGraw-Hill Companies, Inc. All rights reserved. No part of this publication may be reproduced or distributed in any form or by any means, or stored in a database or retrieval system, without the prior written consent of The McGraw-Hill Companies, Inc., including, but not limited to, in any network or other electronic storage or transmission, or broadcast for distance learning.

Some ancillaries, including electronic and print components, may not be available to customers outside the United States.

This book is printed on acid-free paper.

2 3 4 5 6 7 8 9 0 DOC/DOC 0 9 8 7 6 5 4

ISBN 0-07-256396-6

Publisher: *Jane Karpacz*
Sponsoring editor: *Jane Karpacz*
Developmental editor: *Terri Wise*
Senior marketing manager: *Pam S. Cooper*
Media producer: *Lance Gerhart*
Project manager: *Diane M. Folliard*
Production supervisor: *Janean Utley*
Freelance design coordinator: *Sharon C. Spurlock*
Lead supplement producer: *Marc Mattson*
Cover design: *Amy Evans McClure*
Interior design: *Amy Evans McClure*
Cover image: © *Mary Kate Denny/Photo Edit*
Typeface: *10/12 Palatino*
Compositor: *ElectraGraphics, Inc.*
Printer: *R. R. Donnelley & Sons*

Library of Congress Cataloging-in-Publication Data

Spring, Joel H.
  The intersection of cultures : multicultural education in the United States and the global economy / Joel Spring.—3rd ed.
    p. cm.
  Includes bibliographical references and index.
  ISBN 0-07-256396-6 (softcover : alk. paper)
  1. Multicultural edition—United States. 2. International economic relations. I. Title.
LC1099.3.S69 2004
370.117'0973—dc21

2003044507

www.mhhe.com

About the Author

JOEL SPRING is on the faculty of the New School University. He received his PhD in educational policy studies from the University of Wisconsin. His major research interests are history of education, multicultural education, Native American culture, the politics of education, global education, and human rights education. He is the author of many books, the most recent of which are *Education and the Rise of the Global Economy; The Universal Right to Education: Justification, Definition, and Guidelines; Globalization and Educational Rights;* and *Educating the Consumer Citizen: A History of the Marriage of Schools, Advertising, and Media.*

Brief Contents

PREFACE   *xiii*

Part I
MULTICULTURALISM

Chapter 1   What Is the Culture of the United States?   3

Chapter 2   Dominated Cultures   38

Chapter 3   Immigrant Cultures   64

Chapter 4   Multiculturalism in the Global Economy   88

Part II
CULTURAL FRAMES OF REFERENCE

Chapter 5   Cultural Frames of Reference:
Monoculturalism, Biculturalism, and Ethnic Identity   107

Chapter 6   Cultural Frames of Reference: History,
Gender, and Social Class   123

Chapter 7   The Intersection of School Culture
with Dominated and Immigrant Cultures   144

Part III
PERSPECTIVES ON TEACHING
MULTICULTURAL EDUCATION

Chapter 8   Teaching about Racism   165

Chapter 9   Teaching about Sexism   187

Chapter 10   Teaching and Language Diversity   202

Chapter 11   Teaching Ethnocentrism   224

Chapter 12   Conclusion: Cultural Tolerance,
Social Empowerment, and the Intersection of Cultures
in the Global Workforce and Classroom   246

INDEX   I-1

Contents

PREFACE   *xiii*

Part I
MULTICULTURALISM

Chapter 1   What Is the Culture of the United States?   3

Emotion, Multiculturalism, and Consumerism   8
Cultural Freedom and American Character   11
Multiculturalism and American Culture   13
Multicultural Education and American Culture   14
In Search of American Culture   14
Different Ways of Defining U.S. Culture   17
American Culture and the Culture of Economic Success   20
Black Mobility and Assimilation to the Dominant Culture   21
The Culture of Success for Jews, Women, Asians, Latinos/Latinas,
   Lesbians/Gays, and Low-Income Whites   24
Economic Success versus Cultural Diversity   26
E. D. Hirsch and Cultural Literacy   27
The Dominant Culture As White Anglo-Saxon Values   28
Should We Teach the Values of the Dominant Culture?   29
A Lesson on Cultural Differences: Native American
   and English Cultures   30
Conclusion: American Culture and Multicultural Education   34
Personal Frames of Reference   35

Chapter 2   Dominated Cultures   38

Cultural Domination and Voluntary Immigration   39
The Intersection of African and European American Cultures   40
Ethnocentric Education: Dominated Cultures   48
Debating Education Based on Dominated Cultures   50

*Teaching Hawaiian Culture: Alternative or Transition
    to Economic Success*   52
Is "White Trash" a Dominated Culture?   54
Empowerment through Multicultural Education   56
Educating for Cultural Power   59
Conclusion   61
Personal Frames of Reference   61

Chapter 3   Immigrant Cultures   64

Summer Camps for Cultural Survival   66
Shooting at a Convenience Store   71
Rebellion and School Uniforms   73
Muslim Schools: Finding a Safe Haven   75
Wearing Your Knicks Jacket at the Zocalo   77
Transnationalism: The Multicultural Immigrant   79
Varieties of Educational Experience   80
Conclusion: Knowing Immigrant Cultures   84
Personal Frames of Reference   86

Chapter 4   Multiculturalism in the Global Economy   88

Singapore   90
*The European Union: The World's Most Ambitious
    Multicultural Education Program*   92
English Language Imperialism?   95
The Right to Language and Culture in the Global Economy   96
*Conclusion: Educational Rights Amendment
    to the U.S. Constitution*   98
Personal Frames of Reference   102

Part II
CULTURAL FRAMES OF REFERENCE

Chapter 5   Cultural Frames of Reference:
    Monoculturalism, Biculturalism, and Ethnic Identity   107

Monoculturalism and Biculturalism   109
Development of Ethnic Identity   114
Conclusion: Ethnic Identity, Biculturalism, and Monoculturalism   119
Personal Frames of Reference   121

Chapter 6   Cultural Frames of Reference: History, Gender,
    and Social Class   123

Official History and Folk History Defined   124
Official History   125

Folk History   *128*
Gender   *132*
Social Class   *137*
Conclusion   *140*
Personal Frames of Reference   *141*

Chapter 7   The Intersection of School Culture
with Dominated and Immigrant Cultures   144

Inequality and Schooling   *148*
Resistance: The Intersection of School and Dominated Cultures   *149*
Resistance: Native Americans   *152*
*Latinos/Latinas: The Intersection of School, Dominated,
    and Immigrant Cultures*   *153*
Asians: Comparing Dominated and Immigrant Cultures   *154*
Alienation: The Intersection of School and Family Values   *156*
Cultural Conflicts   *158*
Conclusion   *160*
Personal Frames of Reference   *160*

Part III
PERSPECTIVES ON TEACHING
MULTICULTURAL EDUCATION

Chapter 8   Teaching about Racism   165

The Concept of Race   *166*
Racism   *172*
Teaching about White Guilt   *174*
An Anti-bias Curriculum   *177*
The Teaching Tolerance Project   *179*
La Escuela Fratney   *180*
Racism and Mathematics Instruction   *181*
Conclusion: Racism and the Global Market   *182*
Personal Frames of Reference   *184*

Chapter 9   Teaching about Sexism   187

Republican Motherhood   *187*
The Glass Ceiling of the Classroom   *191*
Single-Sex Schools and Classrooms   *194*
*Consciousness Raising According to the Methods
    of Paulo Freire*   *197*
Conclusion   *199*
Personal Frames of Reference   *200*

Chapter 10   Teaching and Language Diversity   202

   Language, Culture, and Power   203
   Cross-Cultural Communications   205
   Communicating Between Japan and the United States   206
   Language and Culture in the United States   207
   Bilingual Education   209
   Research and Corporate Support for Bilingual Education   211
   Problems in Bilingual Education Programs   213
   Language Issues among Asian Americans   214
   The Language of the Corporation   215
   Conclusion: The Multicultural and Language Debate   217
   Personal Frames of Reference   221

Chapter 11   Teaching Ethnocentrism   224

   Models of Indigenous Education: Educating for the Child, Family, and Community   224
   Child Centered (Maori)   226
   Holistic Education (Okanagan)   226
   Three Baskets of Knowledge (Maori)   227
   Stimulating and Language-Based Education (Native Hawaiian)   227
   Linking Native People to the Spirituality of All Life (Cochiti Pueblo)   228
   Asante: Classical Africa   228
   Afrocentric Pedagogy   229
   The Question of Kemet   230
   The Contribution of Egypt to the Development of Science and Mathematics   231
   Holistic Learning   233
   Personal Witnessing   233
   The Conspiracy to Destroy Black Boys   234
   Lessons from History: A Celebration in Blackness   236
   The Rites of Passage Program   238
   What Every Child Needs to Know   239
   Teaching Core Knowledge   241
   Conclusion   243
   Personal Frames of Reference   243

Chapter 12   Conclusion: Cultural Tolerance, Social
Empowerment, and the Intersection of Cultures in the Global
Workforce and Classroom   246

   Nationalism, Internationalism, and Social Empowerment   246
   Cultural Tolerance and Peace   247
   Multicultural Education for Social Empowerment and Social Reconstruction   249
   Multiculturalism and the Global Workforce   252
   Conclusion: The Intersection of Cultures in the Classroom   254
   Personal Frames of Reference   256

INDEX   *I-1*

Preface

In this Third Edition, I have rewritten Chapter 1 and added new material to other chapters. The major additions to this book are model multicultural lessons for elementary through college classes. These lessons appear in each chapter. The lessons serve a dual function. First, they can be used to help teach the content of each chapter in the book. Second, elementary, middle school, and high school teachers can use these lessons in their own classes.

Lesson 1.1 Lesson on Emotions and History
Lesson 1.2 Make a Cultural Flag: Lesson in Cultural Self-Identification
Lesson 1.3 Identifying the *Other*
Lesson 1.4 What Is American Culture?
Lesson 1.5 Entering the Power Elite
Lesson 2.1 Family Multicultural Tree
Lesson 2.2 Family Multicultural Tree: Dominated Cultures and Voluntary Immigrants
Lesson 2.3 Family Multicultural Tree: Social and Economic Advantages
Lesson 2.4 Dominated Cultures in Classroom Instruction
Lesson 2.5 Museum of the American Empire
Lesson 3.1 The Public School Diversity Parade
Lesson 3.2 Map of Migratory Causes
Lesson 3.3 Language Map
Lesson 3.4 Family Multicultural Tree: Educational Mobility
Lesson 3.5 The Completed Family Multicultural Tree: Dominated Cultures and Voluntary Immigrants, Occupations, and Educational Achievement
Lesson 3.6 Design an Educational Program for Immigrant Children
Lesson 4.1 Clothing Labels, Globalization, and Cheap Labor
Lesson 4.2 Should the U.S. Constitution Protect Linguistic and Cultural Rights in Education?
Lesson 4.3 Education in the Land of Oz
Lesson 5.1 Cultural Perspective

Lesson 5.2   What Is Your Ethnic Identity?
Lesson 6.1   Official History Versus the People's History
Lesson 6.2   What Did My Family Teach Me about Race?
Lesson 6.3   What Did My Family Teach Me about Gender?
Lesson 6.4   What Did My Family Teach Me about the Rich and Poor?
Lesson 7.1   Confucius Attends a U.S. Public School
Lesson 7.2   Maori Go to School
Lesson 8.1   Is the Death Penalty a Racist Law?
Lesson 8.2   The Strange Transformation of Malcolm X
Lesson 9.1   Gender in Advertising
Lesson 9.2   Women: The New Traditionalists
Lesson 10.1   No Child Left Behind and English Acquisition
Lesson 11.1   What Did Columbus's Voyage Mean for Africa, Asia, Europe, and the Americas?

I would like to thank the following professors for the feedback they provided during the development of the third edition:

James Garofalo, Aquinas College

Ronald Lelito, D'Youville College

Edmundo Litton, Loyola Marymount University

George Metz, Bluffton College

Michael R. Smith, Niagara University

Winston Vaughan, Xavier University

PART ONE

Multiculturalism

CHAPTER 1

What Is the Culture of the United States?

Globalization is expanding multicultural contacts as people move around the globe in search of jobs, political rights, and social freedom. By *culture,* I am referring to socially transmitted behavior patterns, arts, beliefs, institutions, and all other products of human work and thought. I am also going to make a distinction between the general and dominant cultures of a nation. The *general culture* refers to what the majority of people consider to be cultural characteristics of their society. The *dominant culture* is the culture of the most powerful members of society. It is difficult to clearly define the general and dominant cultures of a nation. I will elaborate on the problems associated with defining these cultures throughout this chapter.

School systems throughout the world are grappling with the problems caused by multicultural and multilinguistic populations. In addition, the newly created European Union is formulating educational plans to unite under the banner of Europeanism, formerly warring nations such as Germany, France, and England. In addition, because of the immigration of foreign workers and members of their former colonies, France and England are trying to solve internal problems of multiculturalism in the schools.

In *Empire,* a study of globalization, Michael Hardt and Antonio Negri dramatically assert, *"A specter haunts the world and it is the specter of migration."* The authors maintain, "Today the mobility of labor power and migratory movements is extraordinarily diffuse and difficult to grasp. Even the most significant population movements of modernity (including the black and white Atlantic migrations) constitute . . . [minor] events with respect to the enormous population transfers of our times."[1]

Media, travel, migration, and interdependent economic systems are creating a global culture based on the production and consumption of brand-name manufactured products. Calling them the "new world teens," market researcher Elissa Moses argues, "Teens who speak different languages all speak the same language of global brand consumption. . . . Teens love brands. . . . Brands are passports to global culture." Asking teens worldwide to identify 75 brand icons, she finds the five most popular, in order, are Coca-Cola, Sony, Adidas, Nike, and

Kodak.[2] Do brand names and consumer desires now define the behavior patterns, arts, beliefs, and institutions of a common global culture?

The *general* culture of the United States consists of behaviors, beliefs, and experiences common to most citizens. Consider Michael Moore's documentary movie *Bowling for Columbine.* His interest is finding something common in American culture that would explain the high rate of gun violence in the United States. Interestingly, he concludes that the high rate of gun violence is not a result of too many guns or that the United States is more violent than other nations. For instance, he suggests the hunting tradition in Canada results in a high ownership of guns. However, incidents of gun violence in Canada are lower than in the United States. Germany has a much more violent history than the United States but today has fewer incidents of crimes being committed with guns.

Moore hypothesizes that fear is a general cultural trait in the United States. Fear drives people to arm themselves and engage in gun-related conflicts. Admittedly, it is difficult to prove or disprove Moore's contention. However, it does provide an interesting way of defining the general culture of the United States. Moore argues that fear as the underlying American trait originated with the European invasion of North America. Invaders were afraid of Native Americans. They worried that Native Americans would destroy their settlements and all foreigners. Consequently, they engaged in a program of violent genocide to clear North America of its original inhabitants. Fear of Native Americans was followed by fears of violent slave rebellions. The enslavement of large numbers of Africans required regimens of violence wherein slaves were tortured, lynched, and mutilated to discourage them from running away from or overtaking their masters. The end of slavery resulted in continued fears among the white population that the freed slaves would seek revenge. In turn, the black population, after the long history of slavery, feared continued violent actions against them. People were afraid during the violent racial clashes that dotted the history of twentieth-century America. Then after World War II, the Cold War created fears of the end of the world by nuclear destruction. Schoolchildren were trained to climb under their desks as protection against a nuclear holocaust. And then the fears of the Cold War were replaced by fears of terrorists plunging airplanes into buildings and launching biological attacks. The culture of fear was highlighted in December 2002 when a group of unknown people placed empty black boxes labeled "FEAR" throughout a New York City subway station and caused massive transportation delays. Fear related to cultural differences makes the resolution of cultural and linguistic differences difficult in the United States.

Fear of difference, along with a belief in the culture of consumerism, often appears in discussions of race and culture in my classrooms. Of course, I try to create situations that result in displays of emotion. You cannot separate ideas and learning from emotions. You might think you can but any inner exploration will find emotions attached to ideas and beliefs. Dealing with emotions is an important aspect of teaching. I wrote down the following interchange after an interesting classroom exchange of ideas, beliefs, and emotions.

* * *

"They shou...
raised in sub...
The l...
immig...
ha...

...ecome Americans," declared Eric, a white student born and
...my class examined the effect of immigration on U.S. schools.
...sked students how they would introduce a recently arrived
...culture, one student responded, "Take'm to a mall. Get'm a
...ne food court and go shopping at the Gap."
...sponded, "let's divide this class into groups and each group
...definition of what it means to be an 'American'. We'll call this
...the general culture of the United States."

...now what would result from the exercise. My father was a Native
...nd my mother was of English and German descent. Did my father
...at it meant to be an American? I don't think the Americanism of my
...hat Eric had in mind. On the other hand, my mother's family pio-
...e West in the nineteenth century. Was she the embodiment of what it
...o be an American?

...entually, I wanted to describe the general culture of the United States
...nd raise the issue of whether schools should reflect the American culture or
other cultures.

"That's only for whites! Your freedom is not my freedom," Carla, an
African American woman, angrily blurted out when the first group defined
Americanism as a commitment to freedom and liberty. "*You* can talk about
freedom. I define being American as learning how to oppress other people."

Well, I thought, my father would agree with Carla, and my mother would
agree with the group.

"Look at you," an obviously hostile European American female named
Linda said to Carla, "you're all dressed up. I know you drive a nice car. You
could be back in Africa swinging from a tree."

"That's racist," Shawn, a white student, yelled, pounding his desk. I could
feel the class slipping out of control. We were moving deeper and deeper into
people's strongest emotions. Discussions of multicultural education can cause
students and communities to retreat behind walls of hatred and fear.

"Look," I said, trying to soothe feelings and engage in a multicultural conversation, "my father would agree with Carla. America has meant oppression
to many Native Americans. On the other hand, my mother would agree with
Linda. She claims my father would still be shooting bows and arrows at deer
rather than driving a car if it had not been for white people. Besides the issue
of whether my father would have been happier hunting as opposed to owning
a car, we can see that people have different perspectives about America as the
land of liberty and freedom."

"Carla, how did you feel about the comment 'swinging from a tree'?" I
asked.

"Just white trash talking," Carla answered. "It was ignorant and stupid. Besides, I have white blood in me. Am I African or European? How do you define
race? I would rather think of myself as African."

"I'm not white trash," Linda snapped back. "Just because my family's poor
doesn't mean we're white trash. At least we're not niggers."

A loud moan came from the class. Shawn leaped to h. "I can't believe a future teacher would use that word."

"She called me white trash," Linda shouted back. "What's the difference between calling someone white trash or nigger? Why don't you object to me using 'white trash'?"

"It's not the same thing. The 'N' word is unacceptable," responded Carla, unable to repeat the racial slur. "I don't know what white trash means."

"White trash are ignorant and poor whites," Carla explained. "They're rednecks. Drive out to the trailer parks. You'll see plenty of white trash. Cars and junk all around their trailers. Bunch of racist slobs."

"We had a white trash part of our fashion show in high school," giggled Paula, a white student. "We dressed in flour-sack dresses with straw hats and overalls. We made jewelry from crushed beer cans and car parts. It was a gas."

"It seems," I interrupted, "like we have a lot of issues, such as 'they should all be Americans,' 'only whites have freedom,' 'niggers,' and 'white trash.'"

By now I was emotionally involved. One could easily characterize my childhood as white trash. After the divorce, we lived off my mother's meager income as a low-level government clerk supplemented with a small child-support check from my alcoholic father who continued his enlisted career in the U.S. Navy. For Native Americans, and other groups, the military is an equal opportunity employer. Certainly, crushed beer cans symbolized my father's life.

"I'm feeling upset by the exchange that just took place," I continued. "I think we need to balance this emotional outburst with a little bit of thought. Also, we're going to have to talk about some of the language that was used."

Wanting to reestablish my authority over the class, I turned to the chalkboard and composed a list of questions:

- What is the general culture of the United States?
- Are there oppressed cultures in the United States?
- How should we define "culture" and "race"?
- What is the meaning of terms such as "nigger" and "white trash"?
- What is the purpose of multicultural education?

"I wanna talk about that last question," said Linda, as I completed the list. "Why do we have to take this course? It's just another chance for people to beat up on whites. I'm tired of being picked on. Coloreds get all the benefits."

Quickly, I turned to Carla wondering how she would react to Linda's statement. "Carla, why do you think we're studying multicultural education?"

"To end white domination of education!"

"See," Linda smirked. "It's all anti-white."

"Wait a minute," said Chang-Rae Lee, a second-generation Korean student, "it's to help kids from different cultures do well in school. You got to know about the kids' cultures to be able to teach them."

"What's your culture, Chang-Rae?" I asked.

Wearing a baseball hat with an official team logo, baggy jeans, and a T-shirt honoring a heavy metal band, Chang-Rae answered, "American."

"That takes us back to the first question. What is American culture?"

"You know. Baseball, hot dogs, cars, that sort of thing," replied Chang-Rae.

"So teachers only needed to know about American culture to teach you?" I asked. "What about Korean culture?"

"I don't want to learn about Korean culture in school. I want to learn to earn. Get a good education, make money, marry, live in the suburbs, drive a good car, that's my dream. That's the American way."

"And if you married a Japanese woman?" I inquired, trying to provoke Chang-Rae.

"My parents would throw me out of the house. My grandfather might kill me."

"Why's that?"

"Why's that?" Chang-Rae repeated. "The Japs colonized our country, forced my people to live in Japan and work as slaves, and forced our women to be prostitutes. They still discriminate against Koreans living in Japan. My family hates Japs."

"So, do you think it would be important for teachers to know something about Korean history and culture?"

"The problem," Chang-Rae replied, "is that teachers think all Asians are the same. Koreans have done okay in school. But many Chinese students have difficulty with English. They need extra help."

"So knowing something about language issues and cultural differences might help in teaching."

"I guess. But only if it helps students make money," Chang-Rae laughed.

"That's white culture. Make money. That's all whites think about," interjected Alice Rogers. "Multicultural education should promote other cultures, not teach white culture."

I empathized with Alice Rogers. We shared a similar past. We both came from divorced homes with Native American fathers. While my father was Choctaw, hers was Cherokee. There were family rumors that her father was related to Will Rogers, the great Cherokee comedian of the 1920s and 1930s. Last semester, in my educational history class, she declared her intention to be Native American. "After all," she said, "I have a choice. My mother or my father. I hate what schools did to destroy Cherokee culture. I like Cherokee culture better than white culture."

Before I could respond to Alice's remark, Bernardo Montillo interrupted, "That's right. I like Puerto Rican culture—better family relations, good music, more fun. White culture's all uptight. But you need white culture to make money."

"See," Linda responded. "More dumping on whites. You Puerto Ricans, why did you come to the U.S. if you hate it?"

"Puerto Rico is part of the United States, stupid," Bernardo shot back. "Imagine you teaching my kids and you don't even know that Puerto Rico is part of the U.S. I bet you don't even know our history."

"Bernardo, do you think Latino/Latina culture is better than the general white culture of the United States?" I asked, trying to change the direction of the discussion.

"I said Puerto Rican culture. I don't know about Mexican culture. I don't think all Latino culture is the same."

"I don't think," remarked Anne Gabbard, a white 40-year-old student who was returning to college to pick up a teaching certificate, "we can deal with these issues until we define culture. Then we can talk about multiculturalism and American culture. Personally, I think all cultures have something to contribute. Multiculturalism should teach tolerance. And a lot of you need a lesson in tolerance!"

"You can say that because you're white," Carla responded. "Whites have to be taught to tolerate others. Blacks are forced to tolerate whites. We've no option. You got the power."

"What power do I have? I'm a poor working mother trying to get a teaching certificate," countered Anne. "Black kids beat me up all the time in elementary school. They had the power. Seems like you gotta lot of power with that mouth. You should learn to tolerate whites."

"Hold it," I shouted, waving my hands in an effort to regain control and reduce the growing tension in the classroom. "Why is there so much emotion in this discussion of multiculturalism? Can't we just discuss this in an objective way and figure out how best to educate kids?"

As the class gathered their books and headed for the door, Linda closed the discussion with the assertion, "Just teach them to be Americans. Then there's no problem with multiculturalism."

EMOTION, MULTICULTURALISM, AND CONSUMERISM

Classroom discussions of multiculturalism are, I would argue from my teaching experience, inherently emotional. Emotions are embedded in the very concept of culture. After all, emotions are part of behavior patterns, arts, beliefs, institutions, and human work and thought. However, not all emotions involve fear, hate, and anger. There are the emotions of love and compassion. Ideally, I would rather live in a world filled with love and compassion than hate and anger.

In the above classroom discussion a range of beliefs and emotions were presented by students. There were also some complex and unanswered ideas, such as defining American culture. In a limited form, this classroom scenario represented the intersection of cultures in the context of the world movement of populations. The classroom was truly haunted by "the specter of migration." There were the continuing conflicts over "imagined memories" of historical events. In fact, these historical events are key to understanding why multiculturalism is an issue in U.S. schools. The above classroom discussion reflected the following historical events:

1. The violent conflict between Native Americans and Europeans after the European invasion of the Americas.
2. The forced migration and enslavement of Africans.

3. Japanese imperialism, which included the conquest of Korea, Taiwan, Manchuria, and eventually Southeast Asia during World War II.
4. The U.S. conquest of Northern Mexico and Puerto Rico.

Note that all of these events involved some level of violence. Emotions of anger and hate seem to be heightened as cultures intersect when there is some historical connection to acts of violence. Intersections of cultures do not have to be generated by acts of violence. There can be peaceful intersections of culture resulting in voluntary migrations. However, I would like to highlight the following idea:

> *Emotions of anger and hate seem most prevalent when cultural intersections are a result of war, invasions, or forced dominations. Past eras of violent confrontations remain alive in human consciousness and sustain feelings of anger and hate.*

Past wars, invasions, and forced dominations still haunt human memory and shape behavior. As author William Faulkner observed, "The past is never dead. It's not even past." Memory includes remembrance of actual events in a person's life and memories created by historical literature, novels, conversations, and media. While people alive today never actually experienced the U.S. Civil War, most people have images of the war that were created by exposure to history lessons, mass media, and other sources. These images are referred to as *imagined memories*. These imagined memories carry with them a host of emotions.

For instance, some southern states still struggle over the official display of the Confederate flag. The Confederate flag symbolizes a central and violent event in U.S. history that no living person experienced. The flag is associated with death of more than 900,000 soldiers and the torture and killings of enslaved Africans. Images and emotions of the Civil War still stalk the consciousness of Americans. Recently, I parked behind a car with Confederate flag and National Rifle Association decals splashed across its rear bumper and trunk. One large sticker proclaimed, "Born in the North I will die in the South." What these symbols and words exactly meant to the driver is not clear. However, they did seem to show that the driver had her/his imagined memories of a violent war and the South's attempt to maintain legal slavery. Most African Americans would consider the Confederate flag a symbol of racial hate and react in anger to its display.

In contrast, there are many instances in American cultural traditions where "love" plays a more important role in cultural intersections than anger and hate. In the classic 1957 American musical *West Side Story*, Maria, whose brother Bernardo belongs to the Puerto Rican gang known as the Sharks, falls in love with Tony, the former leader of the Anglo-American gang, the Jets. Based on William Shakespeare's *Romeo and Juliet*, their love is doomed to a tragic end. On a broader canvas, the war between the two youth gangs calls forth the memories of the 1898 Spanish–American War when the United States forcefully conquered Puerto Rico and attempted to Anglicize its culture. In contemporary terms, it calls forth the hope that love will subdue the continued anger between these two cultural groups. In Warren Beatty's magnificent 1998 political movie satire *Bulworth*, a senatorial candidate abandons all cautions and speaks the "truth" to the electorate. He proposes that love should prompt interracial marriages that would result in ending tensions between whites and blacks.

Multicultural love is the central theme of one of the top 100 television ads as selected by Bernice Kanner, advertising columnist for New York magazine. Advertising the major global icon of American culture Coca-Cola, the 1971 ad shows a multicultural group of children standing on a hilltop, holding bottles of the product, and singing:

> I'd like to build the world a home and furnish it with love
> Grow apple trees and honey bees and snow white turtle doves.
> I'd like to teach the world to sing with perfect harmony
> I'd like to buy the world a coke and keep it company.
> I'd like to see the world for once all standing hand in hand
> And hear them echo through the hills for peace throughout the land.[3]

Admittedly, the above Coca-Cola song is designed to sell the soft drink by associating it with cultural harmony and world peace. Market researcher Elissa Moses found that Coca-Cola is the most widely known brand icon among global youth. For many, Coca-Cola is the icon of American culture. This TV ad plays on a theme that can be found throughout the history of the United States, namely, the hope of creating multicultural and interracial harmony.

Besides the violence of the U.S. Civil War there was also hope highlighted by the activities of abolitionist groups opposing slavery and wanting to create a land of racial equality. Besides the tensions and anger generated by the Indian wars and the conquest of Northern Mexico and Puerto Rico, there has also been a long history of attempting to reduce the racial and cultural stresses caused by these events. Besides the beatings, lynchings, and discrimination suffered by people from Asia, there has been a counterstruggle to build bridges of understanding and equality.

The National Association for Multicultural Education represents an important and significant organizational attempt to overcome the anger, fear, and hatred sometimes occurring through the intersection of cultures. For instance, the goals for the National Association for Multicultural Education are to:

1. Respect and appreciate cultural diversity.
2. Promote the understanding of unique cultural and ethnic heritage.
3. Promote the development of culturally responsible and responsive curricula.
4. Facilitate acquisition of the attitudes, skills, and knowledge to function in various cultures.
5. Eliminate racism and discrimination in society.
6. Achieve social, political, economic, and educational equity.[4]

In summary, I would like to highlight following major contradiction in American culture:

> A central paradox of American culture is the simultaneous existence of behaviors associated with the emotions of love connected to desires for cultural and racial harmony and with the emotions of anger and hate resulting from violent cultural and racial confrontations. This explains the often recognized contra-

diction displayed in American culture between bigotry and racism, and tolerance and acceptance. Both hate and love live unhappily at the center of American culture.

CULTURAL FREEDOM AND AMERICAN CHARACTER

American culture also contains a belief in freedom and liberty. This belief represents another paradox of American culture when contrasted with its history of slavery, domination, and imperialism. Any survey of American political thought finds freedom a central concept in defining American culture. Freedom is also a key element in defining the cultural experience of Americans.

In a classic American immigrant story, *Jasmine,* the main character leaves India and comes to the United States and lives through a series of adverse conditions.[5] Despite the problems she encounters, she praises American culture because it provides the freedom for people to make choices about who they want to be. In contrast, India is presented as a place where one is born into one's social position and the combination of rigid cultural traditions and limited opportunities restricts personal development. In the United States, Jasmine discovers that she can break out of the limitations of a restrictive culture and have the chance to define her own life and character.

Jasmine's story highlights the fluidity of a multicultural society in the context of the American experience. The intersection of cultures breaks down cultural boundaries and allows for a greater range of cultural choices. Jasmine discovers that in the United States she can retain those aspects of Indian culture that she likes while abandoning some cultural traditions. For instance, she embraces what she considers to be the powerful and independent model of the American woman while rejecting the traditional subservient role of Indian women. In the United States, she discovers the freedom to make that choice and as a result undergoes a cultural transformation. She ends up marrying a midwestern banker of European decent with a disability.

Cross-cultural marriages in the United States highlight the fluidity of multicultural boundaries and the personal freedom to make cultural choices. Sometimes parents object and try to stop children when they marry outside their culture or religion, but it is still possible to cross cultural boundaries. This cultural fluidity dates from the time of the European invasion of North America when some Native Americans decided to take on the manners of Europeans and some Europeans decided to join tribal communities.

It is important to add personal freedom to the concept of American culture. Americans believe and act with the knowledge that they have the ability to shape their own cultural characteristics. They are free to move between cultures, adopt the cultural characteristics of others, and create their own hybrid cultures. Along with economic opportunities, this form of cultural freedom attracts immigrants to the United States. It could be said that America is the land of consumer and cultural opportunities.

In summary, American culture evidences the following complex characteristics. It is important to note that the list below is not intended to represent the

Lesson on Emotions and History

Grades: Middle School through College

Objective:
To understand the emotions caused by multicultural issues.

Lesson:
Display some representation of a Confederate flag. Emphasize that this was the flag flown by the Confederate government during the U.S. Civil War.

1. Ask students to quickly write down their feelings when seeing this flag displayed on the back of a car or truck.
2. Ask students to voluntarily relate their feelings to the rest of the class.
3. Begin an open class discussion exploring why they feel and think certain ways about the Confederate flag.

Teachers: It is important in this exercise that the teacher try to understand student feelings and ideas. It is never certain where this discussion will lead. The teacher should play a creative role in guiding the discussion down the path of personal and mutual understanding. There are no precise rules. For the teacher, this type of reflective decision making about how and when to direct the conversation can be very rewarding.

Outcome: Students and the teacher should leave this discussion still engaged in reflection about their own ideas and feelings.

full range of American cultural characteristics. It is only a summary of the characteristics identified so far in this text. We will be exploring other approaches to identifying American culture later in this chapter.

1. Obsession with shopping and accumulation of consumer goods or what might be called "mall culture."
2. Fear of violence resulting from America's violent history.
3. Anger and hate resulting from violent multicultural confrontations associated with war, invasions, or forced dominations.
4. Love and compassion resulting from a desire to achieve racial and cultural harmony.
5. Fluidity of cultural boundaries allowing freedom for movement across cultural boundaries and cultural hybridity.

MULTICULTURALISM AND AMERICAN CULTURE

What does multiculturalism mean in the context of defining American culture? Many Americans identify with a specific culture while being part of American culture. The lines separating cultures are blurry and very difficult to specify. Also, in the English language, the word "culture" is applied to periods of time, social classes, communities, subjects, and modes of expression, such as modern culture, English culture, the culture of poverty, the culture of New York, and musical culture. In this context, culture refers to all products of human thought and work within a defined group.

The multiplicity of cultures makes cultural identification extremely difficult. For instance, according to our original definition of culture, Native American culture is all behavior patterns, arts, beliefs, and institutions socially transmitted by Native Americans. What does this mean given the existence of over 500 tribes in North America? Most likely, before the European invasion tribal members never identified with a concept of Native American that included all North American tribes. With the arrival of Europeans, tribal members began to distinguish themselves from the invaders. This process involved the very important concept of the "other." Often, individuals and groups achieve self-identification by comparing themselves to other individuals and groups. Prior to the European invasion, the *other* for indigenous peoples was other tribes. After the invasion, the *other* became other tribes and Europeans. Consequently, Native American people could feel a cultural unity in comparing themselves to Europeans. Today, the American Indian Movement, a Native American advocacy group, claims that all tribes share some similar cultural characteristics in comparison to Americans of European descent. Therefore it is important to highlight the following idea:

> Identification of cultural differences depends on the existence of the *other* for purposes of comparison. Consequently, the *other* plays a major role in personal cultural self-identification.

Multiculturalism involves overlapping cultures. For instance, in the twenty-first century, Cherokee culture might be considered a subset of Native American culture just as French culture is a subset of European culture. In other words, Cherokees share some cultural traditions with other Native Americans while having their own unique cultural traditions. The definition of this shared Native American culture depends on comparison with an *other* such as Europeans, Chinese, etc.

In the same manner, the culture of poverty on a global scale can be divided into cultures of poverty in different nations. Also, the characteristics of a culture of poverty depend on the existence of an *other* such as the culture of the rich. One can only define the characteristics of these two economic cultures by comparing them to each other.

Imagine drawing circles on the chalkboard showing how cultures could be subsets of other cultures and all cultures part of human culture. While much of the culture of a rural Mexican village is different from the culture of a small Iowa town, both cultures share a larger culture created by the mass media. In fact, the culture of television and popular music may be the current glue of global culture.

MULTICULTURAL EDUCATION AND AMERICAN CULTURE

The complex nature of multiculturalism in the United States poses a real problem for educators. Initially, multicultural education was thought of as a method for resolving conflicts between different cultures and preserving minority cultures. In the United States, the multicultural education movement was born during the civil rights struggles of the 1950s and 1960s to provide equal opportunity for African Americans, Native Americans, Mexican Americans, and Puerto Ricans. Later, it expanded to include issues of gender, social class, sexual preference, and immigration.

I decided to use the concept of "Intersection of Cultures" to represent the central problem for multicultural education. Multicultural education might not be relevant for a village isolated for centuries from all outside influences. However, an outsider appearing in that village's school would generate the following multicultural-education questions:

1. Should methods of instruction be adapted to the outsider's culture?
2. Should the curriculum reflect the outsider's culture?
3. What educational methods might be used to reduce conflicts between the original habitants and the newcomer?
4. Should the school try to preserve the immigrant's culture or should it try to assimilate the immigrant to the culture of the village?
5. Should the school teach the immigrant the language of the village?
6. Should the school try to preserve the immigrant's culture and language?

IN SEARCH OF AMERICAN CULTURE

For educators in the United States it is difficult to answer the above multicultural-education questions because of continuing cultural conflicts, the fluid borders between cultures, the overlapping nature of different cultures, and the problem of

Make a Cultural Flag: Lesson in Cultural Self-Identification

Grades: Elementary through College (The sophistication of this lesson will vary with ages of students.)

Objective:
For students to understand the complex nature of their cultural self-identification.

Lesson:

1. Students are asked to make a paper flag that represents their identity by using words, icons, drawings, and cutouts. Young students can simply be asked to make a flag that represents themselves. Older students can be asked to make a flag representing their personal cultural identification.
2. After completion of the flags, students are asked to describe their flags to the rest of the class.
3. Students are asked to discuss differences and similarities between the individual flags.
4. Students are asked:
    a. Is there a common culture among students as represented in the flags?
    b. What are the significant cultural differences in the classroom as represented by the flags?

Teachers: Similar to the statement in Lesson 1.1, teachers should creatively, and with the goal of understanding student perspectives, lead class discussions.

Outcome: Students should leave the class reflecting on the multicultural nature of the classroom and their own background.

Identifying the Other

Grades: High School through College

Objective:
To help students understand the concept of the *other* and the role the *other* has in forming their cultural self-identification.

Lesson:

1. Have students create their personal cultural flags according to Lesson 1.2.
2. Have students now make a paper flag that represents the opposite of their own flag by using icons, words, and cutouts.
3. Have students explain to the rest of the class the flag of their *other*.
4. Ask students whether creating the flag of their *other:*
   a. Helped them to understand the decisions they made in creating their own personal cultural flag.
   b. Evoked any emotional feelings about the flag representing the *other*.

Teachers: Similar to the statement in Lesson 1.1, teachers should creatively, and with the goal of understanding student perspectives, lead class discussions.

Outcome: Students should leave the class reflecting on the role of the *other* in their self-identification.

defining the general culture of the United States. For instance, if multicultural educators choose to assimilate immigrants into American culture then they first must define that culture. One possibility is to simply define American culture as the sum of all cultures. In this concept of American culture, all cultures melt together to form a single culture. This construct of American culture is called the *Melting Pot.* All cultures, including Native American culture, melt together to create a common culture.

During the early part of the twentieth century, Americanization programs in public schools attempted to blend all immigrant cultures into the existing American culture. Under Americanization programs, students' names were changed to sound more "American," and students were urged to forget the culture and language of their parents. The Melting Pot idea was what Eric probably had in mind when he suggested that immigrants "should all become Americans."

However, during the civil rights movements of the 1950s and 1960s, it became evident that the Melting Pot never occurred, particularly for minority groups struggling to achieve equality of economic opportunity. Many cultural groups still stood outside the gates of the culture of economic success. What many of these groups wanted was expressed by Chang-Rae when he said, "Get a good education, make money, marry, live in the suburbs, drive a good car, that's my dream. That's the American way."

Consequently, I thought it would be best to begin by exploring that aspect of American culture associated with economic success. This requires describing American culture in relationship to equal economic opportunity. In this context, a possible goal of multicultural education is to *provide all cultural groups with an equal chance to succeed in the economic system.*

DIFFERENT WAYS OF DEFINING U.S. CULTURE

Before exploring the culture associated with economic success, I want to emphasize that economic success is not the only way of defining U.S. culture. In subsequent sections, I will be talking about approaches that define U.S. culture according to something called "cultural literacy" and by white Anglo-Saxon traditions. In addition, one needs to examine the flip side of the coin, which are the cultures that are considered dominated by mainstream U.S. culture. I will do this in Chapter 2. And, of course, there is the argument that U.S. culture is really a consumer culture. Also, there are clearly recognized immigrant cultures. These will be discussed in Chapter 3. Therefore, my approach to defining U.S. culture and its relevance to schools and multicultural education will include the following:

- The culture of economic success.
- Cultural literacy.
- White Anglo-Saxon values.
- Dominated cultures.
- Immigrant cultures

What Is American Culture?

Grades: Middle School through College

Objective:
For students to develop their own concepts of American culture.

Lesson:

1. Select two students to lead the class discussion. One student should call on other students, while the other student writes responses on the board.
2. The class is asked what they think represents American culture. Answers might refer to sports, media, brand names, food, literature, attitudes, etc.
3. Responses are written on the board.
4. When there are no more responses, the whole class should participate in grouping the items into differing categories, such as sports, food, media, etc.
5. The final question for the class is: How do these responses define American culture?

Teachers: The teachers should directly participate in the lesson by offering suggestions about American culture. The teacher should also participate by helping to categorize the items. The teacher must be careful not to dominate the discussion. The teacher might want to sit in the back of the class while the two students are soliciting responses.

Outcome: For students to leave the class thinking and talking about the nature of American culture.

Before exploring the culture of economic success, it is important to recognize the connections between education, gender, race, and economic success. As indicated in Table 1–1, income increases with educational level. There is a steady increase in income from those with less than a ninth-grade education to those with professional degrees. However, women earn less than men at each level of educational attainment. As shown in Table 1–1, a female high school graduate can expect lifetime earnings of $1 million while a female with a bachelor's degree can expect $1.6 million. On the other hand, a male high school graduate can expect lifetime earnings of $1.4 million and a male holding a bachelor's degree, $2.5 million. Comparing women and men's earnings, a man with a high school diploma will earn $400,000 more in a lifetime than a woman with a high school diploma. A man with a bachelor's degree will earn $900,000 more in a lifetime than a woman with a bachelor's degree.

Race is related to income. Table 1–2 indicates racial differences according to household median income. According to the table, white household incomes and per capita incomes are significantly above those of African Americans and Hispanics. The average (1999–2000) white median household income is $44,079 as compared with African Americans at $29,644 and Hispanics at $30,831.

The census data used in Table 1–3 indicates that at almost every level of educational attainment, white, non-Hispanic workers enjoyed higher estimated lifetime earnings. The exception is for those with advanced degrees with white, non-Hispanic and Asian and Pacific Islander workers having equal estimated lifetime earnings of $3.1 million. Otherwise there are significant differences. For instance, white, non-Hispanics with Bachelor's degrees earned an estimated $2.2 million throughout their lifetime while blacks and hispanics with the same educational attainment earned $1.7 million.

TABLE 1–1   Educational Attainment and Estimated Lifetime Earnings of Full-Time, Year-Round Workers by Sex and Educational Attainment (in 1999 dollars)

	Estimated Lifetime Earnings	
Educational Attainment	Women	Men
Not high school graduate	$0.7 million	$1.1 million
High school graduate	1.0	1.4
Some college	1.2	1.7
Associate's degree	1.3	1.8
Bachelor's degree	1.6	2.5
Master's degree	1.9	2.9
Doctoral degree	2.5	3.8
Professional degree	2.9	4.8

Source: This table is adapted from Figure 6 of Jennifer Day and Eric Newburger, *The Big Payoff: Educational Attainment and Synthetic Estimates of Work-Life Earnings* (Washington, DC: U.S. Bureau of the Census, July 2002), p. 6.

TABLE 1–2   Median Income of Households by Race and Hispanic Origins,
2-year average, 1999–2000

Race and Hispanic Origins	Median Income of Households
White	$44,079
Black	29,644
Hispanic (of any origin)	30,831

Source: U.S. Census Bureau, *Money Income in the United States–2001* (Washington, DC: U.S. Printing Office, 2001), p. 6.

TABLE 1–3   Estimated Lifetime Earnings by Educational Attainment, Race,
and Hispanic Origin (in 1999 dollars)

Educational Attainment	Estimated Lifetime Earnings			
	White, Non-Hispanic	Black	Hispanic (of any race)	Asian and Pacific Islander
Not high school graduate	$1.1 million	$0.8 million	$0.9 million	$0.8 million
High school graduate	1.3	1.0	1.1	1.1
Some college	1.6	1.2	1.3	1.3
Associate's degree	1.6	1.4	1.5	1.4
Bachelor's degree	2.2	1.7	1.8	1.7
Advanced degree	3.1	2.5	2.6	3.1

Source: This table is adapted from Figure 7 of Jennifer Day and Eric Newburger, *The Big Payoff: Educational Attainment and Synthetic Estimates of Work-Life Earnings* (Washington, DC: U.S. Bureau of the Census, July 2002), p. 7.

These tables suggest that economic success in the United States is related to level of education, gender, and race. It is an economic advantage in the United States to be white and male and an economic disadvantage to be black and female. However, there are economically successful black women. Is culture a factor in overcoming disadvantages related to race and gender?

AMERICAN CULTURE AND THE CULTURE OF ECONOMIC SUCCESS

What is the culture of economic success in the United States? To answer this question, I turned to recent studies of the mobility of women and minorities into the power elite in the United States, namely *Blacks in the White Establishment?: A Study of Race and Class in America* and *Diversity in the Power Elite* by Richard Zweigenhaft and G. William Domhoff.[6] Both of these studies examine the link between education and cultural change as it is related to economic mobility. The term *power elite* refers to those decision makers who have an important impact on the lives of most citizens. The authors identify the power elite as the directors and officers of the largest banks and corporations as ranked by *Fortune* magazine, members of the president's cabinet, high-ranking military officers, and members of Congress. Included in this power elite are the "1 percent of Americans who in 1992 possessed 37.2% of all net worth [in the United States]."[7]

Regarding culture, I think the most important finding is that *members of the power elite share a single culture and entrance into the power elite requires learning that culture.* Therefore, the power elite is diverse, but not multicultural. The power elite is diverse because there are black, Asian, Latino, Latina, Jewish, female, gay, and lesbian members. On the other hand, the power elite shares a single culture which, in this sense, means that it is not multicultural. Zweigenhaft and Domhoff conclude *that the culture of the power elite is the culture of upper-class white Christians.* The culture of the power elite is learned in the family or at school. Therefore, I would like to highlight the following concept:

> For many upwardly mobile students, schooling is the main source for learning the culture of the power elite. Within this context, I define the *dominant American culture* as the culture of the power elite.

BLACK MOBILITY AND ASSIMILATION TO THE DOMINANT CULTURE

The characteristics associated with black entrance into the power elite are the following:

1. Middle-class and working-class backgrounds.
2. High level of education, particularly education at elite institutions.
3. Adoption of white elite culture.
4. Light skin color.

First, it is important to emphasize the relatively small number of blacks in the power elite. For instance, 12 percent of the population was black in 1995, while only 3.6 percent of the positions on *Fortune* magazine-rated corporate boards were held by blacks. This percentage was a marked increase from the zero membership in 1964.[8] During the 1950s and 1960s, pressure from the civil rights movement forced corporations to open their doors to black leaders. The first black members of *Fortune* 500 corporate boards were Samuel R. Peirce, who joined U.S. Industries, and Asa T. Spaulding, who joined W.T. Grant. Zweigenhaft and Domhoff describe them as "highly educated . . . assimilated into the mainstream (that is to say, white) culture, and . . . not prone to rock the boat."[9] Samuel Peirce came from a wealthy Long Island family and earned BA and law degrees at Cornell University. Asa Spaulding came from a middle-class southern family and was educated at New York University and the University of Michigan. Ironically, both Peirce and Spaulding were conservative in contrast to the militancy of the civil rights movement that was responsible for them gaining access to corporate boards. Spaulding told *Time* magazine that he lived cautiously in contrast to civil rights leaders. "No sir," he said, "I didn't get out and picket or demonstrate anywhere during the civil-rights drive."[10]

Other entrants into the power elite included Clifton Wharton, Jr., and William T. Coleman, Jr., who joined corporate boards in 1969. Wharton's father was the first career black ambassador. Because of the family's diplomatic experience, Wharton was trilingual. He graduated from the prestigious Boston Latin High School and then attended Harvard. He received an MA at Johns Hopkins and a PhD in economics at the University of Chicago. Coleman came from a solidly middle-class family with six generations of teachers and Episcopal ministers. In 1971, Hobart Taylor, Jr., born into a wealthy Texas family and graduating with a law degree from the University of Michigan, was appointed to the board of Standard Oil of Ohio. Peirce, Spaulding, Wharton, Coleman, and Taylor typify the well-educated and solid middle-class and wealthy backgrounds of blacks selected for membership on corporate boards.

Black members of the president's cabinet have come from a very narrow slice of the black community. Since 1966, there have been 10 black members of the cabinet and 7 of those members came from wealthy families. All of them went to college and seven attended elite schools.

Another factor that characterizes black entrants into the power elite is skin color. Light skin combined with assimilation to white culture made it easier to enter the elite. For instance, General Colin Powell, named chairman of the Joint Chiefs of Staff in 1989, was described as "light-skinned and blunt-featured" by interviewer Henry Louis Gates in a *New Yorker* profile. Responding to an interview question about why polls indicated that he received more support from whites than blacks, Powell answered, *"I ain't that black . . .* I speak reasonably well, like a white person. I am very comfortable in a white social situation . . . they [whites] do not find me threatening."[11]

Gradations in skin color were a factor in promotions according to a study by the U.S. government's Glass Ceiling Commission. Using a skin color rating chart, Skin Color Assessment Procedure, developed by two psychologists, Zweigenhaft and Domhoff concluded that black members of the power elite had lighter skin color than the general black population.

Given the importance of family background, how does a person from a poor black family enter the power elite? The answer for Zweigenhaft and Domhoff is to attend an elite secondary school and learn the culture of upper-class whites. Their conclusion is based on a study of black participants in the "A Better Chance" (ABC) program from 1966 to 1975. The program was founded by 16 independent secondary schools to help low-income minority students attend elite prep schools.

In the ABC program, teaching elite white culture was an important part of the summer orientation program held at Dartmouth College. As one headmaster in the ABC program stated, "They couldn't come to Andover or Northfield from Harlem in September and fit, because many of them didn't know a knife from a fork."[12] An indicator of the cultural changes ABC students experienced attending elite prep schools is the development of *biculturalism.* Bicultural refers to the ability to function in two different cultures. In the context of black mobility, bicultural means being able to function in white elite culture and the culture of the home.

For example, Sylvester Monroe's sister told him, "Why don't you leave that St. George's bullshit at St. George's?" Not understanding the importance of bi-culturalism, Sylvester attempted to model the family meal on the ones he experienced at St. George's.[13] After a while, he said, "I dressed, acted one way in Newport, Rhode Island, and when I went home on vacations, I left all of that in Newport."[14] When Alan Glenn went home to Harlem from Hotchkiss, he discovered that "A lot of my friends looked . . . as [though] I thought I was better than they were and thought I was trying to be white."[15]

Often, the effort at biculturalism failed, and a social distance developed between ABC students and their families and neighborhoods. One woman reported, "I had trouble adjusting to my former home. . . . I absolutely hated it. . . . I was angry at them [her parents] for not having been like the parents of my classmates."[16] As Zweigenhaft and Domhoff conclude, "The problem of managing the dual identity of prep school graduate and lower-class black is a difficult one."[17]

Using the language of French sociologist Pierre Bourdieu, Zweigenhaft and Domhoff argue that attendance at prep schools provides the "cultural capital" to succeed in the U.S. economic system. The term *cultural capital* refers to the cultural knowledge needed to maintain one's place in the class structure. Cultural capital includes knowledge of appropriate dress, manners, and social relationships. It also includes a shared knowledge of events, institutions, and the arts, including a shared network of friends. Zweigenhaft and Domhoff conclude that ABC students acquired two important parts of the cultural capital of the power elite: "the ability to talk with anyone about anything, and the ability to benefit from the access to influential people they had gained as a result of attending elite schools."[18]

Graduates of the ABC program believe that learning to converse in any situation was one of their important learning experiences which provided them with the cultural capital to easily fit into the social surroundings of the power elite. "Prep schools," Zweigenhaft and Domhoff stress, "pride themselves on their graduates' ability to interact comfortably with a wide variety of people."[19] ABC student Greg Googer stated that he learned at Phillips Academy "the games, the rules, of what to say, of what not to say, and how to say it."[20] Another ABC graduate, William Foster, described how his prep school training allows him to handle social situations. "I'm able," he said, "to converse with anybody on almost anything. I went to someone's house, a marvelous home, and I felt a little out of place until I saw they had some Oriental prints, and I was saying, 'Isn't this from the such and such dynasty?' The guy perked right up. It worked out well. I felt very comfortable."[21]

For black students, an important aspect of the cultural capital learned at prep schools is the ability to feel comfortable functioning in white culture. A graduate of Miss Hall's, Maccene Brown claims that because of a prep school education, "You're comfortable in the presence of folks who are not of your own ethnic group—and a lot of black people are still not comfortable around white folks."[22] Zweigenhaft and Domhoff conclude, "Perhaps there is no more important cultural capital for blacks than to feel comfortable interacting with whites on an equal basis; this is a major contribution of the ABC program to its graduates."[23]

THE CULTURE OF SUCCESS FOR JEWS, WOMEN, ASIANS, LATINOS/LATINAS, LESBIANS/GAYS, AND LOW-INCOME WHITES

Zweigenhaft and Domhoff found that other groups entering the power elite assimilate to the dominant culture of upper-class Christian white males, similar to the experience of African Americans. Christian is used as a descriptor, because Jews entering the power elite are less likely to practice their religion than other Jews and they tend to marry non-Jews. Culturally, Jews in the power elite avoid Jewish social events and adopt the mannerisms of the gentile upper class. One gentile member of the power elite stated, "I think at the top levels being Jewish will hurt a person's chances. . . . This one man I know is so polished, such an upper-class person, there's no way to know he's Jewish. . . . He's an upper-class type person, the kind who could make it to the top."[24]

Women find that they must assimilate to the male culture of the power elite. Again, the issue is cultural capital, which includes the ability to share social relationships with male colleagues. This tends to be a one-way accommodation of women adapting to men. When Cecily Cannan Selby became the first woman on the board of directors of Avon, she helped her male colleagues relax by smoking a cigar. One corporate manager referred to the sharing of cultural capital as being comfortable. In his words, "What's important is comfort, chemistry, relationships, and collaborations. That's what makes a shop work. When we find minorities and women who think like we do, we snatch them up."[25]

To become "one of the boys," many women find they must learn the male culture of competitive sports. An important aid in a woman's advancement into the power elite is learning golf. Golf is a topic of office conversation and a means of establishing and maintaining social relationships. In *Members of the Club,* Marie Driscoll and Carol Goldberg, both members of corporate boards, state, "We realized the importance of golf . . . but neither of us played golf, we had missed it as an issue for executive women. But golf is central to many business circles."[26]

The knowledge of golf as part of the cultural capital of the power elite was stressed in an article in the business section of *The New York Times.* The *Times* reported as follows:

> To justify spending hours steering dimpled balls into plastic cups, many business people explain that golf is great for building relationships with clients. . . . Comparing the handicaps of a group of corporate chiefs, as reported by *Golf Digest* magazine, to their companies' stock market performance over three years, a clear pattern emerges: If a chief executive is a better-than-average golfer, he is also likely to deliver above-average returns to shareholders.[27]

Entering the Power Elite

Grades: Elementary through College (Obviously, there will be different levels of sophistication in responding to this lesson based on the age of the student, and the lesson should be adjusted to their ages.)

Objective:
To have students identify what they think is the dominant culture of the United States.

Lesson:

1. Ask students what cultural traits they think are required for entering the power elite in American society. For younger students, who might not understand the concept of a power elite, the question might be phrased as identifying the characteristics for success or of being important.
2. The teacher should place different cultural categories on the chalkboard and ask students to identify cultural characteristics for each category. The categories that could be used are:
   a. Dress
   b. Speech patterns and accents
   c. Manners
   d. Religion
   e. Housing
   f. Furniture
   g. Automobiles
   h. Sports
   i. Music
   j. Hobbies
   k. Vacations
   l. Areas of knowledge
3. Students should be asked to compare the above list of the cultural characteristics of the power elite with their own cultural characteristics.

Teachers: Teachers can participate by helping students when they have difficulty with one of the categories. Also, teachers might want to reflect on their own cultural relationship to the power elite.

Outcome: This lesson will give students a clearer understanding of the dominant culture and of cultural differences.

Family wealth and education are the best predictors of the mobility of Asians and Latinos/Latinas into the power elite. If there is substantial family wealth at the time of immigration into the United States, children from these groups have access to a privileged education and social contacts. Generally, wealthy immigrant families already have the cultural capital to function socially with upper-class groups. For instance, Roberto Goizueta grew up in a privileged family in Cuba prior to the rise of the government of Fidel Castro. Educated at Yale University in the early 1950s, Goizueta became CEO of the Coca-Cola Corporation in 1980. Born in Shanghai in 1935, Shirley Young served on the boards of Bell Atlantic and Promus Companies and was vice president of General Motors. Her father was a career diplomat. Chang-Lin Tien, a director of Wells Fargo Bank and a former chancellor of the University of California, was born into a wealthy banking family in Wanchu, China.

As with African Americans, an important attribute for Latinos/Latinas entering the power elite is light skin color. Two sociological studies, Zweigenhaft and Domhoff report, found that in most Latin American countries the more European-looking people tend to be in the higher social classes, while the more Indian-looking are in the lower classes. Another study found that those with medium skin color earned more than those with dark skin color. Zweigenhaft and Domhoff state, "Our own study of the skin color of Hispanics in the corporate elite leads to the same conclusion: it is advantageous to be light-skinned."[28]

Despite political activism for gay and lesbian rights, Zweigenhaft and Domhoff found that most gays and lesbians in the power elite remain closeted. In other words, they do not openly display or refer to their sexual preferences. Similar to other groups, gays and lesbians blend into the culture of the power elite. One study of homosexuals in the corporate elite concluded, "They learn to control and monitor outward appearances, to distort them when necessary . . . they manage their sexual identities at work."[29]

While Zweigenhaft and Domhoff did not include the mobility of poor whites (white trash) into the power elite, I didn't think my students would have much difficulty extrapolating information from their other findings. Obviously, skin color is not an issue for poor whites. On the other hand, cultural capital is an issue. The children of low-income white families, similar to other groups, need to learn the culture of the upper class for mobility into the power elite. Education and social contacts are important means for achieving this goal. President Bill Clinton, who grew up in a poor southern family, gained his cultural capital attending Yale University and studying in England as a Rhodes Scholar.

ECONOMIC SUCCESS VERSUS CULTURAL DIVERSITY

In presenting the findings on assimilation to the dominant culture as a requirement for entrance into the power elite, I feel it is important to stress the difference between cultural unity and cultural diversity. For instance, the ABC program prepares African Americans attending prep schools for cultural unity with the white Christian culture of the upper class. There is no attempt in this program to teach or maintain black culture. In contrast, many programs in Native American schools maintain Native American culture. Often the debate regarding these Native American programs centers on their ability to prepare students for work in a largely white-controlled economy.

I decided to present the following questions to the class after examining the material on mobility into the power elite:

- Should multicultural education focus on preparing students to succeed in the economic system?
- Should multicultural education focus on maintaining diverse cultures?
- Can multicultural education preserve diverse cultures while preparing students for economic success in the dominant culture?

E. D. HIRSCH AND CULTURAL LITERACY

Some educators argue for direct instruction in the dominant culture as a means of equalizing economic opportunity and promoting national unity. These educators are divided over how to determine the dominant culture. Some argue that the dominant culture is reflected in the values that serve as a foundation to basic U.S. institutions, such as the government, family, and economic system. Others argue that determining the dominant culture requires constant research because culture is dynamic and constantly changing.

Reflecting this latter position, E. D. Hirsch argues that research can identify the core knowledge of the dominant culture and that this core knowledge can be taught in schools. For Hirsch, *cultural literacy is knowing the dominant culture.* The goal of schools, he believes, should be teaching cultural literacy based on research into the nature of American culture. By achieving universal cultural literacy, Hirsch maintains, there will be national unity and all groups will have equal economic opportunity.[30]

Hirsch argues that, to be culturally literate, people must have a framework of knowledge to interpret the information that they receive from the outside world. Therefore, from Hirsch's perspective, schools should teach all children the same core knowledge needed to understand the information they receive from reading and other sources. Hirsch's concept of cultural literacy is relative to a particular period of time. The cultural knowledge required for literacy in the 1990s was different from that needed in the 1890s. Hirsch argues that the core knowledge for cultural literacy should be determined through research. In his original work, core knowledge, listed in the appendix of his book, involved 5,000 names, phrases, dates, and concepts which are a product of the research done by Hirsch and his colleagues—Joseph Kett and James Trefil—at the University of Virginia.

If the information Hirsch believes is necessary for cultural literacy were common to all people, then there would be no reason for teaching it. All people sharing the same culture would have the same cultural information. But all Americans, according to Hirsch, do not share the same cultural information.

The major divisions between people regarding cultural information follow so-cial class lines. According to his argument, the group that is suffering the most from lack of cultural literacy are the poor. Obviously, as Hirsch admits, the poor do have a culture that contains cultural information. The problem is that their cultural information does not create the type of cultural literacy needed for par-ticipation in the dominant institutions of U.S. society.

Consequently, Hirsch claims, a program of cultural literacy will help alle-viate poverty in the United States. In an argument that might be challenged by people who believe that poverty is caused by economic conditions, Hirsch states that poverty is perpetuated by the lack of proper cultural literacy. Hirsch claims that cultural literacy programs in public schools will help the poor gain employment and climb out of a state of poverty and, in addition, will ease the transition of immigrants to American culture.

In addition to claiming that cultural literacy will help the poor, Hirsch argues that cultural literacy provides the cultural unity that is necessary for maintaining social order. He believes that modern industrialism requires a specialization of labor that tends to destroy a feeling of national unity. Consequently, Hirsch asserts that public schools should play a major role in building national cultural unity. For this reason, he emphatically rejects ethnocentric programs that teach from the per-spective of a particular culture, such as instruction based on the cultural perspec-tive of African Americans or Mexican Americans. He believes that schools might teach tolerance of other cultures but at the same time they should teach a common culture to all students. Hirsch's argument rejects an emphasis on cultural differ-ences. In fact, he argues for the ending of cultural differences by, for example, in-tegrating Native American children into mainstream American culture.

THE DOMINANT CULTURE AS WHITE ANGLO-SAXON VALUES

In contrast to Hirsch's research of contemporary culture, Arthur Schlesinger, Jr., ad-vocates teaching the values of the so-called Founding Fathers of the United States. Author of many U.S. history books and *The Disuniting of America,* Schlesinger ar-gues that the institutions and culture of the United States are primarily the product of English and European values and that these core values should be the source of national unity. Schlesinger argues, "For better or worse, the white Anglo-Saxon Protestant tradition was for two centuries—and in crucial respects still is—the dominant influence on American culture and society."[31] This white Anglo-Saxon Protestant tradition, he argues, came from Britain. In his words, "The language of the new nation, its laws, its institutions, its political ideas, its literature, its customs, its precepts, its prayers, primarily derived from Britain."[32]

Historically, Schlesinger contends, the culture of the United States was uni-fied by the common use of the English language and core values derived from this white Anglo-Saxon Protestant tradition. These core values, he states, in-clude mutual respect, individual rights, tolerance of differences, and individual participation in government.[33] Similar to Schlesinger, Thomas Sobol, former New York Commissioner of Education, believes in a curriculum that unites different cultural groups around common values. Sobol states, "The democratic ideals and values to which we still aspire . . . the rule of law, freedom of speech, minority rights, tolerance of dissent, respect for individuals, and more—derive from British political and legal traditions."[34]

In California, State Superintendent of Education Bill Honig defended a new social studies curriculum by an appeal to the teaching of core values. Honig stated in 1991, "This country has been able to celebrate pluralism but keep some sense of the collective that holds us together. . . . Democracy has certain core ideas—freedom of speech, law, procedural rights, the way we deal with each other."[35]

Schlesinger, Sobol, and Honig recognize that U.S. history contains many examples of the violation of these principles by federal and state governments. They recognize that, at various times in history, federal and state governments supported slavery, committed genocide against Native Americans, and denied equal rights and opportunities to many ethnic groups. But, they argue, it was these core values that provided the impetus for correcting these wrongs. The abolition of slavery, the extension of political rights to women, and the civil rights campaigns by African Americans, Mexican Americans, Native Americans, Puerto Ricans, and Asian Americans reflect these core values. These civil rights movements, according to Schlesinger, were based on the core values of the white Anglo-Saxon Protestant tradition.[36]

Given this perspective, it is hardly surprising that those calling for the teaching of core values would object to the teaching of minority cultures. Schlesinger attacks education based on African American culture as distorting the importance of Africa in the development of Western traditions and in the development of African American culture. Because of the variety of African cultures from which African Americans are descended, Schlesinger argues, it is hard to identify a common African heritage for African Americans. In addition, many African cultures are more oppressive than white Anglo-Saxon Protestant culture, as proved by the fact that slavery continued in Africa for many years after it was abolished in the United States.[37]

In addition, Schlesinger rejects the idea of teaching history for the purpose of building a sense of self-worth among children. In his words, "The deeper reason for the Afrocentric [education based on African and African American values] campaign lies in the theory that the purpose of history in the schools is essentially therapeutic: to build a sense of self-worth among minority children."[38] With regard to the teaching of the history of Africa, Schlesinger rejects the direct connection between African heritage and African American culture and dismisses the practice with the statement: "There is little evidence, however, that such invention of tradition is much more than a pastime of a few angry, ambitious, and perhaps despairing zealots and hustlers."[39]

SHOULD WE TEACH THE VALUES OF THE DOMINANT CULTURE?

It is important to understand the difference between determining the dominant culture by Hirsch's research of contemporary culture and Schlesinger's examination of historical values. Also, I know that many people object to the educational goal of economic success and teaching the dominant culture of the United States. Two major difficulties come to the fore:

- A lack of understanding of the nature of cultural differences.
- Uncritical acceptance of the dominant culture.

The intersection of Native American and English culture illustrates these issues by highlighting the values of the dominant culture and questioning the worth of the dominant culture to human happiness.

A LESSON ON CULTURAL DIFFERENCES: NATIVE AMERICAN AND ENGLISH CULTURES

Understanding the nature of cultural differences is crucial for understanding the problems in the intersection of cultures and in multicultural education. A study of cultural differences requires an examination of differing values about work, property, the environment, the family, and political and social organizations. Treating only the superficial qualities of cultures does not prepare a person to interact with another culture. For a student to learn only that Indians lived in wigwams and ate roots and berries is not preparation for interaction with Native Americans.

The differences between English and Native American cultures provide a good illustration of this point. For this discussion, I am relying on the work of ethnohistorian James Axtell and my own research on the cultural transformation of the Choctaws. Axtell pioneered the concept of the intersection of cultures while studying the cultural changes that took place among Native Americans and the French and English in North America.[40] My own work on the Choctaws examines the effect of formal schooling on cultural changes and power relationships within the tribe.

Many Europeans preferred to join Indian tribes and live like Indians. They were known as "white Indians."[41] Many other English colonists, however, were racially prejudiced and argued against intermarriage.[42] Native Americans considered their own culture to be superior and few preferred to live like English colonists. What Native Americans found particularly unattractive were English cultural values regarding work and property. For the English, work was a duty to God and, except on Sunday, was something to be sought. For Native Americans this was a startling concept. From their perspective, work should only involve the sustaining of life and not the accumulation of additional property. Why should one try to increase the amount of work? Wasn't work something to be avoided? For Native Americans it did not make much sense to try to organize a society that required increased amounts of work. In contrast, the English considered Native Americans to be lazy.[43]

Related to the concept of work is the concept of property. English culture valued the personal accumulation of wealth. The goal of increased labor was to accumulate property. High status was given in English society to the person who worked hard and became rich. Within the Protestant ethic, wealth was considered a sign of being blessed by God. Native Americans, on the other hand, believed in the sharing of property as opposed to personal accumulation.[44] In describing this concept of property to students at the University of California in 1880, John Edwards, a missionary teacher to the Choctaws, commented, "One result of this [sharing as opposed to accumulation of property] is that they have no need of poorhouses. . . . You perceive that this militates very strongly against accumulation of property."[45]

Without a desire to accumulate wealth, Native Americans could not justify working beyond the requirements of maintaining their own existence. In addition, social status was not determined by the amount of wealth. This meant that while the English thought of society in terms of social classes—the rich and the poor—Native Americans thought of social differences in terms of wisdom and the ability to contribute to the welfare of the tribe.

The concept of property is also related to the concept of the family. For the English, an important role of the family was to accumulate property for inheritance by the next generation. The father was the authority figure within the framework of the nuclear English family. In contrast, Native Americans organized their family structures around a clan system in which property was collectively owned and responsibility for bringing up children was shared by all members of the clan. In criticizing the clan system of the Choctaws, Edwards told the students, "One serious difficulty with the system is that it takes from the father his proper place at the head of his family and leaves him comparatively little control of his children. With that Christianity has to contend, and it is gradually overcoming it."[46]

The clan system, as Edwards suggested, supported more permissive child-rearing practices than those practiced by the English. In fact, the English were horrified at the freedom granted to Indian children. For the English colonists imbued with a strong sense of Calvinism, the goal of child rearing was to control a child's "evil" disposition and instill fear of the authority of parents, government, and God. Authority and control were the hallmarks of English child-rearing at this time.[47] About the child-rearing practices of the Choctaws, Edwards complained, "There is very little order or discipline in the family. Each does what is pleasing in his own eyes. A parent may beat a child in anger, but seldom does he chastise him with coolness and in love."[48]

While Native Americans retained a sense of the superiority of their culture, English culture was characterized by racist attitudes which branded Native Americans as savages and inferior, and which justified not only removal of them from their lands but, in some cases, the practice of genocide. The growth of racism in English culture, according to historian Ronald Takaki, begins with the English conquest of Ireland in the sixteenth century. The English justified their conquest of Ireland by calling the Irish "savages." Savage in this context referred to cultural differences. The Irish were considered savages because they lived outside the framework of what the English considered civilization. This implied that the Irish could be educated and brought into the realm of what the English defined as civilization. While the English held out the possibility for the improvement of Irish culture, they considered the Irish lazy, wicked, and as living like beasts.[49]

One of the important functions of identifying another culture as inferior is that it provides a justification for economic exploitation and political control. Therefore, the English believed that the Irish would benefit by being controlled by the superior culture of England. In addition, since the Irish were considered savages, the English believed that it would be in the best interest of the Irish to deny them political and economic rights. Consequently, English colonizers of Ireland passed laws that gave the death penalty to any Irishman carrying a weapon and denied the Irish the right to purchase land, hold a public office, and serve on a jury.[50]

The next step in the development of racist thought is to argue that not only is a particular culture inferior or savage, but that inferiority is inherent in the very being of the people. In other words, it is not possible to "civilize" a group of people by changing their culture. Savagery, within this concept, is biological and it is inherited. A group of people are lazy, stupid, and live like beasts because they are born that way. By branding a culture as inferior and considering that inferiority as biologically inherent, the English could not only justify control and management of a group of people but also their eradication. Genocide is justified with the argument that a group of people are inherently inferior.

With regard to Native Americans, English colonists wavered between these two concepts of savagery. Some English colonists instituted educational projects designed to "civilize" Native Americans. These educational projects were accompanied by a strong sense of the superiority of English culture and the inferiority of Indian culture. This was particularly true with regard to the issue of work. While Native Americans questioned the value of the English work ethic, the English believed that the key to civilizing Native Americans was to turn them into yeoman farmers and instill the English work ethic. Typical of this attitude was missionary educator David McClure's comment in 1772: "The men are ashamed of all kinds of labour, except war & hunting [and] the building of their miserable houses. . . . Such is the pride of these lazy lords of the wilderness."[51]

It is important to understand the relationship between the English concept of "civilizing" Native Americans and economic exploitation. Just as branding the Irish as inferior justified the conquest of Ireland, branding Indian culture as inferior justified the conquest of Indian lands. Turning Native Americans into yeomen farmers as opposed to hunters would reduce the amount of land needed by Indian tribes. Contained on farms, Indian lands would become available to English settlers.

The English construction of the racial concept of savagery was used to justify the physical removal of Indians from their lands. According to this racial concept of savagery, nothing could be done to turn Indians into model English men and women. In the 1820s and 1830s, Andrew Jackson adopted the position that Indians were racially inferior and, consequently, incapable of civilization. The only hope was to move them from their lands to the area west of the Mississippi that became known as Indian Territory. Under Andrew Jackson, the forced march of the Five Civilized Tribes to Indian Territory became known as the "Trail of Tears" because of the forced abandonment of homes and the large number of Indians who died on the trail. It was one of the major acts of geno-cide in human history.[52]

For Native Americans, the intersection of Indian and English cultures was devastating. The two cultures, as I discussed earlier, were sharply divided by different concepts of work, property, family, and relations between different cultures. Most Native Americans could not accept the idea that work was a virtue in and of itself or that their goal should be to accumulate property as opposed to sharing. Most could not accept the idea of an authoritarian nuclear family and authoritarian patterns of child rearing. There was nothing in Native American culture that would lead them to brand another culture as racially inferior.

But these cultural values provided little defense against the values held by English colonists. The English belief in their cultural and racial superiority provided the justification for the conquest of Native American tribes. From the perspective of English culture, Native Americans were lazy and primarily focused on their own sensual pleasures, that is, savages. On the other hand, English culture valued personal denial, hard work, and the accumulation of property, which provided the justification to take away Native American lands.

While the clash resulting from this intersection of cultures continues today, there was some cultural exchange: some Europeans chose to become "white Indians" and some Native Americans adopted European values. By the nineteenth century, social classes developed within Indian tribes. Those Indians who became "civilized" adopted values of hard work and property accumulation. A visitor to Indian Territory in 1842 noted, "Indians have classes as well as white men; some are prudent and turn their annuity to a good account. . . . It is mostly those who are in power and wealth."[53] But even today, traditionalists within Indian tribes cling to values of sharing and permissive child-rearing. The division between traditionalists and "civilized" Indians is an important factor in Native American education. Equally important is the clash with "white" values.

The examination of cultural differences between Native Americans and European Americans raises questions about what cultural values are best for a society. Should we adopt the Native American attitude that the goal of society is to maximize leisure and minimize work? As modern restructuring of corporations forces employees to work harder and longer hours, we might want to reconsider the nature of the work ethic in our society. Should we adopt the Native American attitude that the goal is to share property as opposed to accumulating property? By identifying these cultural differences, multicultural educators are provided an opportunity to evaluate the cultural values that underpin white European civilization.

In summary, the analysis of the intersection of Native American and English cultures highlights the depth and importance of cultural differences beyond those of food, housing, and dress. This analysis also demonstrates some of the basic incompatibilities that can exist between cultures. Given these basic differences: Can we teach tolerance of other cultures? Is this a good thing to do? For example, can Native American children who are raised with traditional values be taught to tolerate the values of European Americans? Should they be taught to tolerate the values of European Americans?

This analysis also highlights one of the basic forces in American history that has complicated cultural relationships. From the sixteenth century to the twentieth, the English and European American belief in the superiority of their culture and people justified acts of conquest, enslavement, and genocide. White Anglo-Saxon Protestant traditions stress the importance of individualism, particularly economic individualism. In this tradition, the goal of equal economic opportunity reflects a belief in individual economic competition and individual accumulation of property. And, implied in the concept of property accumulation, is a belief in the Protestant work ethic. Traditional Native American culture rejects these values.

Professor Leonard Jeffries, an Afrocentrist who has made controversial speeches attacking white people, condemns whites for being "ice people." He argues that European culture is individualist, materialistic, and aggressive. Has European culture, in fact, brought to the world what Jeffries calls the three D's, "domination, destruction, and death"?[54] Are advocates of teaching a core of white Anglo-Saxon Protestant values blind to the possible defects in those values? While Schlesinger argues that these values provided the basis for ending slavery, they also provided the basis for the original support of slavery.

CONCLUSION: AMERICAN CULTURE AND MULTICULTURAL EDUCATION

Traveling in foreign countries, I can often spot other Americans moving along crowded streets. There is something about their mannerisms, dress, and voice that give them the air of Americanism. My identification of them as Americans is highlighted by the surrounding crowds of the contrasting *other*. But I can't spot every American given the complexity of our multicultural society. It is very difficult to precisely define American culture with its overlapping cultural groups and murky cultural boundaries. Maybe, E. D. Hirsch has the right suggestion that we must do research to identify the concepts, icons, and events commonly known by most Americans.

Despite the difficulty in clearly defining American culture most Americans identify themselves with a single or multiple cultural group. African Americans might identify with African American culture while simultaneously considering themselves part of a general American culture. The same thing is true of Native Americans, Irish Americans, Japanese Americans, Mexican Americans, and all the other ethnic groups of the American population. I have identified some characteristics of a *general* American culture such as obsession with shopping, the accumulation of consumer goods, and mall culture; fear and insecurity; anger and hate resulting from historical multicultural confrontations; and a hope that love and compassion will help achieve racial and cultural harmony.

The difficulty in defining American culture complicates the three major issues facing multicultural education: (1) the lingering anger and hostility between cultural groups; (2) the desire by some to maintain their cultures within the framework of a general American culture; and (3) the adjustment of recently arrived immigrants to American culture.

A simplistic resolution of these issues as proposed by Arthur Schlesinger, Jr., would be for the schools to focus on the assimilation of all groups to the dominant Anglo-American culture. If everyone were part of the same culture then, according to this reasoning, cultural differences would not be a road block to equality of opportunity. However, this solution does not address the lingering anger of groups such as African Americans, Native Americans, Puerto Ricans, and Mexican Americans who were raped, tortured, mutilated, and dispossessed of their labor and lands. Simply decreeing that the dominant culture should be the culture of the schools might only fan the flames of revenge.

Also, teaching the dominant culture does not directly address the problem of the cultural adjustment of immigrants. In the nineteenth century, the U.S. government tried a disastrous experiment in cultural change when it tried to destroy Native American culture in one generation by sending Native American children to boarding schools to learn the dominant culture and language. Maybe, immigrants would like to retain their cultural traditions and languages. In the land of the free, should the schools simply impose a culture and language on an unwilling immigrant population?

There are also issues of the content and methods of instruction in multicultural education. The sample lessons provided in this chapter are meant to illustrate classroom techniques for initiating discussions about the meaning of culture and cultural differences. These are important lessons to consider when teaching about multiculturalism.

While I have so far focused on the problems in defining the *general* and *dominant* American culture, I still need to discuss *dominated* cultures. *Dominated* are those groups who unwillingly became part of the United States, such as African Americans, Native Americans, Mexican Americans, and Puerto Ricans. As I suggested throughout this chapter, many cultural tensions are a product of the conditions associated with the oppression of these groups. The next chapter will address several important questions:

- What are the characteristics of dominated cultures?
- Should dominated cultures be preserved as alternatives to the dominant culture?
- Should schools through methods and content of instruction maintain the cultures and languages of dominated groups?

PERSONAL FRAMES OF REFERENCE

1. What culture do you belong to?
2. Does your culture create for you an economic advantage or disadvantage in the United States?
3. What cultural groups in the United States have an economic advantage over your particular cultural group?
4. What cultural groups in the United States have a disadvantaged economic position in comparison to your cultural group?

5. In what ways does your culture reflect the values of English colonial settlers?
6. In what ways does your culture reflect the values of Native Americans?
7. Do you believe that the lack of cultural unity will result in increased social
   and racial conflict?
8. Do you want our nation and/or world unified around a particular set of
   cultural values? If so, which cultural values?
9. Are you culturally literate (in reference to Hirsch)?
10. Do you believe a program of cultural literacy will provide greater equality
    of opportunity for all children?

Notes

1. Michael Hardt and Antonio Negri, *Empire* (Cambridge: Harvard University Press, 2000), p. 213.
2. Elissa Moses, *The $100 Billion Allowance: Accessing the Global Teen Market* (New York: John Wiley & Sons, Inc., 2000), pp. 4, 10–11.
3. Bernice Kanner, *The 100 Best TV Commercials* (New York: Random House, 1999), p, 18.
4. The objectives can be found on the Web page of the National Association for Multicultural Education, http://www.nameorg.org.
5. Bharati Mukherjee, *Jasmine* (New York: Grove Press, 1999).
6. Richard Zweigenhaft and G. William Domhoff, *Blacks in the White Establishment?: A Study of Race and Class in America* (New Haven: Yale University Press, 1991) and *Diversity in the Power Elite* (New Haven: Yale University Press, 1998).
7. Zweigenhaft and Domhoff, *Diversity in the Power Elite,* p. 4.
8. Ibid., p. 99.
9. Ibid., p. 80.
10. Ibid., p. 81.
11. Ibid., pp. 112–13.
12. Zweigenhaft and Domhoff, *Blacks in the White Establishment?,* p. 3.
13. Ibid., p. 59.
14. Ibid.
15. Ibid.
16. Ibid.
17. Ibid., p. 60.
18. Ibid., p. 107.
19. Ibid.
20. Ibid., p. 108.
21. Ibid.
22. Ibid.
23. Ibid.
24. Zweigenhaft and Domhoff, *Diversity in the Power Elite,* p. 26.
25. Ibid., p. 51.
26. Ibid., p. 53.
27. Adam Bryant, "Linking Good Golf and Good Business," *The New York Times,* www.nytimes.com, 3 May 1998.
28. Zweigenhaft and Domhoff, *Diversity in the Power Elite,* p. 122.
29. Ibid., p. 161.

30. See E. D. Hirsch, Jr., *Cultural Literacy: What Every American Needs to Know* (New York: Random House, 1987).

31. Arthur M. Schlesinger, Jr., *The Disuniting of America* (Knoxville, TN: Whittle Direct Books, 1991), p. 8.

32. Ibid.

33. Ibid., p. 80.

34. Thomas Sobol, "Revising the New York State Social Studies Curriculum," *Teachers College Record* 95, no. 1 (Winter 1993), p. 266.

35. Caroline B. Cody, Arthur Woodward, and David L. Elliott, "Race, Ideology and the Battle Over the Curriculum," in *The New Politics of Race and Gender,* ed. Catherine Marshall (Washington, DC: Falmer Press, 1993), p. 55.

36. Ibid., pp. 40–55.

37. Ibid., p. 43.

38. Schlesinger, p. 47.

39. Ibid., p. 34.

40. James Axtell, *The Invasion Within: The Contest of Cultures in Colonial North America* (New York: Oxford University Press, 1985).

41. For instance, my great-great-grandparents became white Indians by marrying into the Choctaw tribe. Axtell describes this phenomenon with regard to white captives of Indian tribes who prefer to remain with the tribe as opposed to returning to European colonial society (Ibid., pp. 302–29).

42. Ibid., p. 304.

43. Ibid., pp. 148–51.

44. Ibid., p. 166.

45. John Edwards, "The Choctaw Indians in the Middle of the Nineteenth Century," *Chronicles of Oklahoma* 10 (1932), pp. 403–4.

46. Ibid., p. 402.

47. See Joel Spring, *The American School 1642–1993,* 5th ed. (New York: McGraw-Hill, 2001), pp. 24–28.

48. Edwards, p. 410.

49. I will elaborate on the racist values inherent in English culture in Chapter 6. An important study of these cultural values can be found in Ronald Takaki, *A Different Mirror: A History of Multicultural America* (Boston: Little, Brown and Company, 1993), pp. 24–44.

50. Ibid., p. 27.

51. Axtell, p. 153.

52. The classic study of this act of genocide is Grant Forman, *Indian Removal: The Emigration of the Five Civilized Tribes* (Norman: University of Oklahoma Press, 1932).

53. Grant Forman, ed., *A Traveler in Indian Territory: The Journal of Ethan Allen Hitchcock, Late Major-General in the United States Army* (Cedar Rapids, Iowa: The Torch Press, 1930), pp. 186–87.

54. Schlesinger, p. 15.

CHAPTER 2

Dominated Cultures

Raiding bee hives to treat his fatal illness, Sequoyah traveled south in 1842 from Indian Territory into Mexico. Twenty years earlier, he had invented a written form of the Cherokee language. Cherokee leaders hailed this remarkable accomplishment as an important step in preserving the Cherokee culture and nation. Sequoyah's set of characters made it possible to print the first Native American newspaper, the *Cherokee Phoenix*, in 1827. Literacy in Cherokee spread through the nation as the newspaper and other printed material united the nation. Besides being the first newspaper written in a Native American language, the *Cherokee Phoenix* was the first bilingual newspaper with columns written in English and Cherokee.[1]

Sequoyah's death in a lonely cave in Mexico symbolized the defeat of early-nineteenth-century resistance to cultural and political domination. Cherokee resistance centered on bilingual education and adoption of white American political institutions, including the writing of a Cherokee national constitution. However, embodied in their resistance were cultural compromises that were repeated by dominated groups through the twentieth century. Efforts to preserve cultural traditions included learning English and adopting the political and social institutions of the conquering European peoples. Consequently, the very nature of resistance changed cultural traditions. Also, Native Americans could abandon resistance and embrace European culture. Some Native Americans selected this option. By the early nineteenth century, a powerful political and economic class had evolved in Cherokee society that dressed, acted, and lived like their counterparts in white culture. This elite created a split in tribal culture that would be labeled by Americans of European descent as progressive. Up to present times, the division between so-called progressives and traditionalists was a major source of tribal tensions with the progressives seeking assimilation into white society and traditionalists hoping to resist cultural domination.[2]

CULTURAL DOMINATION AND VOLUNTARY IMMIGRATION

The story of Sequoyah and Cherokee resistance exemplifies the complexity of cultural domination. There are many groups in the United States that can be described as dominated cultures. I am defining *dominated cultures* as those groups that were forced to become part of the United States through slavery, conquest, or colonization. For instance, Africans were forced to come to the United States as enslaved persons, and Native Americans, Mexicans living in the southwestern part of what is now the United States, and Puerto Ricans were conquered by the U.S. government.[3] Hawaii was annexed despite objection from native Hawaiian leaders. For these groups, this forced domination created somewhat different educational issues than for those who voluntarily immigrated to the United States.

While voluntary immigrants can face discrimination and bigotry, they often see these as part of the price for improving their conditions in the United States. In fact, it can be argued that many immigrant groups, particularly people of color, encounter the same problems of racism and cultural exclusion as dominated groups. The difference is that the cultural perspectives of dominated groups contain a level of hostility toward the institutions which subjugated them, while immigrants enter the United States with the hope that these institutions will provide them with improved living conditions.

In most cases, immigrants come to the United States because they believe they will improve their economic or political conditions. Consequently, voluntary immigrants have different attitudes regarding public schools than do dominated cultures. In contrast to dominated groups, Kevin Brown writes, for voluntary immigrants "cultural and language differences enshrined in public schools are not generally perceived as oppositional or as threats to the identity that they wished to maintain."[4] Therefore, while dominated and immigrant groups might share similar problems of prejudice and discrimination, they often differ with regard to how they see their possibilities for advancement in U.S. society. The experience of African Americans, Native Americans, Mexican Americans, Hawaiians, and Puerto Ricans in U.S. schools has often been negative and has created a level of suspicion, and sometimes hostility, toward the institution. On the other hand, many Asian immigrants find schools a source of hope.

As the brief discussion of Sequoyah and the Cherokee suggests, there are a number of difficult issues facing dominated groups, particularly the tension between assimilation into the dominant culture and maintaining a separate cultural identity. As I argued in the previous chapter, economic success in the United States often depends on assimilation into the culture of the power elite. Therefore, dominated cultures have debated the following educational questions:

- Should schools teach the culture of the dominated group (Native American, African, Mexican, Hawaiian, or Puerto Rican)?
- Or, should schools prepare students for economic success in the dominant culture?
- Should the language of instruction be that of the dominated group?

- Or, should the language of instruction be English?
- Should instruction be bicultural and bilingual?

The above questions are complicated by the cultural changes resulting from the intersection of dominant and dominated cultures. For instance, Sequoyah's invention of a written language and the creation of a bilingual newspaper significantly changed Cherokee culture. In the next section, I will detail how African cultures and languages changed under slavery. For supporters of instruction in the culture of a dominated group, the questions are as follows:

- Should schools teach the historical culture of dominated groups, such as Africans or Native Americans as they were prior to the European invasion?
- Or, should schools teach the culture resulting from the intersection of dominant and dominated cultures, such as African American culture?

The following discussion of the intersection of African and European cultures highlights the issues presented by these questions.

THE INTERSECTION OF AFRICAN AND EUROPEAN AMERICAN CULTURES

A study of the intersection of African and European American cultures provides an understanding of the effect of an extreme form of cultural domination. I am using the term *European American culture* to refer to the culture of slave owners and mainstream "white" culture. Although the English played a major role in the slave trade and provided a racial ideology to justify slavery, not all slave owners were English. For instance, my great-great-grandparents owned enslaved persons, and they were "mixed breed" descendants of Choctaw Indians and French and Swiss settlers. However, it can be argued that English culture was the primary cultural influence in the ownership of African people, as well as in European American culture in the United States in the eighteenth and nineteenth centuries.

The extreme racism required to justify the enslavement of Africans which, like English attitudes toward Native Americans, had its origins in English culture has left its mark on the culture of the United States. Racism was used to justify expansion into Africa in the same manner it was used to justify taking over Native American lands. As late as the 1890s, British leaders such as Cecil Rhodes were making claims of racial superiority to justify English expansion into Africa. For example, Rhodes wrote, "I contend that we are the finest race in the world and that the more of the world we inhabit the better it is for the human race. . . . Africa is still lying ready for us, it is our duty to seize every opportunity for acquiring more territory."[5] In Rhodes's mind, "more territory simply means more of the Anglo-Saxon race, more of the best of the most human, most honorable race this world possesses."[6]

While slavery in the United States ended with the Civil War, the racist thought required to support slavery continued through the twentieth century. Just as the English rationalized the conquest of the Irish and Native Americans by labeling them as uncivilized savages or racially inferior, they justified the

Family Multicultural Tree

Note: This lesson is continued in Lessons 2.2 and 2.3.

Grades: Elementary through College (Levels of understanding will differ based on the age of the students.)

Objective:
For students to understand their cultural history and that of their fellow students.

Lesson:

1. Each student should prepare a family tree indicating the cultural background of each ancestor. The number of generations in the family tree will depend on the student's knowledge of his or her ancestors.
2. Students should be allowed to use their own identifiers of cultural background. For instance, cultural background could be identified by race or national and ethnic origins, such as white, Native American, Irish, Chinese, etc.
3. This project will usually require the student to do some research. This research could simply be limited to discussions with family members.
4. Students should present and discuss their family trees to the class.

Teachers: Teachers should allow a great deal of flexibility in how students construct their family trees. Important discussions regarding the meaning of these family trees will occur in Lessons 2.2 and 2.3.

Outcome: Preparation and class discussions of family trees will help students understand their own and the others' multicultural backgrounds.

LESSON 2.2

Family Multicultural Tree: Dominated Cultures and Voluntary Immigrants

Grades: High School through College

Objective:

1. To understand the difference between dominated cultures and voluntary immigrants.
2. To understand the effect on the cultural self-identification of the student of ancestors who were dominated or voluntary immigrants.

Lesson: Using the family tree created for Lesson 2.1 students should:

1. Label members of family tree as descendants of dominated cultures or voluntary immigrants.
2. Indicate members of family tree who have ancestors descended from both dominated cultures and voluntary immigrants.
3. Indicate which cultures in the family tree have the greatest impact on the student's self-identification of culture.
4. Ask students to present and discuss their cultural self-identification in the context of their ancestors' origins as dominated or voluntary immigrants.

Teachers: It is important for teachers to help students understand the multiple ancestry of many Americans in relation to dominated cultures and voluntary immigrants. For instance, many people who identify themselves as African American also have ancestors who are European and Native American and many Americans who identify themselves as white have Native American ancestors. When there is multiple ancestry related to dominated cultures and voluntary immigration the teacher should ask why the student identifies with one particular cultural tradition in the family tree.

Outcome: The student should gain a clear understanding of the distinction between dominated cultures and voluntary immigration, and the source of his or her cultural self-identification.

Family Multicultural Tree:
Social and Economic Advantages

Grades: High School through College

Objective:
To help the student understand the social and economic consequences of having ancestors who were members of a dominated culture or who were voluntary immigrants.

Lesson:

1. Using the family trees from Lessons 2.1 and 2.2, students should indicate the occupations of their ancestors. In many cases, the student might have difficulty identifying the occupation. For ancestors who were enslaved Africans the indication could simply be "forced and unpaid work."
2. Have students indicate on their family trees the economic mobility between generations based on changes in occupations.
3. Ask students to present to the class the occupational mobility within their family tree.
4. In class discussions have students indicate what they believe was the effect of the dominated cultural or voluntary immigrant status of their ancestors on the occupational status of their parents.

Teachers: Income and social status are often difficult to attach to family trees. Therefore, I suggest just adding occupation. Of course, occupation does not often indicate income or social status, such as the difference between a poor and a wealthy farmer. However, occupation will serve as a rough guide to income and social status and it will be adequate for understanding the effect of dominated and voluntary immigrant status on occupational opportunities.

Outcome: Students should gain an understanding of the possible effects of dominated and voluntary immigrant status on occupational mobility in the United States.

exploitation of African labor by arguing that African civilizations and race were inferior to the English.

The intersection of African cultures and European American cultures within the context of slavery had a lasting effect on the development of African American culture. W.E.B. DuBois commented in *The Souls of Black Folk*, written in the early twentieth century after more than 30 years of freedom from slavery, that the African was forced to come to the United States through a system of slavery and, consequently, ended up being surrounded by a culture that denigrated and discriminated against his very being. Reflecting on the discrimination he experienced during his childhood, he asked, "Why did God make me an outcast and a stranger in mine own house?"[7]

The intersection of African and European American cultures left the African with what DuBois calls a double consciousness that was internally at war with itself. The consciousness created by European American culture competed with the consciousness created by African ancestry. DuBois plaintively wrote, "One ever feels his twoness, an American; Negro; two souls, two thoughts, two unreconciled strivings; two warring ideals in one dark body, whose dogged strength alone keeps it from being torn asunder."[8]

For DuBois, a central problem in the development of African American culture was the reconciliation of these two conflicting cultures. He argued that African Americans do not want to "Africanize" the United States because the United States has too much to offer the world. On the other hand, the African American did not want to "bleach his soul in a flood of white Americanism," because Africans had a message for the world. The African American, DuBois asserted, wanted to be a "coworker in the kingdom of culture." "He simply," DuBois stated, "wishes to make it possible for a man to be both a Negro and an American, without being cursed and spit upon by his fellows, without having the doors of opportunity closed roughly in his face."[9]

DuBois believed that the three gifts the African culture of former enslaved persons could add to European culture were "a gift of story and song," "the gift of sweat and brawn to beat back the wilderness," and "a gift of spirit."[10] The gift of story and song contributed to the growth of American popular music and jazz, which influenced music around the world. The gift of sweat and brawn opened the wilderness of the United States and provided the foundation for its economic growth. The gift of spirit made it possible for the United States to overcome the worst calamities. "Would America," DuBois rightly asked, "have been America without her Negro people?"[11] In identifying "story and song" as a contribution to American culture, DuBois was highlighting one of the major products of the culture of slavery and a core part of African American culture.

The culture of slavery was a product of the conditions of slavery. Enslaved Africans came from a variety of regions, cultures, and language groups in Africa. They not only had to adjust to the institution of slavery but also to the variety of backgrounds and languages of other enslaved people.

While enslaved Africans did not share a single African culture, they did share an African heritage, the experience of enslavement, and the culture they created in the context of slavery. To understand the evolution of African American culture, one must consider the initial conditions faced by enslaved Africans. Transported to the Americas, enslaved Africans were forced to abandon cultural practices related to marriage, family relations, property, child-rearing, friendships, and social status. Literally, enslaved Africans had to create their own culture within the context of domination and enslavement.

In the words of anthropologists Sidney Mintz and Richard Price, "The Africans in any New World colony in fact became a community and began to share a culture insofar as, and as fast as, they themselves created them."[12] This culture had two important facets: the relationship among enslaved Africans and their relationship to the owner or master. The intersection of slave culture and European American culture was in the context of a master-slave relationship. Enslaved Africans had to learn and develop modes of interaction with a master who literally had the power of life and death and who could at anytime inflict severe punishment. Enslaved people were not protected by any legal institution from the arbitrary brutality of the master. The owner could demand sexual relations with any enslaved person and had the power to break up families and wrench children from their parents by selling them.[13]

In the context of this total domination, the intersection of African and European American cultures produced the songs and stories that W.E.B. DuBois recognized as being at the center of African American culture. It is important to note that it was illegal to teach enslaved people to read and write. The fear among owners was that education would cause a rebellion against the slave system. Despite this prohibition, some enslaved people did learn to read and write, but the cultural legacy of slavery was primarily oral.[14] This oral tradition provided a psychological refuge against the degradation of slavery. Enslaved Africans created songs while working, during whatever leisure time was available, and during religious services. The lyrics reflected their effort to cope with inhuman conditions. In *Black Culture and Black Consciousness: Afro-American Folk Thought from Slavery to Freedom*, Lawrence Levine concludes, "The slaves' oral traditions, their music, and their religious outlook . . . constituted a cultural refuge at least potentially capable of protecting their personalities from some of the worst ravages of the slave system."[15]

Created in a context of domination, this oral tradition reflected an obvious distrust and dislike of whites, a hope that they would eventually triumph over the master, and the methods by which they tried to cope with their state of powerlessness. The religious songs of enslaved Africans often portrayed whites as the devil and slaves as the chosen people. As the chosen people, they would eventually triumph over the cruelties of white people. "We are the people of God," "We are de people of the Lord," "I really do believe I'm a child of God," "To the promised land I'm bound to go," and "Heaven shall-a be my home"—refrains like these ran through slave spirituals. On the other side of the coin, slave attitudes toward whites ranged from "You no holy. We be holy" to "No white people went to heaven."[16]

When describing relations with masters and other whites, slave tales outlined a social system based on trickery as a means of self-protection. For instance, inadequate food was a constant problem for slaves. Slaves believed that taking food from the master was not stealing because the master owned the slave and the food consumed by that slave remained in the ownership of the master. On the other hand, taking something from a fellow slave was considered theft, an act "just as mean as white folks."[17]

Typical of stories involving the taking of forbidden food is the tale of Henry Johnson, who lured a turkey into his cabin and killed it. He immediately ran crying to his mistress that one of her turkeys unexpectedly died. She told him to stop crying and get rid of the possibly diseased bird. That night Henry ate the turkey. In another story, an enslaved African ran to his master to tell him that all seven of his hogs had died. When the master appeared at the scene, a group of African slaves informed him with sorrow that the hogs had died of "malitis" and that they were afraid to touch the meat. Reacting with fear for his own health at the word "malitis," the master ordered them to eat the dead hogs. "Malitis" is a word they made up for the "disease" that resulted from a slave hitting each hog in the head with a heavy mallet.

In another story, an African slave took some chickens and began cooking them in his cabin. The master entered the cabin and the slave informed him that he was cooking a possum. The master decided to wait and share the possum. Fearing that the master would discover the chickens, the slave told him that it would take a long time to cook because slaves make their possum gravy by having the family spit in it. In disgust, the master left and the slaves ate the chickens.[18]

Emancipation required an adaptation of slave culture to a world where freedom was tempered by racism. The racism that had justified slavery now became a justification for marginalization and segregation of African Americans. Toni Morrison captures the new world faced by the freed slave in a description of a small statue on a shelf in a white home in late-nineteenth-century Ohio. Denver, a main character in Morrison's novel *Beloved,* notices, as she leaves through the back door of a white family's house after asking for work, the statue of a black boy kneeling with his head thrown back as far as it could go and his gaping mouth full of coins to be used for paying for deliveries and other services. "Painted across the pedestal he knelt on were the words 'At Yo Service'."[19]

Once freed, former African slaves rushed to the schoolhouse. As W.E.B. DuBois wrote, "Public education for all at public expense was, in the South, a Negro idea."[20] Throughout the South, during and after the Civil War, former slaves took the initiative to engage in some form of self-education. Missionary teachers from the North assisted. Former African slaves realized that literacy was necessary for economic and political adjustment to freedom. The history of black education is one of constant struggles against the forces of segregation and lack of support from the majority of the white community. State and local governments controlled by whites were very reticent about giving much money for the support of black schools.

Between 1910 and 1930—the period James Anderson calls the second crusade for black education in the South—segregated schools were paid for by a combination of personal donations of time and money by black citizens, donations by private foundations, and some government money. What is important to note about the second crusade is that black southern citizens paid directly from their own pockets to build schools for their children, while, at the same time, they paid local and state taxes that went primarily to support white segregated schools.[21]

These educational efforts resulted in a dramatic decline in illiteracy. This is one of the important educational stories of the nineteenth and twentieth centuries. At the end of slavery, only 7 percent of the adult black population was literate. By 1950, schooling had raised that literacy rate to an amazing 90 percent.[22]

However, this impressive educational effort conflicted with the African American culture created during slavery. Public schools primarily taught from the perspective of European American culture and language. Emerging from slavery, black culture was a combination of African traditions and adjustments to slavery. Interaction with the dominant culture required a form of biculturalism, where former slaves could move between the worlds of black and white cultures.

Learning the language of the school created a situation of bidialecticalism, where former slaves moved between the speech patterns of black dialect used outside school and "standard" English used in school. The black dialect of slavery was a combination of African languages and the English learned in slavery. Writing about the grammar of black dialect, anthropologist Alma Gottlieb states "[it] can be traced to regular grammatical features in the Niger-Congo languages of West and Central Africa, the mother tongues of African slaves brought to the Western World."[23]

As schooling provided the road to literacy, black culture continued to evolve in the twentieth century under the continued pressure of racism. The music traditions of Africa and slavery produced jazz, blues, rock and roll, and gospel songs. DuBois's recognition in the early twentieth century of the importance of African American music was proved correct as popular music worldwide became and continues to be largely modeled on these traditions. As the United States exported its popular music to the rest of the world, it also exported African American culture. And, in a cultural twist in history, African American jazz influenced the popular music of Africa.

From the oral traditions of slavery emerged the African American literary traditions of the twentieth century, both of which were shaped by a continuing state of oppression. The writings of Langston Hughes, Richard Wright, James Baldwin, and Toni Morrison, to name but a few great authors in the African American tradition, all touched in some way on how black culture is shaped by the race line. The work of contemporary playwrights such as August Wilson and Eugene Lee focuses on the development of modern-day black culture in a racist society. While writing this chapter, I attended a performance of Eugene Lee's *East Texas Hot Links* at the Public Theater in New York City. Set in a "colored" bar in east Texas in the 1950s, the play portrays the betrayal of a black community by an African American who aids the local Klan in the killing of young black men. Reflecting the merging of traditional racism with modern developments, a young black man's hand is found sticking out of newly poured concrete on one of the first interstate highways in Texas. The storytelling and humor in the play reflect a cultural tradition shaped by distrust and anger toward the white population.

While African American humor during slavery often focused on master-slave relations, black humor in the twentieth century often reflects problems of racism and civil rights.[24] For instance, in one popular joke, two black men in

Mississippi are hit by a convertible being driven at a high speed by a white man. One black man bounces up in the air and lands in the back seat of the convertible while the other man lands quite a distance up the highway. The police let the white man go free but arrest one black man for illegal entry into a car and the other for leaving the scene of an accident. In another joke by African American humorist Moms Mabley, a southern sheriff assures a black prisoner, "I'm gonna get you a good lawyer and see that you get a fair trial. And then I'm gonna hang you."[25] Mabley also tells this joke: After walking into a fancy restaurant where white patrons stare at her, she assures them, "I don't want to go to school with you. I just want a piece of cheesecake."[26]

Shaped by slavery and the forces of racism, the culture of African Americans reflects, as Lawrence Levine states, "a deep ambivalence concerning the degree to which they desired to enter the mainstream of white American culture."[27] This ambivalence is present in attitudes toward public schools. On the one hand, schools are seen as a source of the knowledge needed to protect political and civil rights and as a means of economic mobility. On the other hand, public schools are sites of discrimination, segregation, and denial of equal educational opportunity. In addition, schools primarily teach from the perspective of "white American culture," which contains the seeds of racism that justified slavery and segregation.

ETHNOCENTRIC EDUCATION: DOMINATED CULTURES

The African American history exemplifies the problems in choosing the cultural orientation of schooling. I am defining *ethnocentric education* as an education that reflects one cultural perspective. This definition includes the teaching of the culture of the power elite. It also includes schools that reflect the cultural perspective of dominated groups. For instance, Afrocentric is a popular form of ethnocentric education. In the 1990s, public school districts in Miami, Baltimore, Detroit, Milwaukee, and New York City created or considered plans for Afrocentric schools.[28] Advocates of Afrocentric education argue that they can improve a student's sense of self-worth, help students relate to the curriculum, and help students understand the causes of cultural domination.

An important concept in the argument for ethnocentric schools is cultural perspective. For instance, because African American culture evolved in the context of slavery and later forms of segregation and racism, there developed a distrust and suspicion toward white Anglo-Saxon Protestant tradition. Consequently, the Afrocentrist turns to other traditions. As one of the leading Afrocentrists, Molefi Asante argues, "Afrocentrism directs us to . . . meditate on the power of our ancestors. . . . Afrocentricity is the belief in the centrality of Africans in postmodern history."

By meditating on the "power of our ancestors," the focus of history shifts. For instance, U.S. history taught from the perspective of the white Anglo-Saxon Protestant tradition usually begins with Columbus "discovering the New World" and quickly moves to a discussion of English settlement of North America and the evolution of European American culture and institutions. Slavery and African American culture are discussed in the context of European American history.

Taught from an Afrocentric perspective, the story begins in Africa, continues with the landing of the first Africans in Jamestown, and focuses on the evolution of African American culture and institutions. European American culture and institutions are discussed in the context of their impact on African Americans. For instance, colonial history might focus on the transition of Africans during colonial times from indentured servitude to slavery, and the contribution of Protestant thought and English culture to the creation of the status of slavery. Or, consider the history of North America from the perspective of Native Americans. Obviously, the story begins many centuries before the appearance of Europeans on the continent. When Europeans enter the scene, they are viewed as the outsiders and, eventually, invaders. From the sixteenth to the twentieth centuries, the story is of constant attempts to resist the unrelenting greed of Europeans for land and the horrors of the constant atrocities of Europeans against Indians. Native American participation in the civil rights movement was an attempt to win back lost rights and traditions within the framework of the political process established by Europeans.

The impact of the Native American perspective is captured by Dee Brown in *Bury My Heart at Wounded Knee: An Indian History of the American West*. Consider the meaning, from a Native American perspective, of General Philip Sheridan's statement in 1868, when a surrendered Comanche Tosawi said in broken English, "Tosawi, good Indian." Dee Brown writes, "It was then that General Sheridan uttered the immortal words: 'The only good Indians I ever saw were dead' . . . in time they [the words] were honed into an American aphorism: 'The only good Indian is a dead Indian.'"[29]

Therefore, teaching from an Afrocentric, Native American–centered, Mexican American–centered, Hawaiian-centered, or Puerto Rican–centered perspective creates a different view of the world as compared to teaching from the perspective of the power elite. In fact, according to Asante, moving away from a white Anglo-Saxon Protestant-centered curriculum will completely change a student's view of the world. Asante writes, "A new consciousness invades our behavior and consequently with Afrocentricity you see the movies differently, you see other people differently, you read books differently, you see politicians differently; in fact, nothing is as it was before your consciousness."[30]

Supporting ethnocentric education, Jawanza Kunjufu argues that the inherent racism of white-dominated institutions hinders the education of African Americans. In his words, "We must develop programs and organizations to protect and develop African American boys because a conspiracy exists to destroy African American boys. The motive of the conspiracy is racism, specifically European American male supremacy."[31] He proposes an educational program that will prepare African American boys to understand their oppression. An important part of his proposal is to present strong African American male role models to young black boys so that they can break through the conspiracy.

DEBATING EDUCATION BASED
ON DOMINATED CULTURES

Ethnocentric education centered on dominated cultures has generated a great deal of controversy. Some members of dominated communities object because they believe schools should prepare students for economic success in the dominant culture. Similar to the split between progressives and traditionalists in Native American communities, the debate often pits those seeking economic success in the national economy against those seeking to maintain a separate lifestyle.

However, there are gradations of opinion between the two extremes of teaching only the culture of the power elite or only the culture of the dominated group. Some argue that schools should teach both the culture of the power elite and that of the dominated culture so that students will be able to function in both communities. Others argue that schools should utilize the culture of dominated groups in teaching methods and in the curriculum to build self-esteem and positive attitudes toward schooling. In this case, teaching dominated cultures serves as a transition to learning the culture of the power elite. The following represents the range of opinion in the debate over education based on the cultures of dominated groups:

- All schools should teach the culture of the power elite to ensure the future economic success of students.
- All schools should teach the cultural values embedded in established U.S. institutions, such as the Constitution, government, and the dominant economic system, because these cultural values are superior to other cultural values.
- Schools serving children of dominated groups should incorporate their cultural values in the curriculum and instructional methods as a means of building self-esteem and positive attitudes toward schooling. Building self-esteem and positive attitudes toward schooling are essential for success in schooling and in the economy.
- Schools should educate students to be bicultural.
- Schools serving dominated groups should reflect their cultures for the purpose of providing an alternative to the dominant culture of the United States. For instance, some people believe Native American culture can contribute more to human happiness than the culture of the power elite.

It is important to emphasize that the above viewpoints regarding the education of dominated groups reflects divisions *within dominated groups and in the general population.* For instance, there are no available figures on the actual number of African Americans supporting Afrocentric education or assimilation into the culture of the power elite. However, given the economic imperatives of U.S. society, I would speculate that a large percentage of the African American community wants their children to be educated for economic success. It is difficult to determine how many want schools to utilize African American culture in educating children or to teach from an Afrocentric perspective.

LESSON 2.4

Dominated Cultures in Classroom Instruction

Grades: High School through College

Objective:
To understand the issues regarding the role of dominated cultures in classroom instruction.

Lesson:

1. Divide the class into five groups.
2. Each group should be assigned one of the following arguments regarding the culture of classroom instruction:
   a. All schools should teach the culture of the power elite to ensure the future economic success of students.
   b. All schools should teach the cultural values embedded in established U.S. institutions, such as the Constitution, government, and the dominant economic system.
   c. Schools serving children of dominated groups should incorporate their cultural values in the curriculum and instructional methods as a means of building self-esteem and positive attitudes toward schooling.
   d. Schools should educate students to be bicultural.
   e. Schools serving dominated groups should reflect the cultures of these groups for the purpose of providing an alternative to the dominant culture of the United States.
3. Each group should prepare a defense of the assigned position on cultural instruction.
4. Each group should present its arguments to the class.
5. Each group should defend its arguments by responding to the arguments presented by the other groups.

Teachers: There is no objectively correct answer to this debate. The role of the teacher should be to help students understand the arguments supporting each position in this debate.

Outcome: Students should gain an understanding of the arguments regarding the cultural content of classroom instruction.

TEACHING HAWAIIAN CULTURE: ALTERNATIVE OR TRANSITION TO ECONOMIC SUCCESS

Breaking sharply with past efforts to eradicate Hawaiian culture and history, the 1978 Hawaiian state constitution mandates:

> The State shall promote the study of Hawaiian culture, history and language.
> The State shall provide for a Hawaiian education program consisting of language, culture and history in the public schools.
> The use of community expertise shall be encouraged as a suitable and essential means in furtherance of the Hawaiian education program.[32]

These constitutional provisions represent an attitude quite different from the one I experienced attending junior and senior high schools in Honolulu in the early 1950s. In my classes, teachers never referred to Hawaiian culture or language. Public school teachers and administrators acted as if Hawaiian culture and language had disappeared with the only remnants being used in hula dances to greet tourists.

The schools I attended in Honolulu were segregated according to standard and nonstandard usage of the English language. In effect, language segregation meant racial segregation. Since I arrived from the mainland speaking what was considered standard English, I was placed in an English Standard School rather than in "regular public schools." Glancing over photographs in my junior high school annual, the majority of students appeared to have been Japanese Americans followed in numbers by haoles (Hawaiian term often used to identify whites). I had difficulty finding any native Hawaiians among the grinning faces. At that age, I was oblivious to issues of language and racial segregation. The only sense of inequality I had was the frequently repeated rumor among fellow students that pupils could go barefoot to regular schools while shoes were required at English Standard School.

Similar to language development among African slaves, native Hawaiians and contract workers from Asia developed their own language called Hawaiian, Creole, English, or HCE. Often referred to as pidgin English, those speaking HCE attended regular schools.[33] The transition to all standard English schools and the end of segregation began in 1949 when public schools were ordered to begin changing requirements to meet those of English Standard Schools. This transitional period was still occurring in 1953 when I had to travel past several "regular" junior high schools on my way from Waikiki to the English Standard Robert Louis Stevenson Junior High School.

However, the transition to all standard English schools assumed that the school curriculum would continue to ignore Hawaiian culture and languages. As Maenette K. P. Benham and Ronald H. Heck detail in their brilliant study of Hawaiian educational policy, *Culture and Education Policy in Hawaii: The Silencing of Native Voices,* after the arrival of American missionary educators in the 1820s, school policies focused on replacing native culture and religion with white culture and Christianity. Specific policies regarding English only in schools were put into place after the overthrow of the Hawaiian monarchy in the 1890s. In 1893, under the leadership of pineapple and sugar baron Sanford

Dole, U.S. residents in Hawaii declared the end of the Hawaiian monarchy and the creation of a provisional government. Queen Lili'uokalani refused to recognize the provisional government and temporarily abdicated her rule to the U.S. government. She requested that the U.S. government investigate the provisional government. President Grover Cleveland declared the provisional government illegal and refused to annex Hawaii to the United States. Reacting to this decision, Dole and his supporters declared the formal creation of the Republic of Hawaii in 1894. Similar to the creation of the Republic of Texas in the 1840s and its eventual annexation to the United States, the Republic of Hawaii set the stage for takeover by the U.S. government.

Under the Republic of Hawaii, the goal of educating native Hawaiians continued to be centered on destroying traditional culture and languages and all ties to the monarchy. In 1896, the new government of the Republic of Hawaii declared the following:

> The English language shall be the medium and basis of instruction at all public and private schools. . . . Any schools that shall not conform to the provisions of this Section shall not be recognized by the Department [of Public Instruction].[34]

After annexation to the United States in 1898, public schooling continued to be focused on assimilation of native Hawaiians to the dominant culture of the United States. However, unlike early Christian missionaries who focused on the destruction of native culture, the issue was now confused by the development of a new culture resulting from contact with Europeans, whites from the United States, and Asians. Similar to the experience of Native Americans and Africans, the intersection of cultures had fundamentally changed native culture and created a new culture. Was Hawaiian culture to be considered the culture that existed prior to contact with Europeans? Or, was Hawaiian culture now the product of cultural changes?

This new culture was branded as inferior by school administrators, which resulted in the previously discussed segregation into English Standard Schools and "regular" public schools. This attitude was reflected in the official annual report of Superintendent W. E. Givens in 1924. Givens wrote as follows:

> Most of the children come from non-English speaking homes. The first so-called English that they hear is the "pidgin" English of the cane fields, the ranches and the street, frequently mixed with profanity. This jargon is used when conversing with their playmates and improper speech habits are formed before the children attend school. Once these habits are formed the correction of them is not an easy problem.[35]

Therefore, by the time the 1978 Hawaiian state constitution required schools to promote the study of Hawaiian culture, history, and language a great deal of traditional culture had been destroyed and a new culture and language had evolved. And, similar to Native Americans, some native Hawaiians were completely assimilated to haole culture and spoke standard English. Also, prior to the provisions of the 1978 state constitution, the U.S. government recognized Hawaiian Creole English as a language that qualified for funds set aside for bilingual education.[36]

Fortunately for promoters of instruction in traditional Hawaiian language, there existed a privately owned island, Ni'ihau, where traditional culture and language had been preserved. Benham and Heck report that, in 1983, the Hawaiian Board of Education ordered the Ni'ihau school to use Hawaiian as the primary language of instruction with English taught as a second language. In addition, the Kamehameha Early Education Program (KEEP) tried to resolve the conflict between the culture of Hawaiian students and the culture of the school. In 1992, the Board of Education (Hawaii has a state educational system) approved a Hawaiian Language Immersion Program to Grade 12. By 1995, there were 11 Hawaiian immersion schools.[37]

Benham and Heck conclude their book, prior to the epilogue, with a 1991 poem by H. Apoliona. Translated from Hawaiian, the poem reads as follows:

Let us move forward into the future
Carrying with us the best from the past.
The dawn (the time) has arrived for the
Revitalizing and the reawakening of our community.[38]

Critics of educational programs centered on dominated cultures might argue that the teaching of Hawaiian culture and language is an unrealistic response to economic requirements. The focus, these critics might argue, should be on teaching English and the culture of the power elite. From this perspective, restoration of Hawaiian culture and language will just ensure the lower economic status of native Hawaiians. Others, such as supporters of the KEEP program, might argue that adaptation of instruction and curriculum to the culture of the home will increase the success of native Hawaiian students in school and, subsequently, in the economy.

On the other hand, Apoliona's poem suggests a blending of the past and the present by "Carrying with us the best from the past." This suggests that dominated cultures have something to contribute to the dominant culture of the United States. Similar to Native Americans, native Hawaiians have cultural differences with Europeans and haoles that extend beyond dress and manners. There exist fundamental differences in thinking about the world. Benham and Heck constructed a chart highlighting these cultural differences.[39] Produced here as Table 2–1, an excerpt from that chart provides a guide to understanding the profound clashes that can occur with the intersection of cultures.

Should and can these native Hawaiian values be blended with the dominant cultural values of the United States? Are native Hawaiian values superior in promoting human happiness in comparison to the dominant values of U.S. society? Will the teaching and promoting of native Hawaiian values reduce the economic success of students? These are the difficult questions confronting advocates of education based on the cultural values of dominated groups.

IS "WHITE TRASH" A DOMINATED CULTURE?

In *White Trash: Race and Class in America*, Matt Wray and Annalee Newitz argue that whiteness is often excluded from discussions of multiculturalism because it is treated as a norm and it lacks a victim status. As a norm it is used to judge

TABLE 2–1   Excerpts from a Comparison of Cultural Differences

Concept	Native Hawaiian Ways	Western Rational View
Intellect	Na'au: Thinking comes from the intestines; the "gut" links the heart and the mind. Thus, feelings and emotions are not separate from knowing, wisdom, and intelligence.	Separation of intellectual activity (cognitive domain) and emotion (affective domain). Thinking comes from the head/brain.
Relationship	When love is given, love should be returned. Because one is spiritually and physically connected to others, good relationships and reciprocity are highly valued. The connections between people must remain unbroken, harmonious, and correct.	Individuals are disconnected from each other. Because knowledge is seen more as a concrete set of ideas and skills that can be quantified, individual grasp of knowledge is highlighted. This creates a commodity quality to knowledge that leads to individual focused learning and being.
Knowledge	All learning must have aesthetic or practical use. Knowledge must link the spirit and the physical, and maintain relationships.	Knowledge for knowledge's sake has problematized Western education as the bridge between theory and practice has not been resolved.
Analysis	Kaona: This establishes a tolerance for ambiguity often viewed in the use of symbol and metaphor.	Concrete analysis and objectivity clearly explain subject matter.

Source: Excerpts from Maenette Benham and Ronald Heck, *Culture and Educational Policy in Hawaii: The Silencing of Native Voices* (Mahwah, NJ: Lawrence Erlbaum Associates, Inc., 1998), p. 33.

other cultures and, consequently, tends to maintain the assumed supremacy of whiteness. They write, "It has been the invisibility (for whites) of whiteness that has enabled white Americans to stand as unmarked, normative bodies and social selves, the standard against which all others are judged (and found wanting)."[40]

Also, they argue, the tendency is to include only "social victims" in multicultural studies. Often this means the victims of whites. This conceptualization of multiculturalism tends to create an image of all whites as racists and bigots. Consequently, multiculturalism becomes the study of the negative things whites have done to other cultures without any mention of whites who are antiracist and anticolonialist.

How can white culture be included in multicultural studies? First, one must make a distinction between the cultures of various European ethnic groups and the general concept of whiteness in U.S. society. For example, in *How the Irish Became White*, Noel Ignatiev describes the changing social status of the Irish.[41] When Irish immigrants arrived in the United States in the nineteenth century, they were discriminated against by other groups of European descent and placed by these white groups in the same social category as African Americans and Native Americans. The Irish were victims of white prejudice. Ignatiev argues that their change in social status depended on gaining power over African Americans and Native Americans and joining other whites engaged in racist activities.

Therefore, from this perspective, being white in U.S. society means holding a favorable racial position in the social hierarchy. But what about social class? It was suggested in Chapter 1 that the power elite had the privileged culture in the United States and that successful African Americans were often accused by other blacks of acting white. In this framework, the privileged white culture is the culture of the power elite.

In contrast, according to Wray and Newitz, "White trash becomes a term which names what seems unnameable: a race (white) which is used to code 'wealth' is coupled with an insult (trash) which means . . . economic waste. . . . White trash is thus one way people living in the U.S. try to describe class identities."[42]

Also, the term *white trash* highlights the tendency to associate wealth with whites and poverty with other groups, such as blacks. Some blacks are wealthy and some whites are poor. In fact, almost half (48.1 percent) of the poor in the United States are non-Hispanic whites. The overwhelming absolute number of poor in the United States are white. Poverty is being defined as the lowest 20 percent of family incomes.[43]

Does poverty mean that poor whites are a dominated culture? No, if being a dominated culture means being a conquered and colonized culture. Poor whites still exercise racial privilege.

On the other hand, a child from a poor white family trying to enter the power elite might face the same cultural problems as blacks or other dominated groups. Of course, poverty or membership in a dominated group doesn't mean that the family doesn't reflect the culture of the power elite. But, for many children from the poor white families, economic success might depend on learning the culture of the power elite or, as expressed earlier, the culture of the prep school. Language, manners, and ability to fit into any social situation might be important ingredients for the economic success of white children growing up in poverty.

EMPOWERMENT THROUGH MULTICULTURAL EDUCATION[44]

Leaders of the multicultural movement in the 1960s and 1980s, such as James Banks, Christine Sleeter, and Carl Grant, were concerned with empowering oppressed people by integrating the history and culture of dominated groups into public school curricula and textbooks. In general, they wanted to reduce prejudice, eliminate sexism, and equalize educational opportunities.[45]

Empowerment is concerned with ethnic studies and consciousness raising. Within this context, the term *empowerment* means providing the intellectual tools for creating a just society. Usually the concept of empowerment is contrasted with benevolent helping, such as welfare programs, family assistance, and other forms of aid. These programs, it is argued, keep people in a state of dependence. Empowerment gives people the ability to break out of these dependent states.[46]

Ethnic studies can empower dominated and oppressed immigrant cultures by creating an understanding of the methods of cultural domination and by helping to build self-esteem. For instance, the study of African American, Native American, Puerto Rican, Hawaiian American, and Mexican American history serves the dual purpose of building self-esteem and empowerment. In addition, the empowerment of women and people with disabilities involves, in part, the inclusion of their histories and stories in textbooks and curricula.

As one aspect of social empowerment, ethnic studies have influenced textbooks and classroom instruction in the United States. The ethnic studies movement resulted in the integration of content into the curriculum dealing with dominated and immigrant cultures, women, and people with disabilities. Multicultural educator James Banks worries that many school districts consider content integration as the primary goal of multicultural education. He states, "The widespread belief that content integration constitutes the whole of multicultural education might . . . [cause] many teachers of subjects such as mathematics and science to view multicultural education as an endeavor primarily for social studies and language arts teachers."[47]

The other part of social empowerment, consciousness raising, has two sources. "One source," Lee Bell writes regarding her work in empowering female elementary school students, "is the feminist consciousness-raising process of the early 1970s, a process by which individual women explored their experiences . . . through naming their problems and concerns collectively."[48] This form of consciousness raising provides insights into how institutional power relations and socialization can oppress people.

The second source of consciousness raising, as Bell points out, is the work of Paulo Freire. In the United States, his method of instruction is referred to as critical pedagogy. For Freire, critical pedagogy should result in individuals understanding the social, political, and economic factors shaping their consciousness and, consequently, their actions. With this heightened consciousness, the individual is able to participate in changing the course of human events. This participation will lead to a world, Freire argues, where there is political equality and a more even distribution of economic goods. Rather than being a passive actor on the world's stage, the socially empowered person becomes active in working for political and economic justice.[49]

The best example of multicultural education for empowerment is Sonia Nieto's *Affirming Diversity: The Sociopolitical Context of Multicultural Education.* Growing up as a Puerto Rican in New York City, Nieto felt the tension between the language and culture of her family and the language and culture of the school. The school made her feel that there was something deficient in her background. She states, "We learned to feel ashamed of who we were, how we spoke, what we ate, and everything else that was 'different' about us."[50] For Nieto, the goal of multicultural education should be to bridge the gap between the culture of the family and the culture of the school so that children of immigrant and dominated families do not have to suffer the pain and shame that she experienced. In her words, "Our society must move beyond causing and exploiting students' shame to using their cultural and linguistic differences to struggle for an education that is more in tune with society's rhetoric of equal and high-quality education for all students."[51]

Multiculturalism for social empowerment attempts to maintain cultural identity and, at the same time, promotes values of social justice and social action. In her book, Nieto presents a chart displaying the seven characteristics of this form of multicultural education.[52] The first characteristic is that the school curriculum is openly antiracist and antidiscriminitory. An atmosphere is created where students feel safe about discussing sexism, racism, and discrimination. In addition, the curriculum includes the history and cultural perspectives of a broad range of people. Students are to be taught to identify and challenge racism in society.

The second characteristic is that multicultural education is considered a basic part of a student's general education, which means that all students become bilingual and all students study different cultural perspectives. Linked to this second characteristic is the argument that multiculturalism should pervade the curriculum. This third characteristic results in multiculturalism being included in all aspects of the curriculum and in the general life of the school, including bulletin boards, lunchrooms, and assemblies. In addition, the fourth characteristic is that multicultural education is important for all students.

The last three characteristics emphasize the social empowerment aspects of multicultural education. The fifth characteristic is social justice. Nieto argues that schools should recognize their potential for bringing about social change and that students should be engaged in community activities. An emphasis on social justice is important as a means of preparing students to overcome racism and discrimination against various cultures. As part of the quest for social justice, the sixth characteristic emphasizes the process of learning, particularly the asking of the questions why, how, and what if. Obviously, when these questions are asked regarding issues of social injustice they can in turn lead to a questioning of the very foundations of political and economic institutions. This makes multicultural education a combination of content and "process".

The last characteristic reflects the direct influence of Paulo Freire. Multicultural education, Nieto states, should include critical pedagogy. Critical pedagogy becomes the primary method of instruction. With critical pedagogy, in Nieto's words, "students and teachers are involved in a 'subversive activity.' Decision making and social action skills are the basis of the curriculum."[53]

In the framework of this approach to multicultural education, critical pedagogy helps students to understand the extent to which cultures can differ. In addition, these differences are to be affirmed and given equal treatment. Also, critical pedagogy will help students to understand cultural domination and how they can end it.

Missing from multicultural education for social empowerment is an analysis of the intersection of different cultures. It is assumed that an understanding of oppression and discrimination will provide a common theme in critical pedagogy that will prepare all students to struggle for social justice. But there are important and deep differences in values between cultures. Does social justice mean giving a person an opportunity to achieve within the framework of English or Native American values? Or, does it mean creating a whole new set of values for the world?

EDUCATING FOR CULTURAL POWER

Lisa Delpit is more interested in directly instructing children of dominated cultures in the culture of power. She believes that advocates of social empowerment often fail to reveal to children the requirements for economic advancement. She does not reject the importance of critical thinking, but she does think children should be directly told about the standards for acceptable speech and behavior for social mobility.

Working at the University of Alaska, she criticized what she called "liberal" educators for primarily focusing on native culture while instructing native Alaskans. These liberal educators, she claimed, were damaging students by not preparing them for success in the broader society. She was also critical of traditional instructors for ignoring native traditions. From her perspective, traditional culture needed to be considered when preparing students to achieve in the real world.

Delpit encountered the same issues when working with teachers of black children in Philadelphia schools. White teachers often thought they knew what was best for black students. Usually this meant some form of progressive instruction designed to enhance critical thinking and imagination. While not denying the importance of these goals, Delpit found white teachers neglecting the instruction of black students in standard English. One complaining black parent told her, "My kids know how to be black—you all teach them how to be successful in the white man's world."[54] Several black teachers suggested to Delpit that the "'progressive' educational strategies imposed by liberals upon black and poor children could only be based on a desire to ensure that the liberals' children get sole access to the dwindling pool of American jobs."[55]

There are five important aspects, according to Delpit, to preparing dominated children for access to power:[56]

1. "Issues of power are enacted in classrooms." It is important to examine, Delpit argues, the power of teachers and government over students, textbook publishers, and curriculum developers. This examination can be considered preparation for understanding the exercise of power in the world of work.
2. "There are codes or rules for participating in power; that is, there is a 'culture of power.'" In the classroom, this means direct instruction in linguistic forms and presentation of self, including ways of talking, writing, dressing, and interacting.
3. "The rules of the culture of power are a reflection of the rules of the culture of those who have power." For Delpit, the culture of the school is the culture of the middle and upper classes. Therefore, it is important for children from dominated groups to participate and learn school culture.
4. "If you are not already a participant in the culture of power, being told explicitly the rules of that culture makes acquiring power easier."

Museum of the American Empire

Note: This lesson is based on the 2002 opening of the British Empire and Commonwealth Museum. This museum includes photos, artifacts, and representations of the cultural impact of the British empire on England and their colonies.

Grades: Middle School through College

Objective:
To understand the impact of the American empire on American culture.

Lesson:

1. Divide the class into groups of four or five.
2. Have each group design a museum collection that represents the following aspects of the American empire:
   a. Conquest and appropriation of Native American lands.
   b. Louisiana Purchase.
   c. Annexation of Texas from Mexico.
   d. Conquest of Mexican lands now known as Arizona, Colorado, New Mexico, Nevada, and California.
   e. Purchase of Alaska.
   f. Conquest of Puerto Rico.
   g. Conquest of the Philippines.
   h. Annexation of Hawaii.
3. Ask groups to design one section of the museum to reflect the current impact of the American empire on American culture.

Teachers: Teachers should play an active role in helping each group think about materials that could be included in the museum collection. Of course, the sophistication of the museum collection will depend on the grade level of the students.

Outcome: Students should gain an understanding of how American imperialism has impacted American culture.

5. "Those with power are frequently least aware of—or least willing to acknowledge—its existence. Those with less power are often most aware of its existence." From Delpit's perspective, white liberal educators are uncomfortable admitting they are part of the culture of power. On the other hand, students from dominated groups are aware of white power and they would like the parameters of power clearly stated.

CONCLUSION

Dominated groups, as Lisa Delpit suggests, are caught in a cultural bind. Economic success in U.S. society may depend on assimilation to the culture of the power elite at the expense of traditional culture. Should schools focus on the cultural imperatives of the economic system? Or, should schools maintain traditional cultures?

Whatever the answers to the above questions, dominated cultures will continue to resent their history of victimization by colonialism, conquest, enslavement, and racism. Consequently, some members of these groups are, understandably, angry toward the dominant culture of U.S. society. These feelings can contribute to student resistance and resentment to the actions of public schools. Sometimes, this resentment creates an antischool culture that contributes to school failure and dropping out. For instance, a Native American student might ask, Why should I try to achieve in a white man's school when whites are responsible for killing my people and taking away our land? How should public schools deal with this anger and resentment?

PERSONAL FRAMES OF REFERENCE

In a broad perspective, your beliefs regarding multicultural education reflect your general vision for the future of the world. You might want to consider the following questions in the context of your personal beliefs regarding global culture:

1. Do you want to receive an education that will empower you with the intellectual tools to change the world?
2. Do you believe that public schools should provide an education that will empower people with the intellectual tools to change the world?
3. Do you believe that the purpose of multicultural education should be empowerment or simply toleration?
4. Do you believe that ethnocentric forms of education will improve the conditions of dominated cultures in the United States?

Notes

1. See Grant Forman, *Sequoyah* (Norman: University of Oklahoma Press, 1938).
2. For a history of the evolution of Cherokee culture in the early nineteenth century see William G. McLoughlin, *Cherokee Renascence in the New Republic* (Princeton, NJ: Princeton University Press, 1986).

3. For a brief history of this conquest see Joel Spring, *Deculturalization and the Struggle for Equality: A Brief History of the Education of Dominated Cultures in the United States,* 4th ed. (Burr Ridge, IL: McGraw-Hill, 2004), pp. 1–34.

4. Kevin Brown, "Do African American Males Need Race and Gender Segregated Education?: An Educator's Perspective and a Legal Perspective," in *The New Politics of Race and Gender,* ed. Catherine Marshall (Washington, DC: Falmer Press, 1993), p. 111.

5. Quoted by Jawanza Kunjufu, *Countering the Conspiracy to Destroy Black Boys* (Chicago: African American Images, 1985), pp. 2–3.

6. Ibid., p. 3.

7. W.E.B. DuBois, *The Souls of Black Folk* (New York: Signet Classic, 1969), p. 45.

8. Ibid.

9. Ibid., pp. 45–46.

10. Ibid., p. 275.

11. Ibid., p. 276.

12. Sidney Mintz and Richard Price, *The Birth of African American Culture* (Boston: Beacon Press, 1976), p. 14.

13. Toni Morrison captures the full psychological impact of this system in her Pulitzer Prize–winning novel *Beloved* (New York: Penguin Books, 1988).

14. See James Anderson, *The Education of Blacks in the South, 1860–1935* (Chapel Hill: University of North Carolina Press, 1988), pp. 4–32.

15. Lawrence W. Levine, *Black Culture and Black Consciousness: Afro-American Folk Thought from Slavery to Freedom* (New York: Oxford University Press, 1977), p. 54.

16. Ibid., pp. 33–34.

17. Ibid., p. 125.

18. Ibid., pp. 81–135.

19. Morrison, p. 255.

20. Quoted by Anderson, *The Education of Blacks,* p. 6.

21. Spring, *Deculturalization,* pp. 35–59.

22. Levine, p. 156.

23. Alma Gottlieb, "Tenacious African Link," *The New York Times,* 19 January 1994, A20.

24. Levine in *Black Culture and Black Consciousness* devotes an important chapter (pp. 198–367) to African American humor in the twentieth century. *Certainly, humor is a key to understanding the attitudes of a culture.*

25. Ibid., p. 363.

26. Ibid., p. 365.

27. Ibid., p. 444.

28. Anthropologist John Ogbu found that a number of black youths believed that doing well in school required "acting white." See John U. Ogbu, *Minority Education and Caste: The American Cross-Cultural Perspective* (New York: Academic Press, 1978) and "Class Stratification, Racial Stratification, and Schooling," in *Class, Race, & Gender in American Education,* ed. Lois Weis (Albany: State University of New York Press, 1988), pp. 183–209. Also, Jawanza Kunjufu makes this argument in *To Be Popular and Smart: The Black Peer Group* (Chicago: African American Images, 1988).

29. Dee Brown, *Bury My Heart at Wounded Knee: An Indian History of the American West* (New York: Henry Holt, 1970), pp. 171–72.

30. Molefi Kete Asante, *Afrocentricity* (Trenton, NJ: Africa World Press, 1989), p. 7.

31. Kunjufu, *Countering the Conspiracy to Destroy Black Boys,* p. 32.

32. Maenette K. P. Benham and Ronald H. Heck, *Culture and Educational Policy in Hawaii: The Silencing of Native Voices* (Mahwah, NJ: Lawrence Erlbaum Associates, Inc., 1998), p. 198.
33. Ibid., p. 102.
34. Quoted in Ibid., p. 107.
35. Quoted in Ibid., p. 148.
36. Ibid., p. 197.
37. Ibid., p. 199.
38. Ibid., p. 210.
39. Ibid., p. 33.
40. Matt Wray and Annalee Newitz, *White Trash: Race and Class in America* (New York: Routledge, 1997), p. 3.
41. Noel Ignatiev, *How the Irish Became White* (New York: Routledge, 1995).
42. Ibid., p. 8.
43. Doug Henwood, "Trash-O-Nomics," in Wray and Newitz, pp. 177–193.
44. The title for this section is taken from Christine Sleeter's *Empowerment through Multicultural Education* (Albany: State University of New York Press, 1991).
45. See James Banks, "Multicultural Education: Historical Development, Dimensions, and Practice," *Review of Research in Education 19*, ed. Linda Darling-Hammond (Washington, DC: American Educational Research Association, 1993), pp. 3–50; and Sonia Nieto, *Affirming Diversity: The Sociopolitical Context of Multicultural Education* (White Plains, NY: Longman Inc., 1992).
46. Ibid., p. 5.
47. Ibid.
48. Lee Bell, "Changing Our Ideas About Ourselves: Group Consciousness Raising with Elementary School Girls as a Means to Empowerment," in Sleeter, p. 230.
49. For an analysis of Freire's ideas in the context of other educational philosophies see Joel Spring, *Wheels in the Head: Educational Philosophies of Authority, Freedom, and Culture from Socrates to Paulo Freire* (New York: McGraw-Hill, 1994).
50. Ibid., p. xxiv.
51. Ibid., pp. xxv–xxvi.
52. Ibid., pp. 280–81.
53. Ibid., p. 281.
54. Lisa Delpit, *Other People's Children: Cultural Conflict in the Classroom* (New York: The New Press, 1995), p. 29.
55. Ibid., p. 29.
56. Ibid., pp. 24–26.

CHAPTER 3

Immigrant Cultures

Imagine your parents announcing when you were 8 years old that the whole family was emigrating to a nation with a different culture and language. For a child, immigration can have serious psychological consequences resulting from a loss of familiar surroundings, culture, and friends. Envision your first day of school surrounded by teachers and students who do not speak English and being given textbooks written in a language you cannot read. How would you do on your first test? Would your classroom performance result in you being labeled learning disabled or a slow learner? Would you fall behind your fellow students in basic subjects, such as math and science, as you learn the language of your new country?

The psychological and social consequences of this scenario of emigration from the United States is described by Ann Kimmage in her autobiography, *An Un-American Childhood.*[1] Returning from school to their home in Queens, New York, on a warm spring day in 1950, Ann, who was 8 years old, found her mother hurriedly packing suitcases. Her mother said they were taking a little trip. Awakened later that night, Ann was hustled onto a train bound for Mexico City and, after hiding in a rural Mexican farmhouse, Ann's family arrived at their new home in Prague, Czechoslovakia. At the time, Czechoslovakia was ruled by a communist government and was considered a political enemy of the United States.

Ann's experience can be compared to that of children of political refugees to the United States. In this case, Ann's father was a high-ranking official of the U.S. Communist Party during a militant anticommunist period in U.S. history. Ann's life was being determined by the political beliefs of her parents. She did not ask to immigrate to Czechoslovakia. At age 8, she did not completely understand the political issues surrounding her family's immigration.

Ann's primary concern as a child was being accepted in her new homeland and not with her parents' politics. Similar to many other children, Ann did not like the feeling of being an object of attention for curious strangers. Describing her feelings during those first days on the streets of Prague, Ann wrote, "Pedestrians scrutinized my mother and me when we walked in the streets, straining to hear the English words we exchanged with each other. The stares made me wonder if something was wrong with the shape of my nose or the arrangement of my clothing. . . . I hoped that if my mother bought me one of the long salty rolls the other children were eating, the Prague pedestrians would not pay so much attention to me."[2] Consequently, Ann's major concern was fitting into her new culture.

Ann's first days at school were traumatic. She was scolded for not bringing cloth slippers. Her parents didn't know that students were required to wear cloth slippers at school in order to keep the floors clean. She was given a wooden desk with an inkwell filled with blue ink. On the classroom bulletin boards were unfamiliar portraits of Joseph Stalin, Klement Gottwald, the president of Czechoslovakia, and announcements and pictures of the communist youth group, the Young Pioneers. Lacking a knowledge of how to use a wooden pen and an inkwell, her papers were covered with large ink spots. She mechanically copied the incomprehensible Czech words the teacher wrote on the chalkboard. On the playground, other children pointed at her clothes and freckles. She tried to understand their words. "When I tried to get them to understand me," she wrote, "they laughed."[3]

Recognizing the difficulty of her situation, Ann decided her top priority was learning Czech. In her words, she worked at learning Czech like "a starved animal. . . . I knew that English was my past, but Czech had to become my present. English separated me from my classmates, but Czech would bring me closer to them."[4] Learning Czech was also key to learning the culture of her classmates. Fighting against the loneliness created by language and cultural differences, Ann embraced the customs and language of her new country.

Similar to the experiences of many immigrant children, Ann's quest for acceptance by her schoolmates resulted in gradual alienation from her parents. A cultural divide developed as Ann learned to talk, think, and act as a Czech citizen. After a while, Ann's interest in books written in English disappeared and was replaced by a voracious desire to consume Czech literature. Her father, Abe Chapman, was a scholar of American literature who hoped his daughter would share his love of Walt Whitman and other American poets. Dismayed by the changes in Ann's language and cultural style, her parents reduced her allowance every time she misused an English word or substituted a Czech word for an English one. Ann wrote, "My parents did not know how to preserve my interest and skill in using English for they could not compete with the importance of Czech in my daily life."[5]

The story of Ann's adjustment to the social and psychological problems associated with emigration did not end with her Czechoslovakian experience. When Ann was 15, her parents decided to pursue a new political ideal by emigrating to China. After leaving the familiar surroundings of the United States and learning to love Czech culture and language, Ann arrived by train in Beijing to find herself again the object of curiosity and lacking an understanding of the language and culture of her new country. However, the stay was brief and Ann did not have time to undergo another cultural adaptation. There is a wonderful photograph from this period of Ann sitting in a tree holding a white flag. The Chinese government had decided that grain production could be increased if all sparrows were killed. Like other attempts to manage the environment, this one was doomed to failure. While there were fewer sparrows eating grain, there were now more insects saved from the mouths of sparrows to destroy crops. Ann's job, along with that of other Chinese youth, was to sit in trees waving flags to keep sparrows flying until they died of exhaustion.

Ann Kimmage's experiences highlight some of the following problems facing immigrant children:

- Psychological stress of loss of familiar surroundings and friends.
- Psychological stress caused by being an outsider in a new culture.
- Psychological stress resulting from ridicule by other children because of language, dress, and other cultural differences.
- Desire to learn the language and culture of the new country so that the immigrant child will be accepted by other children.
- Increasing tension between parents and children as children embrace the language and culture of their new home and forget the language and culture of their homeland.

SUMMER CAMPS FOR CULTURAL SURVIVAL

Appalled by their children's rush to assimilate to American culture, many immigrant groups have established summer camps to teach traditional languages and culture. There are Hindu summer camps in New Hampshire and New York and Muslim and Jain Camps in California and Texas. Balu Advani, president of the Hindu Heritage Summer Camp in Rochester, New York, explained, "Most of the kids are children of affluent parents who are too busy working and don't have time to really educate their kids about Hinduism."[6]

In the 1990s a group of economically successful Sikhs from the Punjab region of northern India bought Camp Robin Hood, a former summer camp serving children of wealthy American families. The well-educated Sikh parents immigrated during the last 30 years and have been economically successful in business and in professional careers, such as medicine and engineering. The Sikh religion was founded by the mystic Nanak (1469–1539) who fused elements of Hinduism and Islam. Over the last 50 years, the Sikh community has been engaged in a political struggle with the Moslems in Pakistan and the Hindus in India.

Worried that their children were learning rap songs and the Ten Commandments, while failing to know Sikh scriptures, Sikh parents hope that Lohgrah Retreat, Camp Robin Hood's new name based on Sikh defense against Mughals at Fort Lohgrah in the 1600s, promotes Sikh culture and religion. The camp's website declares, "The battle here and now is against the armies of ignorance and hatred, and the lure of assimilation." Mandeep Singh Dhillon, 28, one of the camp's founders, told *New York Times* reporter Laurie Goodstein, "We have kids whose families have become so integrated that some of these kids have never had a Sikh friend before coming to camp. . . . These kids are American now. They're Americans who follow Sikhism. So we want to give them that exposure so they can understand their religion and be proud of their heritage."[7]

The Public School Diversity Parade

Grades: High School through College

Objective:
To help students understand the complexity of the multicultural issues facing schools and the issues between cultural groups.

Lesson:
Ask students to imagine that they are school administrators in charge of the Public School Diversity Parade. The school board has asked them to conduct a meeting to deal with the following controversy. They are to prepare for the meeting by researching the history and the economic and cultural concerns of low-income whites, Mexican Americans, Native Americans, Puerto Ricans, Chinese Americans, and Korean Americans. Their job as school administrator depends on how well they handle this meeting. The school board is watching them. Will they cancel the diversity parade or will they save it? What will they recommend?

Each student should write recommendations to the school board.

Controversy Surrounding Diversity Parade

Beth Sue charged out of the trailer ready to kill. It was the third day in a row the clanging and pounding across the street from the trailer park had awakened her from a badly needed sleep. Her two back-to-back, 8-hour, minimum-wage jobs left her with little time to keep her life together, let alone sleep. Only a few days of sickness kept her from work the previous year and she was able to earn the grand total of $20,800. But she was able to manage with the low-rent, one-bedroom trailer and some free food from the local church. Her major worry was getting sick or medical costs for her daughters.

It took her an hour by bus to get to the first job washing dishes. Fortunately, the second job at the laundry was only a block away from the first. Still it meant 18 hours for work and travel. With the remaining 6 hours she had to worry about her 8- and 10-year-old daughters, Carla May and Ann Carol. At least, she had trained them to do the shopping, cooking, and cleaning. Her husband had died in a drunken car crash after going on a spree when he was laid off. She didn't blame him. He had tried. But no matter how hard he worked, his jobs never lasted.

She came to an abrupt stop at the gate of the trailer park. Across the street in an empty lot several groups of what appeared to her as foreign-looking men and women were working away at strange-looking structures.

What them Asians doin' here? she wondered. Walking over to a group working on a tall construction of a man, she asked, "What you doin' waking

(continued)

everyone up? This is a peaceful place. Why don't you go back to where you belong?" Debbie Chang, a pleasant-looking woman, smiled and answered, "We're making a figure of Confucius for the Public School Diversity Parade."

"I don't care what you build. I need sleep. What's those others doin'? You all look kind'a funny to me. Are you Americans?"

Debbie, who had been active in the Asian American rights movement, had had many encounters with people like Beth Sue. She knew and understood the anger of the white working poor. Pointing at a group constructing a flatbed float, Debbie calmly said, "That's the Mexican American group, La Raza, over there building a float for Aztec dances. Over there," she pointed to a group at the far end of the lot, "Park Lee and his group are building a float to celebrate the end of Japanese oppression in Korea. Though they may have some problems because some Japanese corporations found out what they were planning and they are threatening to withdraw funding from the parade."

"That looks un-American," Beth Sue said gesturing at a painted banner hanging on the lot's fence. The banner read, "INDEPENDENCE FROM U.S. TYRANNY NOW!"

"Well," Debbie admitted, "that's created some problems. You'll notice on the back fence is a banner reading, "STATEHOOD NOW! The Puerto Rican group got into a fight over their diversity banner. They've split into two groups."

"They should go back to their island. They're just livin' off hard-working white people like me," Beth Sue complained.

"Well, things aren't that simple," Debbie tried to explain. "Puerto Rico is part of the U.S."

Suddenly, Beth Sue let out a blood-curdling scream. A man was hanging from a tree by a rope that was attached to a length of wood that pierced the skin of his chest. Drops of blood splattered on the ground.

"That's the American Indian Movement doing the Sun Dance. It is pretty gruesome," Debbie admitted. "But it is their religion."

"Religion," said Beth Sue. "That's pagan. That's Satan for sure. I gotta tell Pastor Ben. This is goin' to send us all to hell. And they're doin' it right next to my trailer. It's goin' put a curse on us all."

Pastor Ben suddenly appeared and fell down on his knees. His church was only a few blocks from the lot. And he had heard about the Aztec dances and Sun ritual. "Holy Jesus save us from these idolaters. Satan is after our souls."

Pastor Ben stood up brushing the dirt off his knees. "I want you to know that me and the other God-fearing men and women of this town are going to stop this parade. No Satan is goin' march through the streets of our town."

"Where's the float for us whites?" Beth Sue asked looking around the lot. "Ain't we part of America?"

Debbie blushed. She hadn't thought of whites as part of diversity. "Well, I guess it's because you're the majority. This parade's for you. To educate your people," she replied.

"You mean no one needs to learn about us?" Beth Sue was surprised by her own question. She had never thought about it that way. "What about those Koreans? What do they know about me?"

That evening a large group attended the school board meeting. Beth Sue had taken off from her dishwashing job when she heard that her daughters' teachers wanted them to dress up like Islamic women for the parade. Since there weren't any Moslems living in the community, the teachers decided to recruit some boys and girls of European descent. Also present were members of La Raza and the American Indian Movement, and of the Chinese American, Korean American, and Puerto Rican communities. Pastor Ben and other Christian leaders were present. In the back sat members of the public relations departments of the two Japanese firms located in the community. School board members were nervous because the Japanese corporations were a major source of school funding.

Teachers: This is a complex assignment requiring a careful understanding of intercultural history and relationships. The teacher should spend some time explaining the decision-making process in school districts.

Outcome: Students should learn the complexity of multicultural issues facing school districts.

At the 60-acre summer camp, the day begins with morning prayers followed by lessons in chanting and Sikh spiritualism. *Times* reporter Goodstein observed two evenings of a group discussion on the topic "Why am I a Sikh?" Time is also spent learning traditional dances and Sikh history.

Similar to Ann Kimmage's concern about being an object of curiosity and ridicule, Sikh boys worry about religious dress codes, particularly the requirement of long hair and the wearing of a turban. The tenth guru of the Sikh religion requires males to wear five symbols: uncut hair, a comb, a steel wrist bangle, a sword, and short breeches under their pants. These requirements can cause difficulties in modern U.S. society, particularly trying to pass through airport security with a sword.

Riding in a New York City taxi with a turbaned Sikh driver who happily gave me literature on the Sikh religion, I asked, "Are you wearing a sword?"

"Yes," the driver replied, "I have a small sword inside my clothing."

Amazed, I stared at the gleaming modern skyscrapers along Fifth Avenue while reflecting on the cultural contrast between my Native American heritage and my driver's sword, turbaned hair, and, I assumed, short breeches under his pants.

However, wearing turbans and long hair does not allow Sikh boys to blend into the culture of their peers. The camp tries to maintain this tradition by holding turban-tying contests. Inder Paul Singh, an 18-year-old student at the College of William and Mary, states that in his early teens other kids teased him about his long hair worn in a bun on top of his head and covered by a knotted scarf. Frequently, Sikh boys complain about being called "rag head" and having their turbans pulled off. Many of the boys attending the Lohgrah Retreat refuse to wear long hair and turbans.

A feeling of cultural alienation from their parents pervades the attitudes of Sikh youth. Singh said, "A lot of the guys had questions about our identity, about whether we want to be Sikhs, why we have to keep our hair and tie turbans, because we are so different from everybody else."[8] The most poignant indication of the cultural gap between generations came from a boy who said he felt like an actor in a play written by his parents.

The opposite situation of parents' complaints about loss of cultural traditions are Sikh children in search of their cultural roots. Mandeep Singh Mundi, 17, complained that his parents, successful businesspeople living in Johnson City, Tennessee, refused to let him grow his hair and wear a turban because they wanted to blend into the local community. Rebelling against their strictures, Mundi lied to his parents that he was attending college registration and drove to the Lohgrah Retreat. "This camp has really changed my life," Mandeep said. "It turned me from the person my parents wanted me to be, this assimilated American guy, into someone who's proud of his culture."[9] Mandeep announced that he intended to grow his hair while attending college.

The experience of Sikh parents and children raises a number of complicated and conflicting issues regarding the schools' response to cultural differences. Consider the following questions:

• Should schools help immigrant students assimilate to U.S. culture by ignoring cultural differences? (Remember that some immigrant students do not want their cultural differences highlighted because they simply want to blend into the world of their classmates.)

- Or, should schools help immigrant students gain acceptance by their classmates by teaching about cultural differences? (A boy wearing a turban might gain greater acceptance if his peers understood the religious reasons behind the practice.)
- Should schools help to maintain the culture and religion of immigrant groups? (There is a difference between maintenance and transition. *Maintenance* of culture is exemplified by Mandeep Singh Mundi who wants to retain Sikh cultural practices. *Transition* refers to recognition of immigrant cultures as a step in assimilation.)

SHOOTING AT A CONVENIENCE STORE

Stepping into his car on a November night in 1994, after buying milk at a convenience store in the inner city of Windigo, Michigan, Cha Shou C., a Hmong immigrant, was hit in his upper hip by a stray bullet from a street shooting. After surviving war in Laos that killed one-third of the Hmong population and living in a refugee camp in Thailand, Cha now experienced the trauma of inner-city life in the United States. Cha's story of tragedy and achievement is told by Donald Hones and Cha Shou in the well-written and fascinating study of immigrant lives, *Educating New Americans: Immigrant Lives and Learning.*[10]

Cha Shou's immigrant experience is in sharp contrast to the well-educated Sikhs who have been successful in business and professional careers. The Hmong people lack a written language and the majority of immigrants to the United States were illiterate. Their history is characterized by continuing oppression by other nationalities. In the nineteenth and twentieth centuries, the Hmong fled discrimination and oppression in China and settled into a peasant life in the mountain regions in Laos, where they were subjected to humiliating treatment by Laotian authorities. Historian Meyer Weinberg reports that in the company of Laotian officials they "were not permitted to stand . . . and if they approached an official they had to literally crawl, head down, and wait patiently until he [the official] recognized their presence."[11] During the Vietnam War, the U.S. government enlisted the Hmong in a secret war in Laos. After U.S. defeat and withdrawal, the Hmong in 1975 began immigrating and in 1990 the U.S. census reported 100,000 Hmong living in the United States.[12]

The educational problems facing Hmong adults and children were staggering. Three out of four Hmong entering the United States in 1975 were illiterate in their own language and the average education was 2 years of schooling. Only a small fraction, 0.9 percent, of the immigrant population could speak English or write in English. Hmong illiteracy and lack of knowledge of English sharply differed from the immigrant Sikh graduates of India's institutions of higher education where English is the standard language. As a result of language and educational problems, only about 16 percent of Hmong found employment by 1984 and almost half of these jobs were temporary and without fringe benefits.[13] Typical of the employment patterns of Hmong immigrants, Cha Shou worked as a pizza delivery driver at the time he was gunned down.

Major cultural changes in Cha Shou's life began in Thai refugee camps in 1979 with the study of English and with conversion to Christianity. Traditionally, the majority of Hmong worshiped ancestors with a small percentage practicing Buddhism. His conversion to Christianity and inability to attend the spirit ceremony at his father's funeral alienated him from part of his family. Life in the refugee camps was hard. Hmong refugees constantly feared reprisal from Laotian and Thai communists. Camp life left deep psychological scars in children and adults. After immigrating to Chicago in 1982, Cha worked at low-paying jobs while preparing for entry into the ministry of an evangelical church. After receiving ministerial training in Milwaukee in 1983, he moved to Windigo.[14]

Visiting Cha's ministry, the evangelical Salvation Church, Donald Hones found the Sunday school class of Hmong children doing language lessons by reciting Hmong letters and sounds and corresponding letters and sounds in English. The lesson was conducted by Cha in Hmong. After the recitation, Cha asked the children to silently read a passage from the Bible. After the period of silent reading, he listed keywords on the chalkboard, such as fellowship, offering, lamb, and sin. He then asked the children to explain the meaning of the words.

In contrast to the cultural style of U.S. public school classrooms, Cha allows the children to talk among themselves about answers to questions. Typically, U.S. classrooms emphasize individualism in learning as opposed to group learning. The Sunday school provides an opportunity for children to improve their English and the only opportunity to practice literacy in Hmong.

As a result of the shooting and surrounding publicity, school administrators in the area became aware of Cha's interest in teaching and they asked him to work as a bilingual assistant at the Horace Kallen School and to be a liaison to the Hmong community. The Horace Kallen School focuses on the education of immigrant children from a variety of countries, including Laos, Vietnam, Iraq, Mexico, and Haiti. It provides English as a second language classes and uses bilingual assistants. Cha is an assistant to Ana Torres, a second-generation Cuban, who believes that instruction in English provides the cultural glue for uniting her multilingual classroom. Torres told Hones, "If there is an Arabic girl who wants to talk to a Vietnamese boy, they are all going to have to speak in a common language. It pulls them all together."[15] Regarding Cha's assistance, Torres reports, "This is my second year working with him. Now that we have spent this much time together I can't imagine teaching without him. . . . He knows on days when I am struggling for words or something he will fill in. . . . The way he works with children is just beautiful."[16]

This brief description does not do justice to the depth and complexity of Cha's life in Laos and Thailand, his cultural changes, and the analysis of immigrant education as it appears in *Educating New Americans: Immigrant Lives and Learning*. Cha's life reflects many of the struggles of the Hmong community in the United States. Today, many Hmong complain about the inadequate education provided by local schools. Low-paying jobs force the Hmong to live in low-income areas with low-quality schools.

For the Hmong, the most important issue in adapting to their new country is learning English. Many are disappointed by the poor quality of ESL (English as a Second Language) classes and the lack of bilingual instruction. However, like Cha, Hmong parents are trying to improve their educational opportunities through active involvement in community and school affairs. Quoting a report on Hmong students in Fresno, California, Meyer Weinberg reports, "Even the most successful Hmong high school students . . . feel they need much more writing instruction to continue their education effectively. Once they are mainstreamed out of ESL, they receive no further special help with their English writing skills."[17]

In addition, Hmong children face problems of cultural adjustment similar to those of Ann Kimmage and Sikhs. Typical comments by Hmong students include the following: "They called us names, imitated our talk, and shoved us around." "Experienced for the first time [on entering elementary school] what it was like to be discriminated against and hated simply because we looked different . . . It made me realize I would be surrounded by hatred and hostility." "Racism was the first shocking thing I observed on arrival [in the U.S.]. . . . Racism was probably the hardest challenge and most difficult obstacle that I've encountered in the United States."[18]

Similar to Sikhs, Hmong youth utilize different strategies for dealing with cultural change. Citing studies of Hmong youth, Hones and Cha Shou C. identify three strategies:

- Desire to assimilate to the dominant culture.
- Desire to hold on to traditions.
- Rebellion against dominant culture and traditional culture.

The Hmong experience highlights the problem of language and education among immigrants from Asia. Many non-Asian educators assume that Asian immigrants are model students who have little difficulty achieving in U.S. schools. In fact, many Asian immigrant students arrive with a limited educational background and little understanding of English. Consequently, they have difficulty adjusting to U.S. schools. It is important that teachers of immigrant children attend to the following:

- The educational background of students prior to immigration.
- Functional illiteracy of students in English.

REBELLION AND SCHOOL UNIFORMS

Asian gang members? In 1992, the Los Angeles county probation department called for a truce between the law enforcement agencies and the notorious youth gangs, the Crips and Bloods. "It does seem to be a legitimate effort on the part of some of our gangs," said Burt Davila, the director of the county probation department's specialized gang-supervision programs.[19] In Long Beach,

California, the Crips and Bloods had recruited the children of Cambodian immigrants. Long Beach has the largest concentration of Cambodians.[20]

To counter the growth of youth gangs, the Long Beach school district requires school uniforms, a policy that President Bill Clinton hailed in his 1996 State of the Union address as a means of curbing violence and increasing discipline. Clinton suggested that schools would keep teenagers from "killing each other over designer jackets."[21]

Those Cambodian youth that joined gangs like the Crips and Bloods represent those immigrant youth whom Hones and Cha Shou C. identified as choosing to rebel against assimilation and tradition. Similar to the Hmong, Cambodians entered the United States with the psychological burden of war and life in refugee camps. In many ways, their experiences are worse than those of the Hmong. Under French rule until 1949, a large percentage of the native population was denied access to educational institutions. After independence, the number attending school increased dramatically. For instance, between 1955 and 1970 the number of school-age children in primary schools jumped from one-third to three-fourths.[22]

But then came the Khmer Rouge and the "killing fields." Motivated by a belief that the ideal communist state could only be achieved by returning to a peasant society and throwing off all remnants of European culture, the Khmer Rouge forcibly moved urban dwellers to rural villages, destroyed books and libraries, and systematically killed all former leaders and intellectuals. Escaping with little but their lives, Cambodians flowed into Thai refugee camps and from there, like the Hmong, to the United States. Cambodians entering the United States between 1980 and 1986 averaged fewer than 5 years of education with less than 1 percent having received schooling beyond high school.[23]

Similar to the Hmong, Cambodian immigrants lived in areas with high crime rates and had difficulty finding employment. In 1981, 95 percent of Cambodians in Long Beach were living off government relief programs. By 1991, 51 percent of Cambodians were still living in poverty.[24] A major problem facing Cambodians in gaining employment was difficulty in speaking English and illiteracy in English. A major focus of the Cambodian community's concern, like that of the Hmong, was English literacy.

Cambodian children faced psychological problems resulting from the horror of the killing fields, life in refugee camps, transition to a new culture, learning a new language, and rejection by their American peers. Living in Stockton, California, Sokunthy Pho wrote:

> I hated my parents for bringing me and my sisters . . . to America because we were always being picked on by the white kids at our school. . . . They spat at us, sneaked behind us and kicked us. . . . We didn't respond. . . . Instead, we kept quiet and walked home with tears running down our brown cheeks.[25]

It is a miracle that all Cambodian children didn't rebel and join the Crips and Bloods. Despite the weight of these psychological and social factors, the majority of Cambodian students are succeeding in school. However, there is still a high dropout rate. For instance, the Lowell, Massachusetts, school district reported that between 1986 and 1987 15 percent of Cambodian students dropped out.[26]

There are two important lessons for teachers from the experience of Cambodians in American schools:

- Teachers should know the political and social conditions that immigrant groups left behind. In the case of Cambodians, very few U.S. teachers know and understand the horror of the killing fields, the traumatic flight to refugee camps, and the difficulties of camp life. This requires more than a simple knowledge of customs of other countries. Teachers need to understand the psychological impact of political and social upheavals.
- Teachers must attend to the problem of English literacy. Many U.S. teachers assume an Asian face means a literate student capable of academic success. Consequently, the literacy problems of Cambodian students are neglected.

MUSLIM SCHOOLS: FINDING A SAFE HAVEN

"My father's family survived in Bosnian society as a minority for centuries," said Saffiya Turan, founder of the Noor Al Iman, a Muslim school in South Brunswick, New Jersey. "To survive, you have to know who you are."[27]

Muslim immigrants face problems of relocation and a hostile environment in the United States where followers of Islam are stereotyped as bomb-throwing terrorists by images in the media. Worried about the reaction of many Americans to Muslim culture and religion, Islamic groups have created national organizations and programs to explain Islam to other religious and cultural groups. In addition, Muslim schools are flourishing as centers for cultural and religious preservation.

However, Islamic schools have adapted to U.S. culture. At the Al Noor school in Brooklyn, New York, students study a standard U.S. academic curriculum enriched by Arabic and religious classes. In addition, the student body is culturally heterogenous. There are the children of American-born converts mixed with an immigrant population from Asia, Africa, the Middle East, and India. Consequently, instructional materials reflect the varied backgrounds of the children. For religious, cultural, and Arabic instruction, the Al Noor uses books from Egypt, Yemen, and Jordan.

The mixed cultures require a constant stress on the differences between old country cultures and religion. Souhair Ayach, who teaches Islamic studies at the Al Iman school in Queens, New York, finds discussions wandering from religious issues, such as the divine source of human genius, to secular topics, such as arranged marriages. "Is there something in Islam that, like, says a girl should get married at a young age, or is it just tradition?" a teenage girl asked her one day. Avoiding a direct answer, the teacher responded, "Here you have to have education because you need a good job, a respectable job, to make your living. So it's better if you marry early, but under some circumstances it's better to develop your life first."[28]

LESSON 3.2

Map of Migratory Causes

Note: While visiting a museum in Budapest, Hungary, I encountered a section devoted to the large numbers of Hungarians who immigrated to the United States in the 1890s. The section emphasized the terrible economic conditions in Hungary that caused immigration to the U.S.

Grades: Middle School through College

Objective:
To understand the multiple reasons for global migration to the United States and other countries.

Lesson:
This lesson should be done with the whole class using a large world map on a chalkboard or other means of displaying a world map.

1. Draw lines or connect with yarn or string the United States with other major regions of the world.
2. Have students list on the lines the migratory groups from each region of the world.
3. Divide the class into world regions for the purpose of investigating the reasons for migration from these regions.
4. List reasons for migrations and dates of migration along the lines leading to the United States after each group has completed its investigations.

Teachers: Teachers should help students identify migratory groups and reasons for migration.

Outcome: Students will understand the economic, political, and social conditions that cause people to migrate to the United States.

Muslim schools try to maintain traditional moral values, particularly related to the separation of sexes. At the Al Iman school in Queens, New York, students sit in rows separated by sex. Girls wear headscarves and all children are uniformed with girls wearing shapeless robes, and boys wearing blue sweaters and gray trousers. Students are punished for bringing toys, comics, cosmetics, or jewelry to school. In addition, the school forbids wearing nail polish and "pursuing acts of romanticism," such as flirting with other students.

However, Muslim schools have adapted to the questioning nature of U.S. culture. "Overseas, you aren't taught to ask why," commented Abir Catovic of the Noor ul Iman School of South Brunswick, New Jersey. "Here you've got students who ask why, and you'd better be prepared to answer more than just, 'Because it says so.'"

While Muslim schools provide some protection from the perceived immorality of U.S. culture, many Muslim parents consider sending their children home. "Many are thinking of sending them back," said Abdulhakim Ali Mohamed, the iman of the Al Farooqu mosque. "We tell them that's not a solution. If you take them back, you have to go back with them."[29]

The problems faced by Muslim immigrants highlight the importance of U.S. teachers understanding the following:

- The moral traditions of immigrant groups.
- The religious traditions of immigrant groups.
- Media stereotypes of religious and cultural groups.

WEARING YOUR KNICKS JACKET AT THE ZOCALO

The religious procession climbed up the hill as worshipers dressed in Knicks jackets, assorted T-shirts proclaiming the name of a favorite band, and dresses and shoes bought in New York department stores sang to the Chinantla's patron saint, Padre Jesús: "Padre Jesús of Chinantla please send your blessings to the so many of us in New York."[30] In the crowd were many who formed the underclass of New York workers as busboys, hospital workers, and maids. There were also nurses and successful businesspeople. Maintaining ties to their hometown, they return annually for a week of fiesta.

Unlike Hmong or Cambodian immigrants, Mexican immigrants can more easily migrate to and from their hometowns and the United States. Mexican law now allows migrant workers to retain their Mexican citizenship and confers it on children born outside of Mexico. Travel across the border is aided by proximity to the United States and cheap international plane fares. International phone cards allow easy contact with family and friends in the immigrant's former home.

Similar to immigrants from small towns in the Dominican Republic, Haiti, and Ecuador, Mexican immigrants often live a double life. For those from Chinantla, this double life means work and community in the vast and complex world of New York and the intimacy of the small Mexican village. Their lives,

LESSON 3.3

Language Map

Grades: Middle School through College

Objective:
To identify the languages spoken by immigrants to the United States.

Lesson:

1. Divide the class into groups based on the regions indicated on the world map of migratory causes from Lesson 3.2.
2. Each group will investigate the different languages spoken in their assigned world region.
3. These languages should be listed alongside the reasons for migration to the United States.

Teachers: Teachers should play an active role in helping students identify the languages of immigrant groups.

Outcome: Students will understand the complexity of language issues faced by U.S. schools.

minds, and pocketbooks straddle the border. In New York, Chinantacans have raised money to provide their hometown with a new water system, new schools, and street lights. Some, after years of hard work at menial tasks, return to build homes or open small stores. Pension and Social Security checks are received by those who decided to retire at home. During the summer, children and grandchildren return to fill the town's zocalo with sounds of English and the latest in U.S. clothing styles.

"People say New York is a pigsty," a retiree living in Chinantla told *New York Times* reporter, Deborah Sontag. "They say we work like slaves here. I say my thanks to God and to New York every night. We made ourselves here. And we remade Chinantla. Were it not for New York, Chinantla would be dead, like a corpse."[31] In contrast, Fabiola Villagomez remarks, "I had imagined this city to be a palace, something beautiful. Not so much cruelty, racism, or the ugly things in this country."[32]

Why New York? Robert C. Smith of Barnard College, who studies Mexicans living in New York City, believes Mexican immigration from Chinantla and the Mixtec region, spanning the states of Puebla, Guerro, and Oaxaca, began in 1945 when two brothers, Pedro and Fermin Simon, hitched a ride with a tourist in Mexico City. Originally, the two brothers tried to sign on as guest workers in Texas to pick fruit. Instead, they ended up in Times Square mopping floors in a restaurant. Restaurant work was considered preferable to migrant farm labor. Through kinship networks and friends, other residents in the Mixtec region heard about New York. Currently, there are 330,000 Mexicans living in New York City. Underscoring the cohesiveness of this population is New York City's nine Mexican soccer leagues with 262 teams and 5,000 players. Two of the teams represent Chinantla.

The pressure to leave Mexico increases as Mexican wages plummet. An illegal immigrant from the Mexican state of Oaxaca complains that he could only make $3 a day at construction work and "you cannot do anything with that. You cannot eat."[33] Unwilling to give reporter David Gonzalez his name because of his illegal status, the man now works in a factory painting clothing at $3 an hour, which is below the legal minimum wage. Gonzalez interviewed another illegal immigrant who earned $6 an hour making salads in a restaurant. "It was definitely worth coming here," he said. "I have a house in Mexico. My family is better off. I'm not ready to leave New York. I like it."[34]

Many of these immigrants hope their children will benefit from U.S. schools. According to Deborah Sontag, "The sons and daughters of peasants who sign their names with inky thumbs, they are also the ones whose American children are almost all headed to college, in college, or graduates."[35]

TRANSNATIONALISM: THE MULTICULTURAL IMMIGRANT

The biculturalism of Chinantla's residents characterizes the growing number of immigrants who maintain close ties with their homelands. Like Chinantacan, they are aided by cheap airfares and modern communications technology. They live bilingual and bicultural lives in the new global economy. "At the same time as they are keeping their old links, many are successfully integrating themselves into the United States," Robert C. Smith, a sociologist at Barnard College and expert on transnationalism told *The New York Times* reporters Deborah Sontag and Celia Dugger. "They're redefining what it means to be American."[36]

"I believe people like us have the best of two worlds," said Fernando Mateo, who commutes weekly between his New York and Dominican homes. "We have two countries, two homes. It doesn't make any sense for us to be either this or that. We're both. It's not a conflict. It's just a human fact."[37] Mateo's immigrant mother flew back to Santo Domingo for his birth so that he could have Dominican citizenship. His early life was split between a small New York apartment and a pink house under a mahogany tree in Santo Domingo. Fluent in Spanish and English, Mateo's biculturalism is symbolized by his custom-made lapel pin of entwined Dominican and U.S. flags. Because of the transnationalism of many Dominicans, Santo Domingo now offers varying aspects of U.S. culture, such as pizza parlors and bagel shops, and a parochial high school whose student body is 20 percent New York–born.

Born in New York and attending Pennsylvania University, Vinit Sethi agreed to let his mother arrange a traditional marriage with Anshu Jain, an Indian woman who had never been to the United States. Wearing a golden turban with strands of emeralds hanging from his neck, Sethi married a woman he had never kissed or held hands with and who refuses to say his given name because, as she explained, "For a wife, your husband is God. And you don't call God by his first name."[38]

Sethi grew up in a tightly bound Indian community of Indian gemstone merchants in New York. Sethi's father and family frequently travel to India. Scattered between city and suburbs, this Indian-merchant community meets for ski trips, social events, and learning traditional Indian dances and music. Family leaders worry that their children will succumb to the temptations of U.S. life and break with traditional practices. Shyama Devi Kotahwala, the Kotahwala matriarch, fears that her children will be "spoiled [by the] culture of America" and marry outside the Hindu religion or, even worse, marry an American.[39]

VARIETIES OF EDUCATIONAL EXPERIENCE

Immigrant groups arrive with a variety of educational backgrounds. For instance, studies of Chinese immigrants in New York City found a vast range of educational achievement. Those living in Chinatown arrived with primarily working-class backgrounds and limited exposure to formal learning. One study found that the roughly 85 percent of Chinatown residents in New York, Boston, and San Francisco had not attended secondary school. The children of these immigrants often struggle in school because of language problems. On the other hand, many wealthy and well-educated Chinese immigrants, who in New York tend to live outside of Chinatown, often send their children to elite universities. The educational level of immigrants reflects their social class back-grounds. In the case of Chinese, some come from peasant backgrounds with lit-tle access to higher education. On the other hand, some come from professional classes and are engineers and college teachers.[40]

Therefore, the educational needs of immigrants must be assessed according to their social and educational backgrounds. These backgrounds vary widely within each immigrant group and among immigrant groups. For the purposes of this discussion, I am going to focus on variations among Asian Pacific im-migrants. However, similar differences will exist between immigrants from other areas, particularly from countries of the former Soviet Union. Table 3–1 indicates variations in social class backgrounds as defined by employment.

As indicated in Table 3–1, a significant percentage of Asian Indian and Chi-nese immigrants are well-educated professionals. However, despite the high percentages of professionals, at least 18 percent of Asian Indians and 31 percent of Chinese immigrants come from low-income service and laborer backgrounds. In contrast, only 8 percent of Cambodians are professional while 40 percent have service and laborer backgrounds.

These variations in employment backgrounds are reflected in levels of ed-ucational achievement as indicated in Table 3–2. Again, there is a wide varia-tion in educational attainment within and between immigrant groups. As indi-cated in Table 3–2, 39 percent of Asian Indians immigrate with bachelor's,

TABLE 3–1 Occupational Attainment of Asian Pacific Immigrants

Occupation	Asian Indian	Cambodian	Chinese	Korean	Pacific Islander
Professional	28%	5%	19%	13%	6%
Service	8	18	19	17	16
Laborer	10	32	12	13	18

Source: Adapted from Meyer Weinberg, *Asian-American Education: Historical Background and Current Realities* (Mahwah, NJ: Lawrence Erlbaum Associates, Inc., 1970), p. 5.

TABLE 3–2 Selected Levels of Educational Attainment of Asian Pacific Immigrants

Educational Attainment	Asian Indian	Cambodian	Chinese	Korean	Pacific Islander
Doctoral or professional degree	14%	1%	6%	5%	1
Bachelor's degree	25	5	20	22	6
High School diploma	12	12	15	25	31
Less than high school	15	64	29	20	32

Source: Adapted from Meyer Weinberg, *Asian-American Education: Historical Background and Current Realities* (Mahwah, NJ: Lawrence Erlbaum Associates, Inc., 1970), p. 7.

Note that columns do not add up to 100 percent because figures for "some college" and "Master's Degree" were not included.

Family Multicultural Tree: Educational Mobility

Note: This lesson is a continuation of the creation of a family multicultural tree begun in Lessons 2.1, 2.2, and 2.3.

Grades: High School through College

Objectives:

1. For those students with ancestors who were voluntary immigrants this lesson will highlight the importance for teachers of knowing the educational level of immigrant families and children.
2. To help understand the differences in educational progress among generations between ancestors who were dominated or voluntary immigrants.

Lesson:

1. Add to family trees developed in Lessons 2.1, 2.2, and 2.3, the completed educational level of each ancestor.
2. In class discussion, compare the educational progress of dominated and voluntary immigrants for each generation.
3. In class discussion consider the advantages and disadvantages of the educational achievement of ancestors who were voluntary immigrants.

Teachers: Sometimes it is difficult to determine the grade level of previous generations. Consequently, students could indicate some education, literate, elementary school, or any other indication of schooling and knowledge.

Outcomes: Students will gain

1. An understanding of the educational advantages or disadvantages of dominated cultures and voluntary immigrants.
2. An understanding of the effects of prior schooling on lives of voluntary immigrants.

The Completed Family Multicultural Tree: Dominated Cultures and Voluntary Immigrants, Occupations, and Educational Achievement

Grades: High School through College

Objective:
To analyze and understand the interrelationship between generational differences in educational and economic progress, and dominated cultures and voluntary immigrants.

Lesson:
Using the completed family tree from Lesson 3.4, the class is asked to compare the economic and educational advantages of dominated cultures and voluntary immigrants.

Teachers: This is a difficult and important assignment. Teachers should be aware that some voluntary immigrants have greater advantages than others. This can be raised as a question for class discussion.

Outcome: Students will understand the economic and educational progress of families based on the educational levels of voluntary immigrants and the problems facing dominated cultures.

doctoral, or professional degrees. If master's degrees had been included, the table would have indicated that 59 percent of Asian Indian immigrants have some form of college degree. Despite this high level of educational attainment, there are still 15 percent of Asian Indians who immigrate with less than a high school education. Cambodian immigrants have a low level of educational attainment with 64 percent having less than a high school education. Among Chinese immigrants there is almost an even split between those with a bachelor's, professional, or doctoral degree (26 percent) and those with less than a high school education (29 percent).

Knowledge of English is an important factor for immigrant occupational and educational success. Again, proficiency in English varies among and within immigrant groups as indicated in Table 3–3.

The level of English proficiency among Asian Indian immigrants is a result of policies imposed by British colonialists which made English a major language in India and the key to success in Indian higher education. However, despite the fact that among Indian immigrants 57 percent speak English very well, 18 percent well, and 16 percent speak only English (for a total of 91 percent), there are still 9 percent who have difficulty with English. In contrast, 42 percent of Cambodian immigrants and 31 percent of Chinese immigrants do not speak English well or do not speak it at all. These variations in social class, educational achievement, and English proficiency highlight the importance of not casting an immigrant population into a single mold.

CONCLUSION: KNOWING IMMIGRANT CULTURES

Given the variety of educational backgrounds and cultures, teachers must do research about the immigrant children in their classrooms. In *The Inner World of the Immigrant Child,* Christina Igoa provides a list of questions to guide teachers. The following are some of the questions Igoa proposes teachers ask in adapting their teaching to the variety of immigrant experiences. I strongly recommend that all teachers of immigrant children read Igoa's invaluable book.

TABLE 3–3   English Proficiency of Asian Pacific Immigrants

English Proficiency	Asian Indians	Cambodian	Chinese	Korean	Pacific Islander
Very good	57%	24%	32%	29%	43%
Good	18	31	32	28	20
Poor	7	32	22	23	10
Not at all	2	10	9	5	5
Speak:					
Only English	16	3	5	15	25
Total	100	100	100	100	100

Source: Adapted from Meyer Weinberg, *Asian-American Education: Historical Background and Current Realities* (Mahwah, NJ: Lawrence Erlbaum Associates, Inc., 1970), p. 8.

Design an Educational Program
for Immigrant Children

Grades: High School through College

Objective:
To understand the educational problems facing immigrant children.

Lesson:

1. Divide the class into small groups of 4 or 5 students.
2. Ask each group to design an educational program for elementary school children who are immigrants to the United States.
3. The focus of the educational design should be on the following educational problems faced in varying degrees by immigrant children:
    a. Psychological stress of loss of familiar surroundings and friends.
    b. Psychological stress of entering a new culture.
    c. Increasing tensions between parents and children as children assimilate U.S. culture.
    d. Possible psychological problems facing immigrant children from war-torn countries and countries undergoing social and political upheavals.
    e. Differences in educational backgrounds of immigrant children.
    f. Language issues.
4. Each group should present its educational designs for class discussion.

Teachers: Students should be encouraged to consider each of the above issues in their educational design. Each group should be allowed to be as creative as possible in developing its educational plan.

Outcome: Students will develop an understanding of the problems facing immigrant children as they enter U.S. schools.

- Were the children schooled or unschooled before they came into the country?
- Was their education fragmented?
- Are the children dependent on the teacher for learning? Do they have any independent learning skills?
- Did they learn English abroad?
- How much of their own language did they learn, orally, and in writing, receptively and productively?
- What is the status of their parents?[41]

PERSONAL FRAMES OF REFERENCE

1. If you have never emigrated to another country, try to imagine your reaction at the age of 6 to emigration and attendance at a school where no one spoke your mother tongue or understood your culture.
2. Imagine yourself preparing a lesson plan for a class composed of non-English-speaking students who have immigrated from many different countries.
   a. How would you prepare yourself for teaching in a multilingual and multicultural classroom?
   b. What would you do to understand the social background of the students?
   c. What would you do to understand the educational background of the students?
   d. How would you prepare for the possible psychological issues facing these students?

Notes

1. Ann Kimmage, *An Un-American Childhood* (Athens: The University of Georgia Press, 1996).
2. Ibid., pp. 47–48.
3. Ibid., p. 56.
4. Ibid., p. 57.
5. Ibid., p. 62.
6. Laurie Goodstein, "At Summer Camp, Sports, Pillow Fights, Cultural Preservation," *The New York Times*, www.nytimes.com, 18 July 1998.
7. Ibid.
8. Ibid.
9. Ibid.
10. Donald F. Hones and Cha Shou C., *Educating New Americans: Immigrant Lives and Learning* (Mahwah, NJ: Lawrence Erlbaum Associates, Inc., 1998).
11. Meyer Weinberg, *Asian-American Education: Historical Background and Current Realities* (Mahwah, NJ: Lawrence Erlbaum Associates, Inc., 1997), p. 183.
12. Ibid., p. 186.

13. Ibid., p. 187.
14. See Hones and Cha Shou C.
15. Ibid., p. 218.
16. Ibid., p. 219.
17. Weinberg, p. 193.
18. Ibid., p. 191.
19. Millicent Lawton, "Major Role Urged for L.A. Schools in Stopping Gangs," *Education Week on the Web,* www.edweek.org (3 June 1992).
20. Weinberg, p. 165.
21. Jessica Portner, "Uniforms Get Credit for Decrease in Discipline," *Education Week on the Web,* www.edweek.org 14 February 1996.
22. Weinberg, p. 158.
23. Ibid., p. 165.
24. Ibid., p. 165.
25. Quoted in Ibid., p. 166.
26. Ibid., p. 167.
27. Susan Sachs, "Moslem Schools in U.S. a Voice for Identity," *The New York Times,* www.nytimes.com, 10 November 1998, p. 3.
28. Ibid., pp. 3–4.
29. Ibid., p. 5.
30. Deborah Sontag, "A Mexican Town That Transcends All Borders," *The New York Times,* www.nytimes.com, 21 July 1998.
31. Ibid.
32. David Gonzalez, "Mexicans Looking for Toehold on Crowded Immigrant Ladder," *The New York Times,* www.nytimes.com, 28 July 1997.
33. Ibid.
34. Ibid.
35. Sontag.
36. Deborah Sontag and Celia W. Dugger, "New Immigrant Tide: Shuttle Between Worlds," *The New York Times,* www.nytimes.com, 19 July 1998.
37. Ibid.
38. Celia W. Dugger, "Wedding Vows Bind Old World and New," *The New York Times,* www.nytimes.com, 20 July 1998.
39. Ibid.
40. Weinberg, pp. 18–37.
41. Cristina Igoa, *The Inner World of the Immigrant Child* (Mahwah, NJ: Lawrence Erlbaum Associates, Inc., 1995), p. 148.

CHAPTER 4

Multiculturalism in the Global Economy

With the growth of a global economy and the mass migration of workers, issues of diversity and multiculturalism are a major concern to corporations around the world. A headline in *The New York Times* declared, "Business Shuns Areas That Look Too White." The accompanying story described why companies were wary of moving to Iowa because it is predominately white. Summing up the feelings of international corporations about multiculturalism and racial diversity, Max Phillips, the co-chairman of the diversity committee of the Des Moines Chamber of Commerce, told *Times* reporters, "Companies today have offices all over the country, all over the world. And it's a good chance that some of their best people will be other than white. How is that company going to feel about sending somebody to work in Iowa if they're going to lose them in a year or two?"[1]

As the global economy expands, issues of diversity and multiculturalism are important for international corporations. Business is interested in selling products and services to culturally and racially diverse markets and in employing a multicultural workforce. Consequently, global business does not have a stake in maintaining the dominance of European culture. Writing in *Harper's*, David Reiff argues, "The market economy, now global in scale, is by nature corrosive of all hierarchies and certainties, up to and including . . . white racism and male domination. If any group has embraced the rallying cry 'Hey, hey, ho, ho, Western culture's got to go,' it is the world business elite."[2] Back in Iowa, which is 96.6 percent white, Michael Reagan, the president of the Des Moines Chamber of Commerce, was startled to hear an executive from a Maryland biotechnology company that decided not to relocate because of the racial homogeneity of Iowa say, "I think we may be uncomfortable here. We're used to all kinds of different people."[3] In response, Reagan commented, "What was once seen as a great advantage, racial or cultural homogeneity is turning into a disadvantage."[4]

However, the United States is not the only country experiencing multicultural tensions. For instance, a series of events in 1993 involving Moslem schoolchildren in France resulted in the French government abandoning efforts to recognize cultural differences in schools and in the implementation of policies designed to teach all school children traditional French values.

Clothing Labels, Globalization, and Cheap Labor

Grades: Elementary School through College

Objective:
To understand global markets and the movement of companies to countries with low labor costs.

Lesson:

1. Place a world map in front of the classroom.
2. Have students examine the labels on their clothing and shoes to determine where they were manufactured (this might be done at home).
3. Indicate on the world map where the clothing and shoes worn by students were manufactured.
4. Have high school and college students investigate the average wages earned by workers in the countries where their clothes and shoes were manufactured.

Teachers: This is a simple and powerful exercise in understanding our global economy. For older students, issues of the exploitation of workers could be discussed.

Outcome: Students will gain a basic understanding of the global market for goods and the search by manufacturers for the cheapest workers.

Similar to dominated cultures in the United States, many Moslems in France came from previously dominated French colonies. In these colonies, they were economically exploited by the French and were victims of prejudice and discrimination. Other Moslems immigrated to France in search of jobs and discovered that their treatment was similar to that received by Moslems coming from former colonies. In France, Moslems faced the same lack of economic and educational opportunities experienced by dominated groups in the United States.[5] And, similar to dominated groups in the United States, they resisted attempts to destroy their cultural traditions.

The events that caused the French government to abandon educational policies of cultural tolerance involved an Islamic law that requires women to wear headscarves. In one incident, teachers in Nantua, France, stopped work for 1 day in protest against the wearing of headscarves to school by two Moroccan sisters, aged 11 and 13, and two Turkish girls, aged 14. The school's teachers argued that wearing Islamic headscarves was a religious practice that broke the rules of secular state schools. The teachers' actions resulted in the suspension of the four girls. During the dispute, a Moslem preacher in Nantua who told a newspaper that Islamic law took precedence over French law was deported.[6] In another incident, a 17-year-old Moslem student went on a hunger strike for a week in a camping van outside the headquarters of the regional education authority in the town of Grenoble to protest her expulsion for wearing an Islamic headscarf during physical education classes.[7] As a result of these incidents, the French government announced that it would no longer tolerate multiculturalism in the schools. Describing previous educational policies, Bernard Dustitiis, who runs a school serving immigrant children, said, "We had a day of couscous, a day of paella, it was 'viva la difference' much of the time. Now the pendulum is going the other way."[8] The reaction to this previous multiculturalism is captured in a statement by Pierre Lelloche, a conservative deputy from a Paris suburb, "Multiculturalism would be the end of France. You can be what you want to be here—Christian, Jewish, Muslim—but we're all Gauls. The alternative is to create cultural ghettos."[9] In fact, French leaders point to the United States as representing the possible consequences of multiculturalism. An unnamed French government official stated, "We have American cities as warning of what could happen here."[10]

Multicultural tensions will continue to increase with the evolution of the global economy. Two notable attempts to resolve conflicts by creating "unity within diversity" are Singapore and the European Union.

SINGAPORE

Singapore, ranked in 1996 and 1997 by the World Economic Forum as first in its Global Competitiveness Report, followed by the United States as third and Britain as seventh, was established in 1810 by the British East India Company to serve as a trading station in its expanding colonial empire.[11] Similar to their colonies in Africa and the Caribbean, the British created a mixed population by importing workers from China, India, and surrounding Malaysia. Under the leadership of Thomas Stamford Raffles, the East India Company ensured the dominant role of the English language by establishing English-speaking schools for the mixed immigrant population. Raffles's name was attached to the Singapore Free School opened in 1834 which provided an English language education for children from all language groups. In 1868, the school was renamed the Raffles Institute and eventually became an English-speaking primary school. There was no provision made in the nineteenth century for Chinese-, Tamil- (language of the people of southern India and northern Sri Lanka), and Malay-speaking schools.[12]

After Singapore became fully independent in 1965, its educational leaders faced the daunting task of reducing friction between the four language groups, creating a sense of nationhood, and training workers. Racial harmony has been a major problem in Singapore as evidenced by the annual recognition of Racial Harmony Day on 21 July to mark violent race riots that occurred in 1964. In 1955, while Singapore was still part of Malaysia, an educational plan called for equal treatment of all four languages by instituting trilingual and bilingual programs. In 1959, the government had advocated equality between languages in the schools, the adoption of Malay as the national language, and an emphasis on technical and vocational education. Common syllabi in all four languages were issued. In 1962, the University of Singapore was established. In 1963, a common education system was formally organized with 6 years of primary education, 4 years of secondary, and 2 years of pre-university education.

Despite the promotion of multilingualism in the schools, English remains the dominant language of education and business. Students are currently placed in ability tracks in the fourth year of primary school according to their abilities in English, a mother tongue (Chinese, Malay, or Tamil), and mathematics. In each of the three ability tracks, the student continues studying his/her mother tongue and English. More time is spent teaching English than the mother tongue. According to the official curriculum guide, "33 percent of the curriculum time will be spent on English, 27 percent on the mother tongue."[13] The Primary School Leaving Examination at the end of the sixth year is on English, the mother tongue, mathematics, and science. Based on the Primary School Leaving Examination, students are placed in three different courses of study, each teaching English and the mother tongue.[14]

The multilingualism of Singapore's educational system is designed to reduce ethnic tensions rather than actually promoting the use of non-English languages. Malay remains the official language, but English is promoted as a "supra-ethnic language of national integration."[15] English is the language used in higher education. According to linguist Robert Phillipson, "Officially, there is a policy of pragmatic multilingualism . . . but effectively English appears to have been established as the language of power."[16]

The major concern is melting together a diverse population into a cohesive workforce. This means reducing cultural tensions. Deputy Prime Minister Lee Hsien Loong stresses, "National Education aims to develop national cohesion, the instinct for survival and confidence in our future."[17] The goal "to befriend and accept pupils of all races" is important for Singapore to survive as a multi-cultural society. To reduce ethnic friction and to recognize cultural differences, Lee states, "We must create unity in diversity."[18] This can be accomplished, Lee argues, by teaching the common history of Singapore while accepting cultural differences. A goal of National Education is for "All Singaporeans, whether Chinese, Malay, Indian or Eurasian . . . [to] identify with the ideal of a multi-racial, multi-religious society."[19]

The goal of "unity within diversity" assumes unity through allegiance to Singapore's economic development and the use of English. In this context, promotion of diversity is simply for maintaining social peace. There is no real attempt to cultivate cultural differences. Ultimately, the goal of Singapore's schools is to socialize all students for the same global economy.

THE EUROPEAN UNION: THE WORLD'S MOST AMBITIOUS MULTICULTURAL EDUCATION PROGRAM

Similar to Singapore, the European Union, officially organized on 7 February 1992, with the signing of the *Treaty on European Union (Maastricht Treaty)*, is attempting to blend a variety of cultural and language groups into a single economic unit to compete in the global economy.[20] A unique feature is the effort to fabricate a "European culture" that will serve to promote Euronationalism and cultural unity. Individual nationalities, such as French and Italian, are to be nested in Euronationalism resulting in "unity within diversity."

The European Union evolved from the European Economic Community created in 1957 by the Treaty of Rome. A goal of both organizations has been fabrication of feelings of Euronationalism through education and cultural activities. However, the quest for Euronationalism has raised a number of questions. Are there common European values? Is there a common European culture? What, for instance, do Italians, Germans, and the French have in common?

Consequently, one of the problems for the European Union is fabricating a common culture for a group of nations with differing languages and historical traditions. In 1973, in an attempt to identify a common European culture, nine nations of the European Community issued a Declaration on European Identity. While recognizing the variety of national cultures, the declaration identified common legal, political, and moral values. These common values were "the same attitudes to life, based on a determination to build a society which measures up to the needs of the individual" and "the principles of representative democracy, of the rule of law, of social justice—which is the ultimate goal of economic progress—and the respect for human rights."[21]

The Declaration on European Identity highlights the concept of unity within diversity. Unity becomes the overriding principle with differences in languages, cultures, and religion being secondary. In 1985, the European Community established the Adonnino Committee to develop programs for European unity. The committee advocated conventional patriotic methods. Traditionally, governments depended on building patriotism by creating emotional attachments to symbols and music. Often, this involved pledges to national flags, celebrations of national holidays, and anthems. Through the work of the Adonnino Committee, the European Community adopted its own flag, established 9 May as European Day, and approved the use of the fourth part of Beethoven's *Ninth Symphony* as the European anthem.[22]

After the Treaty on European Union, the Adonnino Committee recommended that more effort be placed on common cultural projects. For instance, it suggested that every year one town be declared the "cultural capital of Europe" and that a European Baroque Orchestra and a Youth Orchestra be sponsored. To encourage identification with Europe, as opposed to national cultures, the committee called for the presentation of awards for the best European film scripts, books, and other artistic accomplishments.[23]

The treaty itself declares as an objective the creation of unity within diversity. The goal of diversity can be achieved, according to the treaty, "by education and training of quality and to the flowering of cultures of the member states." Unity can be achieved by bringing "common cultural heritage to the fore." Title IX of the treaty lists the following as the means of promoting unity through a common European culture:

- Improvement of the knowledge and dissemination of the culture and history of the European peoples.
- Conservation and safeguarding of cultural heritage of European significance.
- Noncommercial cultural exchanges.
- Artistic and literary creation, including the audiovisual sector.[24]

In line with these goals, the European Union statement on cultural policy asserts that "Forty years of working together, first with the European Community and then the European Union, has made Europeans increasingly aware of their common culture, the importance of their cultural diversity and the immense riches of their cultural heritage."[25] The document claims that the "growing awareness [of a common European culture] made it almost inevitable that the Treaty of European Unity . . . should contain passages on cultural policy in order to remedy the absence of any framework for Community action in the founding Treaty of Rome."[26]

Supported by the European Commission, the Ariane program is attempting to create a common European literature. One of the important spin-offs of creating a European literature is the treating of European history as a whole without emphasizing national perspectives. This literary goal was achieved with the publication of Baptiste Duroselle's *Europe—A History of Its Peoples.*[27]

In 1996, the European Commission sponsored a conference at Cologne University on *Eurolit: The Study of Literature in Europe.* The conference's prospectus announced the intent of using European literature as a means of creating a European identity. The prospectus states, "Literature will play a privileged role in the European process of integration. Whereas the Treaty of Rome stressed the economic cooperation, the cultural heritage of the citizens of Europe is today considered as *the basis for an authentic common identity* [my emphasis]."[28]

Of course, the so-called literature of Europe is also a national literature of particular member nations. The European Commission resolves this problem by proclaiming the doctrine of unity within diversity. In the words of the conference's prospectus, "The diversity of national literatures is sometimes interpreted as an obstacle to complete integration. However, this variety of regional traditions enriches our life precisely by offering a personal identity to everybody."[29] In other words, the identity of the citizen of the European Union is to be a combination of national identity and European identity. This conviction is highlighted in the conference's prospectus by the statement: "On the other hand the different literatures manifest many common features. The emphasis on these close relationships helps to reinforce the feeling of a European identity beyond national differences."[30] The first working group of the Cologne Conference is titled "The European dimension in literary studies."[31]

The variety of European languages is a major problem in creating cultural unity. Similar to Singapore, the European Union is confronted with a diverse population speaking different languages. Ideally, this problem could be overcome by creating or identifying a single language for communication within the European Union. However, existing nationalism precludes the use of a single language. The European Commission emphasized a multiple language policy in its 1996 White Paper on Education and Training. "The main lines of action at the European level," the White Paper states, "envisaged for 1996 include objectives to: develop proficiency [for students] in three European languages."[32]

With regard to educational policy, the European Union supports the LINGUA program which encourages the exchange of students for the purpose of language instruction among schools in different member nations. Under the LINGUA program, as described to students in a fact sheet distributed by the European Union,

> If you are over 14, you are eligible for a language exchange under the LINGUA scheme and can take part in an exchange under a Joint Educational Project between your school and a school in another EU country. This will include work in a foreign language on a topic of special interest to you and an exchange visit.[33]

Important to building cultural and economic unity is the ability of postsecondary students to study in any country of the European Union. Under agreements signed by member nations all students are guaranteed equality of treatment. This means for the individual student "that the university or college in the Member State where you wish to study (the 'host establishment') must accept you under the same conditions as nationals and not, for example, require you to pay higher course fees."[34] In addition, "If a grant is paid to nationals of the country where you wish to study . . . to cover course fees, you too must be able to receive it."[35] The major condition of this equal treatment is that the student meet the educational requirements of the host establishment and, in some cases, demonstrate a knowledge of the language of the host country. The provisions for equality of treatment of university and college students provides an opportunity for students of member countries to mingle and share cultural perspectives. This opportunity is enhanced by European Union rules that mandate social security protection and health care in the host country. Under these rules, the student is informed: "If you live in the Member State where you are study-ing, you are entitled to all the sickness benefits in kind provided under the leg-islation of that Member State."[36] In addition, "diploma[s] issued in one Mem-ber State is equivalent to that issued in another, so that you may continue some or all of your training in different countries without being disadvantaged (the same applies to a period of study)."[37]

Open to youth between the ages of 15 and 25, the SOCRATES program is specifically designed to promote "the European aspect of education."[38] There are several plans that operate under the general umbrella of SOCRATES. One plan is ERASMUS, which is designed for the exchange of students between educational establishments in different European Union countries. In the ERASMUS plan, the European Union provides grants to cover the cost of moving from one country to another. These grants cover language training, travel, and any higher cost of living encountered in another country. In addition, students do not have to pay tuition, examinations fees, or laboratory and library fees at the host institution. And, to pro-mote multilingualism, special language training is provided including language textbooks before the student travels to the host country. Also, ERASMUS provides travel scholarships to other countries for teachers in higher education to "allow . . . [them] to develop *the European aspect* [my emphasis] of . . . [their] subject."[39]

In addition, grants are provided to teachers in higher education to transfer to educational institutions in other countries. In the COMENIUS plan of the SOCRATES program, school partnerships are created for the specific purpose of promoting a European education. The partnerships are between schools of at least three member states of the European Union. The partnerships focus on European Educational Projects with the aim of building "contacts between pupils from different countries and to promote cooperation between schools."[40] Primary and secondary teachers are offered support to work on European Ed-ucational Projects and to learn other European languages.

The European Union's efforts to create unity within diversity are a direct result of the development of the global economy. To survive, European leaders believe it is necessary to create a unified trading block. This means a concerted effort to overcome cultural differences to achieve a competitive place in the world economy. Certainly, it is the most organized multicultural education program in the world today.

ENGLISH LANGUAGE IMPERIALISM?

As a result of British and U.S. expansionism, commerce, motion pictures, broad-casting, and popular music, English is the primary language of the global econ-omy. The number of global speakers of English is impressive. David Crystal esti-mates that close to 3 billion people or more than a third of the world's population are exposed to English. Of this number, 1 to 1.5 billion are "reasonably competent" in English.[41] Many others know rudimentary English. Of course, there are dialec-tical variations in the use of English. This has resulted in the term "Englishes," which refers to dialectical differences between non-native speakers of English. For instance, as Braj B. Kachru states, "The legacy of colonial Englishes has resulted in the existence of several transplanted varieties of English having distinct linguistic ecologies—their own contexts and uses."[42] In India, instructors of English as a Second Language identify three models of English—American English, British English, and Indian English. Other Asian countries add Australian English to the list. In Africa, dialectical differences exist between English-speaking countries. Worldwide, English is an important part of education for the global economy.

Around the world, students are rushing to take courses in English to get jobs in international business. According to one survey, "The global market for English language teaching and learning will increase over the next 25 years."[43] One of the new growth areas includes countries of central and eastern Europe, and countries of the former Soviet Union. Currently, 10 percent of the population—50 million people—are studying English.

English now dominates international exchanges of knowledge. It is central to technological development. It is the main language of global discussions of education. Kachru writes, "English is considered a symbol of modernization, a key to expanded functional roles, and an extra arm for success and mobility in culturally and linguistically complex and pluralistic societies. . . . It internationalizes one's outlook."[44]

A 1981 study found that 85 percent of scientific papers in biology and physics were written in English. In medicine 73 percent were written in English, while 69 percent and 67 percent of the mathematics and chemistry papers, respectively, were in English. In 1995, more than 90 percent of the scientific papers in computer science and linguistics were written in English.[45]

The current importance of English for economic development and global trade, according to critics, has resulted in a new and important form of social difference. In his book, *The English Language,* Robert Burchfield, editor of *The Oxford English Dictionary,* points out the negative consequences of not knowing English. "English," he writes, "has also become a lingua franca to the point that any literate educated person is in a very real sense deprived if he does not know English. Poverty, famine, and disease are instantly recognized as the cruellest and least excusable forms of deprivation. Linguistic deprivation is a less easily noticed condition, but one nevertheless of great significance."[46]

As students in Hong Kong, Vietnam, Nigeria, and India recognize, a knowledge of English is crucial to obtaining a well-paying job. In these and other countries, social mobility is dependent on a knowledge of English. Should English be the central language and culture of global education? Is the power of the global economy and English usage destroying other languages and, consequently, other cultures?

THE RIGHT TO LANGUAGE AND CULTURE IN THE GLOBAL ECONOMY

Declaring the right of all people to their culture and language, the 1992 United Nations Draft Declaration of Indigenous Peoples Rights is an important example of the effort to protect world cultures and languages from the dominating

and homogenizing force of the global economy. Written originally to protect indigenous cultures, such as those in the Americas, Pacific Rim, Eurasia, and
polar regions, the document, I believe, should encompass all world cultures.
Articles 15 and 16 of the declaration state the following:

Article 15

Indigenous children have the right to all levels and forms of education of the
State. All indigenous peoples also have this right and the right to establish and
control their educational systems and institutions *providing education in their
own languages, in a manner appropriate to their cultural methods of teaching and
learning* [my emphasis].
    Indigenous children living outside their communities have the right to be
provided *access to education in their own culture and language* [my emphasis].

Article 16

Indigenous peoples have the right to have *the dignity and diversity of their cultures, traditions, histories and aspirations appropriately reflected in all forms of education and public information* [my emphasis].[47]

Extended to all, this declaration provides the right of immigrants and dominated groups to maintain their own languages and cultures. However, it is important to note, that this is a *right* and *not a requirement*. As a right, all people
can still exercise the option of assimilation to another culture. In the United
States, dominated and immigrant cultures can still choose to assimilate to the
dominant culture and language. They can also choose to be bicultural. And, if
the declaration were recognized as a human right, they could also exercise the
right to preserve their own cultures and languages.
    A longtime champion of linguistic and cultural rights, Tove Skutnabb-
Kangas proposes a universal covenant protecting linguistic human rights as
part of the protection of cultural rights. Key to her proposal is the definition of
a mother tongue. A mother tongue, she writes, can be distinguished as "the language one learned first (the language one has established the first long-lasting
verbal contacts in)" or "the language one identifies with/as a native speaker of;
and/or the language one knows best."[48]
    Her proposed Universal Covenant of Linguistic Human Rights is given as
the following:

A Universal Covenant of Linguistic Human Rights

Everybody has the right

- to identify with their mother tongue(s) and have this identification accepted and re-
  spected by others
- to learn the mother tongue(s) fully, orally (when physiologically possible) and in
  writing
- to education mainly through the medium of their mother tongue(s), and within the
  state-financed educational system
- to use the mother tongue in most official situations (including schools).

Other Languages

- whose mother tongue is not an official language in the country where s/he is resident . . . to become bilingual (or trilingual, if s/he has 2 mother tongues) in the mother tongue(s) and (one of) the official language(s) (according to her own choice).

The Relationship Between Languages

- to any change . . . [in] mother tongue . . .[being] voluntary (includes knowledge of long-term consequences) . . .[and] not imposed

Profit from Education

- to profit from education, regardless of what her mother tongue is[49]

Of fundamental importance to Tove Skutnabb-Kangas's Universal Covenant of Linguistic Human Rights is the stress on bilingual education if the student's language is not the official national language or the language of global culture and economics, which at this time is English. Bilingualism resolves the problem of maintaining the mother tongue and associated culture, while ensuring that the student has access to the world's knowledge.

Tove's covenant reflects the rights provided by the United Nations' 1991 Declaration on the Rights of Persons Belonging to National or Ethnic, Religious and Linguistic Minorities and the International Labour Organization's Convention No. 169 on the rights of indigenous peoples. The 1991 declaration specifically recognizes the right to learn one's mother tongue. Article 4 states: "States should take appropriate measures so that, wherever possible, persons belonging to minorities may have adequate opportunities to learn their mother tongue or to have instruction in their mother tongue."[50]

Convention No. 169 takes a broader approach by insisting on education in the mother tongue and the dominant or official language of the nation. This approach supports the idea of bilingual education for minority language groups. Regarding education in the mother tongue, Article 28 of the convention states, "Children belonging to the peoples concerned shall, wherever practicable, be taught to read and write in their own indigenous language or in the language commonly used by the group to which they belong. . . . Measures shall be taken to preserve and promote the development and practice of the indigenous languages of the peoples concerned."[51] Learning the dominant or official language is also stressed, in the same article of the convention: "Adequate measures shall be taken to ensure that these peoples have the opportunity to attain fluency in the national language or in one of the official languages of the country."[52]

CONCLUSION: EDUCATIONAL RIGHTS AMENDMENT TO THE U.S. CONSTITUTION

In *Globalization and Educational Rights,* I propose an educational rights amendment to the U.S. Constitution.[53] Most national constitutions written after World War II contain a section on educational rights to ensure equal educational opportunity.

Should the U.S. Constitution Protect Linguistic and Cultural Rights in Education?

Grades: High School to College

Objective:
For students to develop an understanding of the issues surrounding linguistic and cultural rights in education.

Lesson:
Students will debate the three sections of an educational rights amendment to the U.S. Constitution proposed in the concluding section of this chapter.

1. Create two debate teams of four or five students.
2. Assign one team the task of preparing arguments to support the proposed sections of an educational rights amendment to the U.S. Constitution and the other team to developing opposing arguments.
3. Have the two teams debate the issue before the entire class.
4. At the conclusion of the debate invite participation from the rest of the class.

Teachers: Teachers should actively participate in helping the two teams develop their arguments.

Outcome: Students will understand the issues related to linguistic and cultural rights in education.

Education in the Land of Oz

Grades: High School through College

Objective:
For students to understand the relationship between education in developing countries and economic, multicultural, and linguistic issues.

Lesson:
Ask students to play the role of Zed and to develop an educational plan for the Land of Oz based on the following story. Of particular importance are resolving the language and cultural differences, and helping homeless children. Students should consider what representatives from the European Union, Singapore, and the United Nations might recommend..

The Minister of Education to the Rescue

Zed stared out the window at the slow-moving traffic of carts and trucks belching clouds of poisonous exhaust. Across the street, several legless beggars were using calloused hands to push themselves along a cracked sidewalk on homemade platforms made of salvaged wood and wheels. Zed grimaced as one of these contraptions slipped into the gutter, spilling its helpless rider into the dirt road. Ignored by passersby, the beggar struggled to move his body and wheeled carriage back onto the sidewalk. The beggar looked to be 60, but Zed guessed the real age to be 30. Life was not easy in the land of Oz.

Turning away from the window, Zed hurried back to the table heaped with reports. He wanted to be prepared before meeting with representatives from the European Union, Singapore, and the United Nations. The data on Oz was certainly clear. Illiteracy was 90 percent. Sixty percent of the people lived in poverty, which in Oz was a per capita income of less than $1 a day. The top 20 percent in income received 63 percent of the total income. Natural resources, the traditional source of national wealth since colonial days, were rapidly being depleted. Oz needed to develop an industrial base.

Earlier that morning, President Munchkin had called Zed into his office. Munchkin warned Zed, "I expect you as Minister of Education to leave these meetings with a workable education plan. We've got to do something or we'll have a revolution. Remember the last education minister was found decapitated in a ditch. Don't let that happen to you."

Munchkin's warning filled Zed with fear. What existed of the school system was in shambles. First, there were language problems. The western section of Oz spoke the wicked-witch language, while the eastern section spoke good-witch. The wicked-witch and good-witch people were constantly fighting each other. In addition, colonialists had imposed an English-language university on Oz and all the elite spoke English. Should he organize the primary school sys-

(continued)

tem around wicked-witch and good-witch or should all people be taught English? Could the school system reduce cultural clashes between the two groups so that Oz could create a unified workforce?

Also, there was the problem of where to spend limited educational monies. Should higher education be expanded or primary education? What should be taught in primary schools? Would expanding primary education lead to unreasonable demands for more secondary and higher education? What about homeless children? The problems were overwhelming. Glancing at the clock, Zed left his office to attend the meeting.

Teachers: This essay could be given as a group project so that group conversation will stimulate ideas about differing approaches to the problems faced by Oz.

Outcome: Students will have a greater understanding of the economic, multicultural, and linguistic issues involved in global education.

Since the U.S. Constitution does not contain any provision for educational rights, linguistic and cultural rights in education remain unprotected. Below are some sections I have suggested including in an educational rights amendment to the U.S. Constitution:

1. The government will promote with special care and financial resources the educational interests of racial, ethnic, language, religious, and gender groups formerly discriminated against by the public and private educational system. The government will protect these groups from social injustice and all forms of exploitation.
2. Everyone has a right to an education using the medium of their mother-tongue within a government-financed school system when the number of students requesting instruction in that mother-tongue equals the average number of students in a classroom in that government-financed school system.
3. Everyone has the right to learn the dominant or official language of the nation. The government-financed school system will make every effort to ensure that all students are literate in the dominant or official language of the country.

PERSONAL FRAMES OF REFERENCE

This personal frame of reference section was presented as Lesson 4.3.

Notes

1. Dirk Johnson, "Business Shuns Areas That Look Too White," *The New York Times*, 18 April 1994, p. A8.
2. David Reiff, "Multiculturalism's Silent Partner: It's the Newly Globalized Consumer Economy, Stupid," *Harper's* (July 1993), p. 65.
3. Johnson, A8.
4. Ibid.
5. A novel that provides insight into the social conditions of immigrant labor in France is Mehdi Charef, *Tea in the Harem* (London: Serpent's Tail, 1989).
6. "Moslem Girls Banned from School for Wearing Headscarves," *Reuter Wire Service*, 4 December 1993, *Executive News Service, Compuserve*, #1452.
7. "Moslem Girl's Plea Rejected in Headscarf Row," *Reuter Wire Service*, 20 January 1994, *Executive News Service, Compuserve*, #1440.
8. Alan Riding, "France, Reversing Course, Fights Immigrants' Refusal to Be French," *The New York Times*, 5 December 1993, p. 14.
9. Ibid., pp. 1, 14.
10. Ibid., p. 14.
11. Peter Passell, "Singapore Ranked the No. 1 Economy," *The New York Times*, 21 May 1997, p. D3.
12. W. O. Lee, *Social Change and Educational Problems in Japan, Singapore and Hong Kong* (New York: St. Martin's Press, 1991), pp. 153–57.
13. Ministry of Education, "The Education System in Singapore—Primary Education: An Information Guide for Parents," http://www.moe.edu.sg, p. 5.

14. Ministry of Education, "The Education System of Singapore—Secondary Education: An Information Guide for Parents," http://www.moe.edu.sg, pp. 1–4.

15. Robert Phillipson, *Linguistic Imperialism* (New York: Oxford University Press, 1991) p. 29.

16. Ibid.

17. Minister of Education, Singapore, "Speech by Bg Lee Hsien Loong, Deputy Prime Minister at the Launch of National Education on Saturday 17 May 1997 at TCS TV Theatre at 9:30 AM," http://www.moe.edu.sg, p. 3.

18. Ibid., p. 10.

19. Ibid.

20. The European Union's official history is provided in "Chronology of the Union," http://europa.eu.int/en/eu/hist/euchron.htm and "Seven Key Days in the Making of Europe," http://europa.eu.int/abc/obj/chrono/40years/7days/en.htm. Symbolically, the European Union's website is named Europa.

21. "On European Cultural Identity," http://www.helsinki.fi/valttdk/neusem/ruokonen, p. 9.

22. Ibid., p. 16.

23. Ibid., pp. 16–17.

24. Ibid., p. 1.

25. "The Union's Policies—Cultural Policy," http://europa.eu.int/pol/cult/en/info.htm, p. 1.

26. Ibid.

27. "On European Cultural . . . ," p. 16.

28. "Eurolit—Evaluation Conference," http://europa.eu.int/en/comm/dg22/news/eurolen.htm, p. 2.

29. Ibid.

30. Ibid.

31. Ibid.

32. "White Paper on Education and Training Teaching and Learning: Towards the Learning Society," http://europa.eu.int/en/comm/dg22/lbhp.html, pp. 1–2.

33. "Studying in Another Country of the European Union: Support for Community Programmes," http://citizens.eu.int/en/en/gf/st/gi/46/giitem.htm, p. 2.

34. "The Right to Study, Train and Do Research: Equality of Treatment," http://citizens.eu.int/en/en/gf/st/gi/40/giitem.htm, p. 2.

35. Ibid.

36. "The Right to Study, Train and Do Research: Social Security," http://citizens.eu.int/en/en/gf/st/gi/43/giitem.htm, p. 2.

37. "The Right to Study, Train and Do Research: Academic and Professional Recognition of Diplomas and Study Periods," http://citizens.eu.int/en/en/gf/st/gi/42/giitem.htm, p. 1.

38. "Support from Community Programmes: SOCRATES," http://citizens.eu.int/en/en/gf/st/gi/46/giitem.htm, p. 1.

39. Ibid., p. 2.

40. Ibid.

41. David Crystal, *English as a Global Language* (Cambridge: Cambridge University Press, 1997), pp. 60–61.

42. Braj B. Kachru, *The Alchemy of English: The Spread, Functions, and Models of Non-Native Englishes* (Urbana: University of Illinois Press, 1990), p. 1.

43. Crystal, p. 103.

44. Kachru, p. 1.

45. Crystal, p. 102.
46. Quoted by Phillipson, p. 5.
47. "United Nations Draft Declaration of Indigenous Peoples Rights," in *Voice of Indigenous Peoples: Native People Address the United Nations,* ed. Alexander Ewen (Santa Fe: Clear Light Publishers, 1994), p. 166.
48. Tove Skutnabb-Kangas, *Linguistic Genocide in Education or Worldwide Diversity and Human Rights?* (Mahwah, NJ: Lawrence Erlbaum Associates, 2000), p. 502.
49. Ibid.
50. "Declaration of the Rights of Persons Belonging to . . . ," p. 4.
51. "International Labour Organization . . . ," pp. 9–10.
52. Ibid., p. 10.
53. Joel Spring, *Globalization and Educational Rights: An Intercivilizational Analysis* (Mahwah, NJ: Lawrence Erlbaum Associates, 2001).

PART TWO

Cultural Frames
of Reference

CHAPTER 5

Cultural Frames of Reference: Monoculturalism, Biculturalism, and Ethnic Identity

Carrying a mouse in your mouth without harming it is an essential skill for boys passing into manhood among the Plashwits, a pastoral people in Turkestan, reports travel writer and novelist Paul Theroux in an article titled "Unspeakable Rituals."[1] The young boy must also fatten the mouse by feeding it flesh from his own body. Is this an unspeakable ritual? Obviously, it's not unspeakable to the Plashwits. It's Theroux's cultural frame of reference that turns the practice into something exotic and shocking. What about the body sculpture of the Mongoni of Nyasaland? Viewing beauty as skeletal and involving unnatural body curves, they cut chunks of flesh from their calves, buttocks, and face. Would the Mongoni describe the pierced tongues of U.S. youth as an unspeakable ritual? Among the Milne of New Guinea, cats are eaten in a variety of conditions, including smoked, in a sauce, dried, salted, in stews, fried, baked, and poached. Theroux reports, "I mentioned to a man . . . that cats are house pets in much of the world. He laughed at such a novel concept . . . [there] pigs are house pets."[2]

Cultural frames of reference, or what is sometimes called cultural perspective, influence the way a person interprets information from the outside world. In a small hut on the Yucatan Peninsula in Mexico, a Mayan Indian watching a U.S.-produced soap opera on television might interpret the meaning of the program quite differently from an Israeli watching the same program. On the other hand, they might have both been educated at Harvard and share a similar cultural perspective. Differences in cultural frames of reference are evidenced in the uneven spread around the world of U.S. popular culture—a popular culture which might dominate the world. A 1994 *New York Times* survey of the impact of U.S. popular culture found significant variations in what appealed to different national audiences. Spaniards loved the movies *Jurassic Park, Aladdin,* and *The Fugitive* and spent their evenings around the television watching their favorite U.S. television programs, "Beverly Hills 90210," "Melrose Place," and "The Simpsons." Meanwhile, on the other side of the globe, Chinese favored the movies *Terminator 2, First Blood,* and *Rambo* and on television watched "Growing Pains," "Roots," "Dynasty," and "The Colbys."[3]

In a multicultural society, such as the United States, cultural frames of reference are influenced by the intersection of cultures. When people are socialized for a single culture, they filter their information through the lens of that single culture. This is referred to as "monoculturalism." On the other hand, a person growing up in a multicultural society might learn to live in two different cultures. This is referred to as "biculturalism." To a certain extent all people learn to function in different cultural contexts. Students act differently in the classroom, at home, or among peers. However, in this text, *bicultural* refers to a broader cultural context in which the home, classroom, and community are nested.

Children growing up in a dominated culture such as African American, Native American, Puerto Rican, Hawaiian American, or Mexican American learn to live within the contexts of their own cultures and, at the same time, within the dominant white or Anglo culture. The immigrant child is constantly faced with the problem of moving between the culture of the family and the dominant culture of the United States. In addition, immigrants must learn to interact with dominated cultures. At times, the intersection of immigrant cultures and dominated cultures results in explosive situations, such as the conflicts between Korean shop owners and African Americans and Mexican Americans in Los Angeles and New York.

Monoculturalism and biculturalism have a direct effect on interpretations of the actions of others. For instance, there are different filters for interpreting the actions of a hostile white teacher. From the monocultural perspective of a European American, a teacher's hostile actions might be interpreted as simply a function of his or her personality. But from the perspective of a Native American or Mexican American living in the Southwest, the actions might be interpreted as racist. From the perspective of an immigrant student, the actions might be interpreted as a rejection of his or her language and culture.

Related to monoculturalism and biculturalism is identity. In the words of psychologist William Cross, "A person's identity filters incoming experiences so that information 'fits' into his or her current understanding of self and the world in which he or she lives."[4] While this chapter will focus on ethnic identity, identity is not necessarily a function of a person's general cultural background. For instance, one Native American might primarily identify with Native American culture while another Native American might primarily identify with a particular religion. This is the simple truism that not all people of a similar cultural background are the same. Religious or political affiliation might be the primary source of identity, or it might be gender or social class.

Identity can also be shaped by a person's role as a dominator or as a victim of domination. European Americans might have ambiguous feelings about their identities because of the past history of European colonialization and racism. As I will explain later, this ambiguity results in different forms of identity. In contrast, being a victim of domination affects a person's identity and perceptions of the world.

This chapter will focus on the effects of monoculturalism, biculturalism, and ethnic identity on cultural frames of reference. Of course, these are not the only filters. Political and religious beliefs, geography, customs, literature, and other influences also can act as filters. But I am focusing on those filters that are most important in the context of the United States.

MONOCULTURALISM AND BICULTURALISM

In her brilliant book, *Affirming Diversity,* Sonia Nieto captures the monocultural perspective in an interview with a 17-year-old white girl who grew up in rural New England. When asked to describe herself, she responds, "I usually describe myself as like what I believe in or something like that. Rather than like what culture I am, whether I'm Black or White. . . . Culture, what you look like, whether you're Black or White could matter less to me."[5] Nieto reports that the girl had difficulty confronting issues of race and cultural differences. She gave Nieto the impression that she felt that bringing up these things for discussion was rude and racist. Being white and Christian, she rarely faces issues of race and culture. The girl sees herself as the "norm," "just a person." Nieto concludes, "As is the case for most White Americans, she has the privilege of seeing herself as just an individual, an opportunity not generally afforded to those from dominated groups. Being White in the United States is simply not an issue."[6]

In contrast to this monocultural perspective, where race and cultural differences are not important, Nieto interviews a 17-year-old African American boy living in Boston. For him, racial identity is a central issue as he constantly thinks of school achievement and career success as a function of race. As one of the best students in a mainly black school, his bicultural perspective causes him to doubt his self-worth. He is driven to wonder whether the world of whites is better than the world of African Americans. Reflecting the doubts created by his bicultural perspective, he tells Nieto, "If you take those top Black students . . . and you put them in a classroom with . . . White students, where would you rank? . . . Most people think being a [Black] school, it's not being top. . . . I think if we had more White students, Black students would go further."[7]

The girl from rural New England and the boy from Boston exemplify differences in cultural frames of reference. In her experience, the girl from New England never encountered personal situations of discrimination against her race and culture. She never had to learn to live between two cultures and think in terms of differences of treatment between two races. Her monocultural perspective leads to a belief that the United States is a land where everyone has an equal opportunity. Her perspective emphasizes treating everyone as an individual.

In contrast, the boy sees himself as being treated not as an individual but as a member of a particular race. His thinking is dominated by a view of a bicultural and biracial world where inequality is a function of race. He must learn to move between the culture of the dominant society and the culture of the dominated. His bicultural perspective causes him to see any situation as potentially loaded with the meaning of race.

Cultural Perspective

Grades: Middle School through High School

Objectives:

1. To understand the concept of cultural perspective.
2. To understand one's personal cultural perspective.
3. To understand how differing cultural perspectives can result in differing interpretations of social situations.

Lesson:

1. Each student should write down his or her responses to the following situations. The process of writing commits the student to an initial response before class discussion. Students should be assured they will not be required to show their papers to the teacher or other students and that there are no correct responses to these situations. They are meant to be ambiguous and to create a discussion about cultural perspectives.
   a. An African American family enters a restaurant and asks for a table. They are told that they must wait since they do not have a reservation. Shortly after the African American family enters, a European American family enters and is quickly seated at a table. The European American family is *not* asked if they have a reservation. A member of the African American family objects. The European American owner explains that he knows this family and they do not need reservations. The owner suggests that the African American family might want to try another restaurant if they are in a hurry to eat.
   b. A Mexican American, African American, and European American are waiting in line to pay for items in a drug store. The cashier is African American. The Mexican American and African American pay for their goods. However, when the European American steps to the counter, the clerk quickly goes into the back of the store before the customer can pay. The cashier returns in 5 minutes.
   c. An African American is appointed to the U.S. Supreme Court.
2. After students have committed their responses by writing them down, the teacher should ask for volunteers to give their responses to these situations.
3. The responses should be listed on the chalkboard.
4. After listing the responses on the chalkboard, the teacher should ask the class why there are differing responses to these situations. Are the differing responses a result of differing cultural perspectives?

Teachers: Teachers must be open-minded and nonjudgmental in conducting this lesson. Teachers must make an effort to gain a variety of responses to these situations. The goal is to see a real-life situation from a variety of perspectives.

Outcome: Students will gain an understanding of how differing cultural perspectives can result in differing interpretations of social situations.

The development of these differences in monocultural and bicultural perspectives is revealed by psychologist William Cross in his study of young, urban, black and white mothers. The study's goal was to determine how everyday activities in their households reflected bicultural and monocultural themes. He found that white mothers did not prepare their children for a multicultural world. In these white households, television was the primary means for children discovering the existence of people of color. Cross states, "The white mothers were not explicitly white-oriented or racist; the process revealed was one of omission rather than commission."[8]

In contrast to white children, whose only exposure to a multicultural world was television, Cross found that 21 percent of the activities of black children had an explicitly black cultural base with the remainder a general white perspective. He argues that the exposure of African American children to black and white cultures was probably from a black perspective. Therefore, in the framework of his argument, the white child learned to see a primarily white world through a white perspective, while the black child learned to see a bicultural world from a black perspective.

In another study of biculturalism, a group of black and white 7- and 8-year-old boys watch a ball-tossing game between one black and one white player. The five games are controlled to produce the following results: (1) the black boy wins by a small margin; (2) the black boy loses by a small margin; (3) the black boy wins by a large margin; (4) the black boy loses by a large margin; and (5) the game is tied. Each spectator is asked to reward the winners of the games by placing 0 to 15 pieces of candy in a container. The result was that white children showed a preference for white players while, according to Cross, "Black children exhibited a black or white preference . . . suggesting, of course, the operation of a bicultural frame of reference."[9]

This bicultural perspective is exemplified in Ruben Navarette, Jr.'s autobiography, *A Darker Shade of Crimson: Odyssey of a Harvard Chicano*.[10] As a Mexican American, his school career was constantly formed by a bicultural perspective. In fact, his success in school left him straddling two cultures without feeling part of either one. With a near-perfect school record and as valedictorian of his high school class, he was admitted to Harvard. Rather than feeling positive about himself, the acceptance made him realize that the bicultural world in which he lived was filled with prejudice against him. As he perceived the situation, faculty, white students, and white parents considered his admission a result of being Mexican American and not a result of his hard work. "Reverse discrimination," declared white teachers and students. These conditions created a complex situation combining biculturalism with the psychological impact of discrimination.

Before his acceptance to Harvard, Navarette describes the high school principal squeezing into his desk during an advanced placement English class and suggesting that he apply to a state college just in case he was not accepted. The principal did think he had a chance to be accepted. "After all," the principal told him, "your race should help you a lot." With that short statement, Navarette felt that his 4 years of hard work and high achievement were dismissed. Navarette believed that the principal was unaware of the damage of his few words "to the self-image of a young man."[11] After acceptance to Harvard, his liberal white social studies teacher did not congratulate him for his academic success, but told him of his support for affirmative action. Fellow students told him that he was only accepted because he was Mexican.

His achievement created a psychological crisis. "I remember," he wrote, "that . . . one thing that I wanted was for someone, anyone, to put their hand on my shoulder, to hug me and tell me . . . I was qualified, more than qualified, to be accepted by a school like Harvard." He hoped that his days would be free of insults disguised as compliments.[12]

In the middle of despair he had a dream representing his identity crisis in a bicultural world. In the dream, he is rescued by a fellow Mexican American student. The rescue symbolizes support from his cultural background. School achievement separated him from his culture while not gaining him acceptance to white student culture. "I found myself alone," he wrote, " . . . I had painted myself into such a corner through my academic achievement." He had sacrificed his friendships with other Mexican American youth on "the altar of academic success." When confronted with the insults of white students, there were no old friends to support him.[13]

In his dream, an old Mexican American friend entered an advance placement course and told the student body president that Navarette beat him in competition for Harvard because he was smarter. The friend pointed his finger at the shaking and fearful white student and declared him a child of privilege. The friend declared that the ticket for Latinos out of the underclass was in the hands of successful Latinos like Navarette and that no one should challenge his worth. His friend won the debate. The student body president did not concede and his friend beat him up.

But, of course, there were no friends to protect him. His bicultural frame of reference left him feeling alienated from Mexican American culture and distrustful and angry toward white culture. He was caught in a space between the two cultures. In part, he blames the educational system. In his words, "The American educational system's first and most thorough lesson is one of division. Remedial students. Honors students. Gifted students. Better students."[14]

Similar to the biculturalism of dominated students, the biculturalism of immigrant children carries a heavy emotional price. In *The Inner World of Immigrant Children*, Christina Igoa illustrates the problems faced by immigrant children as they learn to be bicultural.[15] Based on her experience teaching immigrant elementary schoolchildren from Pacific Islands and Asia, she found students were emotionally pulled between yearning for their homelands and wanting to be accepted into U.S. society. Their biculturalism is a product of this often painful tension.

Compounding the problems of cultural transition is the psychological trauma of immigration. The reasons for immigration often reflect some existing problem in the home country such as political turmoil, displacement, and poverty. Even before immigration, these problems can cause psychological distress. For example, children of Vietnamese boat people often witnessed incredible human atrocities and suffered extreme physical deprivations. Torn from familiar surroundings, the actual trip can be frightening for a young child. In addition, the child's formal education suffers during the period of transition.

After the psychological strain of immigration, children are placed in classrooms before they know English, without friends, and with no knowledge of the expectations of U.S. schools. In her classroom, Igoa found the first reaction is to withdraw. She calls this the "silent stage." Faced with a new language and culture, immigrant children withdraw into silence. Igoa's objective is to break through this silence by acknowledging their cultural roots and helping them to understand and deal with the psychological pain of immigration.

One of the techniques developed by Igoa involves students in the creation of filmstrips with pictures and text. These filmstrips help the children express their emotional difficulties in the transition to biculturalism. For instance, a filmstrip by a 10-year-old Vietnamese girl, Dung, depicts in the first frame an egg in a nest on a branch of a tree. The next frames show the nest in transition from winter to the following spring when from the egg hatches a beautiful bird. The next series of frames shows the bird flying to Vietnam where it rests on the window of a little girl's house. The little girl brings the bird into the house and nurtures it until maturity. In the last frames, the bird leaves the house and finds a mate. The two birds return each year to visit the girl.[16]

Igoa believes the egg symbolizes the transition to another culture. The egg sits in the nest waiting to hatch into the new culture. This period, representing the silent stage, takes over a year. After the bird leaves the nest, it must fly for a period to gain courage to build a new nest. Symbolically, the bird returns to Vietnam to gain this strength. It is the ties to the old culture that provide the strength for the transition to the new. The bird's new nest symbolizes the bicultural transition. According to Igoa, the "nesting" time provides the immigrant child time to protect his or her values, beliefs, and language from ridicule by members of the new culture.

Both the bicultural perspective of immigrant and dominated cultures and the monocultural perspective of the dominant culture can cause misinterpretation of the actions of others. For instance, the monocultural perspective of a white teacher can lead to misinterpretation of the actions of other cultures. White teachers often misinterpret the avoidance of eye contact by Latino and Native American students as a sign of potential dishonesty. For many whites with a monocultural perspective, looking directly into another person's eyes is an indication of trustworthiness and reliability. On the other hand, many Latino children believe that looking a teacher directly in the eyes is a sign of disrespect. For Native Americans it can be a sign of hostility. A monocultural perspective can also result in teachers missing important cues from their students. Puerto Rican students often wrinkle their noses to ask, What? Sometimes teachers will ignore this form of questioning by Puerto Rican students and assume they understand the lesson.[17]

Members of dominated cultures may also misinterpret the actions of whites. In *Light of the Feather: Pathways Through Contemporary Indian Culture,* Mick Fedullo recounts how Apache youth interpret the stares of "Anglos" as acts of hostility. In an open discussion, Apache youths complained to Fedullo that local townspeople displayed hostility toward them. One young man described being in a restaurant and feeling hostility from the other patrons. As the discussion progressed, Fedullo learned that, among Apaches, staring is a sign of aggression and hostility. The feelings of hostility the youth felt in town and in restaurants were a result of being stared at by "Anglos." As the discussion progressed, the youth began to realize that, for white culture, staring is not necessarily an act of aggression and confrontation. For instance, white tourists might stare at them because they were curious and, maybe, had never seen an Indian. In fact, in some situations, a stare might be a sign of sympathetic appreciation. One result of this discussion was to help the youth to be more bicultural so that he could exist in both the culture of the reservation and the dominant white culture of the town.[18]

Sometimes there is a misinterpretation of actions as two bicultural groups intersect. In New York, there is a history of animosity among Koreans, Puerto Ricans, and African Americans. While many Korean immigrants become bicultural in their interactions with the dominant society, they often have difficulty understanding the cultures of dominated groups. In turn, while African Americans and Puerto Ricans are bicultural with regard to the dominant white society, they have not learned to be multicultural regarding people of Asian descent. The result is conflict, prejudice, and open hostility among these groups.[19] To solve these problems, a bicultural perspective must become multicultural.

In summary, monocultural, bicultural, and multicultural perspectives are important filters in a person's cultural frame of reference. These perspectives filter the actions of others and institutions. The monoculturalism of some members of the dominant society makes it difficult for them to understand the actions, feelings, and needs of people of other cultures. Having never been the victim of racism and prejudice, they can dismiss the importance of cultural differences and argue that all people should be treated as individuals. But members of dominated groups feel that they are not treated as individuals but as members of a group. Often African Americans, Native Americans, Mexican Americans, and Puerto Ricans feel that whites see them primarily in terms of their skin color and not as individuals. As Bessie Delany states, "It always seemed to me that white people were judged as individuals. But if a Negro did something stupid or wrong, it was held against all of us. Negroes were always representing the whole race."[20] For immigrant children, gaining a bicultural perspective involves a painful transition into U.S. society. But, as dramatized by the conflict among Koreans, African Americans, and Puerto Ricans, this bicultural perspective might need to become a multicultural perspective.

DEVELOPMENT OF ETHNIC IDENTITY

What is an ethnic group? As I am using the term, *ethnic group* refers to any group of individuals sharing a common set of beliefs and values. This broad definition encompasses a large number of groups. For instance, the ethnic designation of all people living in France might be French. In addition, this grouping can be broken down according to religion, yielding French Catholic, French Protestant, and French Moslem. Or, the groupings could be by political beliefs, such as French Socialist, French Nationalist, or French Communist.

Ethnic identity provides a means of narrowing the meaning of ethnicity. *Ethnic identity* is defined as "a set of self-ideas about one's own ethnic group membership."[21] In other words, one's ethnicity is dependent on self-definition. People can identify themselves according to their religion, nationality, political affiliation, career, hobby, or primary social activity.

For instance, a study of black gay men found that for some their primary identity was African American, while for others their primary identity was gay. Those who identified themselves primarily as African American lived in black communities, participated in black culture, and had black friends and lovers. They felt alienated from the white gay community. On the other hand, the gay-identified black men most often lived in gay communities, had white lovers, and felt alienated from the black community.[22]

A person's ethnic identity acts as a filter for interpreting the actions of other people. If your primary ethnic identity is Native American, then you might interpret outside events primarily from that perspective. The same thing is true if your identity is primarily tied to conservative politics or a liberal religion.

The concern of this text is with cultural identity. Therefore, my concern is with the development of ethnic identity as related to a particular cultural group. For my purposes, I am going to use the stages of the development of ethnic identity created by William Cross in his study of African Americans. While Cross's study focused on one specific culture, I believe it is applicable to other cultures.

Below is a list of these stages in the formation of ethnic identity:

1. Pre-encounter
2. Encounter
3. Immersion-emersion
4. Immersion
5. Internalization

It is important to note that these stages were developed within the context of U.S. society with the assumption that the dominant culture is a product of white Anglo-Saxon Protestant traditions. I am also taking the liberty of adapting Cross's categories not only to other dominated cultures, but also to all immigrant cultures, including European immigrants.[23]

Pre-encounter

For dominated groups, the pre-encounter stage involves a certain level of self-hatred. African Americans, Native Americans, Puerto Ricans, and Mexican Americans who fall into this category often speak disparagingly of their own people. Often, this self-hatred is a product of stereotypes projected by the dominant culture. These negative stereotypes are internalized and form the person's ethnic identity. These stereotypes could include being lazy, stupid, undepend-able, dirty, and criminal. The dominant society can project these stereotypes through conversation, books, movies, television, radio, magazines, and news-papers.

Encountering these negative stereotypes, members of a dominated group could make them their own. Once internalized, for instance, a Native American might talk about Native Americans as being lazy, stupid, and undependable. Native Americans might also identify their own behaviors with these stereo-types. Identifying themselves as probable school failures, they fail at school.

Media are an important source for these stereotypes. For example, in the 1970s, the Mexican American Anti-defamation Committee and other Chicano organizations conducted a campaign against the Frito Bandito, which was used in television commercials by Frito Lay brand corn chips. The cartoon character was charged with creating a racist image of Mexican Americans as sneaky thieves. These groups also attacked another television character, Jose Jimenez, who, it was charged, created the image of Mexican Americans as being happy-go-lucky and not very bright.[24]

Immigrant children face the same possibilities as members of dominated groups. They can become victims of negative stereotyping because of their speech, manners, and skin color. In some cases stereotyping might not be thought of as negative by the dominant culture. For instance, Asians are sometimes stereotyped as being model students. But being a "model" student, in this case, implies being passive and obedient. Many people of Asian descent object to this identity. In discussing the stereotypes of Asian American women, *The New York Times* reported, "They confront a society that often typecasts Asian American women as meek and submissive, as good workers but bad managers." Setsuko Nishi, professor of sociology at Brooklyn College, states, "It is a stereotype that all Asian Americans face, but one that is particularly strong for women."[25]

European Americans have also faced negative stereotypes. In the 1970s, the Italian-American League to Combat Defamation, the German-American Anti-Defamation League, and the Polish-American Guardian Society were orga-nized to combat negative stereotypes on television and in movies. In the media, Italians were portrayed as being members of the Mafia and cold-blooded killers; Germans were treated as heartless Nazis; and Polish people, the victims of some of the most disparaging ethnic jokes, were portrayed as stupid and in-competent.

Encounter

In the encounter stage, a person is confronted with an incident that forces him or her to question his or her ethnic identity. Members of dominated and immi-grant groups are forced to question the negative stereotypes that they made part of their own identity.

William Cross provides several examples of situations that forced many African Americans to reevaluate their pre-encounter identity, including the death of Dr. Martin Luther King, Jr., being assaulted by the police, watching other blacks being victims of police brutality, watching a racial incident on television, and experiencing racism in employment or education. The previously discussed example of Ruben Navarette's encounter with prejudicial thinking by teachers and fellow high school students after being admitted to Harvard forced him into an identity crisis that required a rethinking of his ethnic identity. In the novel *Jasmine*, Bharati Mukherjee portrays incidents ranging from rape to love affairs that cause the main character, an immigrant from India, to change her identity and become an "American."[26]

The encounter causes members of dominated and immigrant groups to think about their ethnic identity. They begin to see self-hatred as a product of negative stereotypes. They see themselves as part of a larger group experiencing similar social barriers. The encounter causes people to ask, Why do I think this about myself?

Immersion-Emersion

This is an in-between stage, where dominated and immigrant people begin to shed their self-hatred and rush to a new ethnic identity. Native Americans rediscover their traditional culture. Immigrants begin to wear traditional clothes and recapture customs that have been lost. According to Cross, "This stage of being 'in-between' explains why new converts are so attracted to symbols of the new identity (dress codes, hair styles, flags, national colors, etc.), code phrases, party lines, ten-point programs, rigid ideologies."[27]

Suddenly, the Native American who throughout his or her life wore standard American clothes now wears beads, beaded jackets, and turquoise bracelets. The African American wears an "Afro" hairstyle and dresses in a dashiki. People of Italian descent criticize themselves for never learning to speak Italian and rush to buy pasta machines. A second-generation Italian commented to me that her generation in the 1950s abandoned traditional Italian delicatessens because they were considered old-fashioned and bought prepackaged macaroni-and-cheese mixes in the supermarket. In the 1990s, her children want to learn how to make traditional ravioli and rush to delicatessens to buy sun-dried tomatoes while turning up their noses at the prepackaged "pseudo" Italian food found in supermarkets.

Immersion

At this stage there is a complete immersion in a person's ethnic culture. African Americans attend political and cultural affairs that focus on black issues. Afrocentricity becomes an important area of interest. Native Americans organize pow-wows to discuss common problems and join the politically active American Indian Movement. Mexican Americans join La Raza and other organizations focusing on Chicano issues. Puerto Ricans involve themselves in a serious discussion about independence and make sure that their children grow up speaking Spanish and knowing their island culture. Descendants of Greeks, Italians, Russians, Chinese, Koreans, and other immigrant groups join organizations reflecting their cultural backgrounds. All ethnic groups seek out the literature and music of their culture. In addition, there is a rush to create a new ethnic literature reflecting generational changes within ethnic communities.

During this stage there is what Cross calls the "Blacker-than-thou" syndrome."[28] As people are immersed in their ethnic background they begin to judge themselves according to identification with ethnic origin. After immersion in Polish culture, a Polish American might criticize other fellow ethnics for not knowing and living by Polish traditions. One Native American might try to prove by knowledge and practices of traditions that he or she is more Native American than others of Indian descent. There develops an attitude of "ethnic correctness."

For dominated groups, this stage involves a verbalization and acting out of anger against the dominators. Black militants take what Cross calls the "I dare you, whitey" stance.[29] The same stance is taken by other groups. Native Americans marched on Washington on the "trail of broken treaties" and took over the enemies' office buildings. Mexican American students struck public schools in Los Angeles demanding that Chicano foods be served in cafeterias. Puerto Rican organizations struggled to assure bilingual education programs.[30]

The anger associated with the "I dare you, whitey" stance provides the emotional energy to expel the final vestiges of domination of the mind. An understanding develops of the source of internalized negative stereotypes. The immersion in ethnic culture changes people's perspective of events. Italian Americans now think in terms of the importance of Italian art and thought to the development of Western art and literature. The world is now seen through a new lens reflecting a person's ethnic background. As Asante suggests, these new lenses cause people to read newspapers differently, see television programming in a different light, find different meanings in music, and change interpretations of other people's actions.

At this stage, a Native American encountering a U.S. history book that begins with Columbus and focuses on European immigrants will say to himself or herself, That's the white man's history. When told that America is the land of freedom, the African American now replies: That's the white man's point of view; there is freedom for whites but not for me. When reading that schools are a source of equality of opportunity, the Mexican American thinks: Equality of opportunity for Anglos—schooling has segregated my people, attempted to destroy my culture, and is often denied to my people. Now when Puerto Ricans hear about the U.S. government spreading democracy around the world they respond, But we were colonized!

Internalization

Biculturalism and multiculturalism can become the mode at this stage of ethnic identity. Persons come to terms with living within the culture of the United States while having a continuing relationship with an ethnic culture. They have a view of the dominant culture which is both accepting and critical. They identify with certain aspects of U.S. culture such as material abundance and independence while rejecting those aspects of the culture that are racist and oppressive. The Italian American can say, "Yes, American culture has distorted the image of my people by making them all look like gangsters. But, I am an American and I like the material goods that I can get." The African American can say, "Some whites are brutal and mean, but not all. Whether I like it or not, I did grow up in this culture. Things can improve if we keep struggling." The Korean American now realizes that to survive in U.S. society he or she must be multicultural and understand the workings of the dominant culture and the cultures of African Americans, Puerto Ricans, and Mexican Americans.

For dominated groups at this stage, anger becomes focused on specific forms of oppression. Not all whites are condemned. Only those whites guilty of oppression are targets of anger. As 102-year-old Bessie Delany says, "Sometimes I am angry at all white people, until I stop and think of the nice white people I have known in my life. OK, OK, there have been a few. I admit it. . . . Sometimes they are hard to find, but they're out there."[31] Native American leaders criticize the U.S. government while pursuing tribal rights in the court system.

Cross argues that this internalized identity serves three main functions. First, it protects from insults that might come from members of other ethnic groups. A person feels secure in his or her identity and therefore is psychologically prepared to deal with racial and cultural prejudice. Second, it provides a sense of belonging. A person feels that he or she belongs to a larger cultural group. And last, it provides a foundation for dealing with people from other cultures.[32]

CONCLUSION: ETHNIC IDENTITY, BICULTURALISM, AND MONOCULTURALISM

Similar to other attempts to fit psychological and social issues into neat categories, these five stages do not explain all the complexities of ethnic identity. People can be found who demonstrate characteristics from several stages. In addition, I want to emphasize that many people do not identify themselves according to their cultural backgrounds. Identity can be a function of religion, politics, hobbies, or career. Despite these limitations, the five stages provide a way of thinking about differences in identity and the transition from a monocultural to a bicultural perspective.

In Chapter 6, I will relate monocultural, bicultural, and ethnic perspectives to history, gender, and social class. The combination of these factors in a person's cultural frame of reference helps to explain both group identity and individualism. A person's cultural perspective is an individual combination of lenses that filter an understanding of the world. One person can interpret the world through a cultural frame of reference that is female, upper class, bicultural, and at an immersion stage of ethnic identity. In addition, this person's interpretation of the world might be shaped by a particular understanding of history. Another person might share some of these perspectives, but, for instance,

LESSON 5.2

What Is Your Ethnic Identity?

Grades: High School through College

Objectives:

1. To have students understand the concept of ethnic identity.
2. To have students define their own ethnic identity.
3. To have students identify their own stage of development of their ethnic identity.

Lesson:

1. Explain to the class the concept of ethnic identity.
2. Ask students to write down what they consider to be their ethnic identities.
3. Explain to the class the stages in the formation of ethnic identity: (1) pre-encounter; (2) encounter; (3) immersion-emersion stage; (4) immersion; (5) internalization.
4. Ask students to explain in writing the stage of ethnic development they feel they are at.
5. As a model for the class, the teacher writes her/his ethnic identity on the board and stage of formation of personal ethnic identity.
6. Ask for volunteers to discuss their stage of ethnic development.
7. Teachers should list on the board different ethnic identities of class members along with their stages of ethnic development.

Teachers: It is important for teachers to participate in this exercise by indicating to the class their ethnic identity and stage in the formation of that identity. Teachers should also be aware that this exercise is often difficult for many white students who claim not to have an ethnic identity. Teachers should raise the issues of "whiteness" as a form of ethnic identity.

Outcome: Students will have a better understanding of the concept of ethnic identity and how it relates to themselves and others.

be monocultural with a different understanding of history. The sharing of perspectives can give a person a group identity. On the other hand, the unique combination of lenses can create an individual identity.

PERSONAL FRAMES OF REFERENCE

In the context of this chapter, you might want to determine your own cultural frame of reference.

1. Are you monocultural or bicultural? Why?
2. Is an ethnic identity important to you? Why or why not?
3. Can you place yourself in any of the stages of ethnic identity discussed in this chapter?
4. Do you interpret the actions of teachers, police, retail clerks, restaurant workers, and politicians differently from those of other racial and ethnic groups?
5. Do you have any group identities?
6. Is your individual identity separate from your group identities?

Notes

1. Paul Theroux, "Unspeakable Rituals," *Granta* 61 (Spring 1998), pp. 143–57.
2. Ibid., p. 148.
3. "Channel-Surfing Through U.S. Culture in 20 Lands," *The New York Times,* 30 January 1994, pp. H30–H31.
4. William E. Cross, Jr., *Shades of Black: Diversity in African-American Identity* (Philadelphia: Temple University Press, 1991), pp. 198–99.
5. Sonia Nieto, *Affirming Diversity: The Sociopolitical Context of Multicultural Education,* (White Plains, NY: Longman Inc., 1992), p. 61.
6. Ibid., p. 65.
7. Ibid., p. 54.
8. Cross, *Shades of Black,* p. 120.
9. Ibid., p. 121.
10. Ruben Navarette, Jr., *A Darker Shade of Crimson: Odyssey of a Harvard Chicano* (New York: Bantam Books, 1993).
11. Ibid., p. 13.
12. Ibid., p. 18.
13. Ibid., pp. 19–20.
14. Ibid., p. 20.
15. Cristina Igoa, *The Inner World of Immigrant Children* (New York: St. Martin's Press, 1995).
16. Ibid., pp. 66–68.
17. See Nieto, *Affirming Diversity,* pp. 110–11; and Mick Fedullo, *Light of the Feather: Pathways Through Contemporary Indian America* (New York: William Morrow, 1992), pp. 107–21.
18. Fedullo, pp. 112–13.
19. For Korean attitudes regarding African Americans and Puerto Ricans see Thomas Kessner and Betty Boyd Caroli, *Today's Immigrants: Their Stories* (New York: Oxford University Press, 1982), pp. 123–43.

20. Sarah Delany and A. Elizabeth Delany with Amy Hearth, *Having Our Say: The Delany Sisters' First 100 Years* (New York: Kodansha International, 1993), p. 129.

21. Martha E. Bernal and George P. Knight, "Introduction," in *Ethnic Identity: Formation and Transmission Among Hispanics and Other Minorities*, eds. Martha E. Bernal and George P. Knight (Albany: New York State University Press, 1993), p. 1.

22. Cross, pp. 126–27.

23. I want to emphasize that any problems with the adaptation of these categories to other dominated groups, immigrants, and members of the dominant culture are mine and not those of William Cross.

24. Kathryn C. Montgomery, *Target: Prime Time Advocacy Groups and the Struggle over Entertainment Television* (New York: Oxford University Press, 1989), pp. 51–58.

25. "Asian American Women Struggling to Move Past Cultural Expectations," *The New York Times*, 23 January 1994, p. 14L.

26. Bharati Mukherjee, *Jasmine* (New York, Fawcett Crest, 1989).

27. Cross, p. 202.

28. Ibid., p. 205.

29. Ibid., p. 206.

30. Joel Spring, *Deculturalization and the Struggle for Equality: A Brief History of the Education of Dominated Cultures in the United States*, 4th ed. (Burr Ridge, IL: McGraw-Hill, 2004), pp. 100–125.

31. Delany, p. 10.

32. Cross, p. 210.

CHAPTER 6

Cultural Frames of Reference: History, Gender, and Social Class

Cultural frames of reference provide both a group identity and an individual identity. Perspectives that a person shares with other people provide a group identity, while a particular combination of cultural perspectives contributes to an individual identity. Historical images are important factors in establishing group and individual identities. History is related to a person's identity and understanding of his or her place in society. History is an image of the past that guides a person's future actions. It is one filter for interpreting impressions from outside. As I will discuss later, a distinction must be made between official history and folk history. Official history is the history presented in textbooks. It is a public presentation of one's identity. Immigrant students from Vietnam might see an official presentation of themselves in a world history textbook or they might find themselves totally missing. In either case, the students are affected by this public presentation. Folk history, on the other hand, is the oral history within the family and community. It is the history told at the dinner table. Folk history can sometimes be a corrective to neglect or distortion of an identity found in official history.

Of particular importance to multicultural education are attitudes about institutions, particularly the school. For dominated cultures in the United States, the school can be both a hope for future improvement and a hostile institution. For immigrant children the school might be viewed as a key to success and assimilation into U.S. society. Attitudes toward the school are a product of folk history. For instance, Native Americans have developed ambivalent attitudes toward the school because of the history, as I will explain later, of the U.S. government using education as a method for destroying traditional Native American culture.

Gender is a major influence on perspective. For dominated groups, the gender issue is sometimes secondary to the issues of racial and cultural discrimination. For immigrant groups, gender issues can divide families, particularly over the issue of female independence. Immigrant men might resent the increased independence both of their wives and of their daughters. In some situations, there is a concern about strengthening gender roles. This is particularly true in Afrocentric education which, in part, is designed to provide positive male role models for young black boys.

A person's social class in the United States has an important impact on his or her perspective regarding education. Public school districts in the United States range from those lacking textbooks, adequate facilities, and regular teachers to elite districts with small classes, college-type curricula, and an abundance of learning resources. Social class is also important in dominated cultures, but, as was sometimes the case with gender issues, racial and cultural prejudice might be more important.

OFFICIAL HISTORY AND FOLK HISTORY DEFINED

History creates images of the past that influence cultural frames of reference. It is also a source of a person's identity. Who we are is a product of history. We are history. If a peoples' images of their country's past is one of glory and humanity, then they might feel more willing to take up arms to protect it. If the image is of a country that terrorized and exploited other people, then a person is less willing to protect it. If people find their cultural history applauded, they are more likely to have a positive identity and a sense of pride about themselves and their culture. On the other hand, being neglected or demeaned results in a negative identity.

Monocultural and bicultural perspectives are related to a person's historical knowledge. A monocultural and Eurocentric history of the United States focuses on the expansion of Europeans in North America and the development of European American institutions. An African American or Native American learning this historical perspective might see the country through a Eurocentric lens. On the other hand, a bicultural perspective understands that dominated and dominant groups can have different perspectives about history.

Official history is the history given in textbooks and in displays in museums and historical societies. It is a history that gives a public demonstration of who you are. Official history gives a person a public identity. For those with a monocultural perspective, official history is a history of European culture and institutions. For the bicultural person, official history should provide both an image of Americanism and of ethnic identity.

Folk history is the history passed on by word of mouth. It is the history given at the dinner table. Many times folk history and official history are in conflict. Official history might present an image of the United States as a land of freedom, whereas the folk history of dominated groups presents an image of freedom for whites only. Sometimes, folk history simply fills in the spaces missing in official histories. Recent immigrant children might find little in the official history about themselves, but their relatives and friends can tell them the history of their country and immigration.

Folk history also plays an important role in developing attitudes about U.S. schools. As I will discuss in this section, African Americans, Native Americans, Puerto Ricans, and Mexican Americans have had many negative experiences in their history of relations with public schools. Unlike official history, which presents the public school as a benign and helpful institution, these folk histories present the potentially destructive and negative aspects of public schooling.

OFFICIAL HISTORY

Recent changes in the ethnic composition of textbooks are the result of political pressure from civil rights and ethnic organizations. This is important to understand because official history does not fall out of the sky. It is the product of decisions by publishers, authors, and public officials. For many years, dominated groups were completely neglected in textbooks. But, even though there is now a greater inclusion of the history of dominated groups, these official histories can be disputed. For instance, should public school history textbooks use the term "genocide" in reference to the treatment of Native Americans by the U.S. government? Should public school textbooks explain that the Founding Fathers intended the United States to contain a primarily white population and that they wanted an opportunity to increase the population of white Europeans in the world? Should U.S. history textbooks attempt to unite citizens around a core set of white Anglo-Saxon Protestant values as advocated by Arthur Schlesinger, Jr.? And, in opposition to Schlesinger, should textbooks present history from differing cultural perspectives?

The content of textbooks has always been a political battleground. When the United States joined forces with England during World War I, history textbooks in U.S. schools were changed to present a more positive image of England. Prior to these changes, England, because of its wars with the United States, its support of the Confederacy during the Civil War, and its colonial empire, was treated negatively.[1] During the 1950s and 1960s, civil rights groups forced important changes in the content of textbooks.

To appreciate the efforts of civil rights groups, consider the results of a 1950s study of the content of elementary school readers. The study combined all the characteristics of American life present in these readers and called this compilation "Textbook Town." In Textbook Town, everyone was white and lived in suburban houses with manicured lawns. All fathers wore suits to a business or professional job. The mother had no occupation outside of housework and only left the house on shopping and family recreation trips. The children were all happy and well adjusted and spent their time doing minor chores or playing. The only emotional crisis in Textbook Town was the illness of a family pet. Otherwise, everyone was happy, parents never fought, and siblings always joyfully played together. The author of the study, Frank Tannenbaum, wrote, "To the lower-class child it looms as a 'never-never world' that may excite in him vague dreams for attainment, but which will probably elude him forever."[2]

When civil rights groups protested the white middle-class content of textbooks, publishers responded by "sun-burning" textbook photographs. Sunburning involves the simple process of taking a previous textbook photograph and coloring some of the people brown. By the late 1960s and 1970s, civil rights groups were able to achieve a greater inclusion of the histories of dominated people and their accomplishments. Textbooks began to include people of color, women in roles other than housewives, and people living in cities.[3]

In the 1990s, the textbook issue changed from one of inclusion of dominated groups to the issue of what form this inclusion should take. Differences over how dominated groups should be presented in official histories is illustrated by Terrie Epstein's response to New York State Commissioner of Education Thomas Sobol's defense of teaching core values. Epstein, a professor of social studies education at the University of Michigan, quotes a poem celebrating the United States presented by Robert Frost at the 1960 inauguration of President John F. Kennedy. As an example of a particular perspective on American history, the poem never mentions Africans or Native Americans while listing the deeds of Europeans in North America. Frost has God nodding "His" approval at the "great four" (Washington, Adams, Jefferson, and Madison) as they fashioned a new government. Obviously, the African slaves and Native Americans of the time did not view these men as the "great four."[4]

As Epstein argues, there is more interpretation in the writing of history than there is something called "truth." History is the product of the perspective of the historian. As an example of the importance of historical interpretation, Epstein analyzes the treatment of Malcolm X and the black power movement in two high school history books. One book is written by a conservative historian, Daniel Boorstin. The perspective in this textbook, Epstein writes, places Malcolm X and the black power movement against a "historical backdrop of violence perpetrated mainly by African Americans who wantonly destroy themselves or others like them, along with their communities."[5] The second textbook was written by Winthrop Jordan, who is an expert in the history of race relations and believes in the power of social movements to bring about positive change—a political perspective which is almost the exact opposite from the one held by Boorstin. From Jordan's perspective, Epstein writes, Malcolm X and the black power movement "are set against the background of interracial violence as well as within the broader context of African-American political thought . . . [the author highlights] the positive as well as the negative consequences of the black power movement for African Americans and European Americans alike."[6]

These two different interpretations demonstrate differences in historical perspective. They also indicate the potential effect of different forms of official history on the reader. In the first version, a European American reader might carry away images of African Americans engaged in acts of terror and forming political movements that will disrupt society. An African American reader might internalize an image of African Americans as violent, and their social and political efforts of little value. In the second version, a European American reader might carry away an image of both whites and blacks being violent, and of the black community being provoked by the racial violence of the white community. In addition, the white reader encounters a serious discussion of African American political thought, something dismissed in the first version. The

Official History Versus the People's History

Note: A high school history textbook, since it is approved by government officials, represents the best example of official history.

Grades: High School through College

Objective:

To understand the difference between official history and other forms of history.

Lesson:

High school students doing this lesson could use their own history textbooks while college students can obtain high school history textbooks from their college's curriculum library.

1. Borrow from library sources copies of Howard Zinn's *A People's History of the United States: 1492 to Present* (New York: Harper Perennial, 2001).
2. Divide the class into small groups of four or five students.
3. Assign each group a specific historical period such as colonial America, the revolutionary era, slavery, Civil War, etc.
4. Have each group compare its high school texts to Zinn's book by listing differences in emphasis and interpretation.
5. Have each group list differences between the two histories on the chalkboard.
6. In class discussion have students reflect on the possible effect of official history on student attitudes about the United States.

Teachers: Teachers should constantly stress throughout this exercise that historical interpretations reflect the political and social bias of the historian. Official history is meant to create a single and national interpretation of history.

Outcome: Students will have a better understanding of how historical interpretations can affect a person's world view.

African American reader learns to appreciate the impact of black political movements and might consider them as a possibility for future action.

For Asian Americans, neglect in textbooks could have a negative effect on self-identity. Similar to dominated groups who at one time could not find themselves in textbooks, people of Asian descent and recent Asian immigrants have a hard time finding themselves in texts. A 1993 study of 47 world history, world culture, and world geography texts for elementary and secondary schools by the National Project on Asia in American Schools found that more than 75 percent did not adequately treat the histories of Asian civilizations. Even some of the 25 percent of the books given a "highly recommended" and "recommended" rating failed to adequately cover Asian history. The study found that the texts gave only superficial treatment to Asian religions and social values. In addition, the treatment is depersonalized, with little mention being given of Asian leaders. The books focus on political and military history, while neglecting social, intellectual, and artistic history.[7]

In summary, official history is often a product of political struggles over images. These images have an effect on a person's future decisions. Historical perspective influences personal perspective. The question for the reader is whether public school books should present a monocultural or a bicultural and multicultural perspective. A person's position on this debate reflects his or her general position on the debate about multicultural education. Those people adhering to the position of teaching core values or cultural literacy would want official history to be from a monocultural perspective, with the history of dominated cultures being presented from this perspective. Those people supporting ethnocentric education would want history taught from the monocultural perspective of their ethnic group. For instance, an Afrocentric or Native American–centered school would teach history from an African American or Native American perspective. Those arguing for a social empowerment approach to multiculturalism would want multiple perspectives of history taught to all students. A student would learn to see history from the standpoint of many cultures. And, for those advocating cultural literacy, history should be taught from the perspective of the dominant culture.

FOLK HISTORY

Sipping her iced tea, Elenore Cassadore, Apache elder and bilingual teacher, expressed the feelings of some tribal members regarding schools. "But there's a lot of parents and grandparents," she said to Mike Fedullo, "you don't know, and they probably wouldn't want to know you . . . all they remember about school is . . . all these Anglos trying to make them forget they were Apaches; trying to make them turn against their parents, telling them that Indian ways were evil."[8]

Cassadore's sentiments are similar to those expressed by Ruben Navarrette's father. Reflecting on the discrimination and prejudice encountered by Mexican Americans in public schools, Navarrette writes, "For sixty years, he

What Did My Family Teach Me about Race?

Grades: High School through College

Objectives:

To understand:

1. The role of the family in shaping racial attitudes.
2. How the racial composition of the family might shape family lessons about race.

Lesson:

1. Ask students to write a short essay about their families' attitudes about race. This essay could include discussions of the following situations:
   a. The reactions of family members to racial issues.
   b. Family discussions or nondiscussions of racial issues. The fact that race might never have been a topic of family discussion is important because it might reflect a denial or avoidance of racial issues in the United States.
   c. Family encounters with members of other races. The lack of family encounters with members of other races is important because it suggests racial isolation, which does influence the thinking of children about race.
2. The essay should be written from the perspective of the racial composition of the family. For instance, consider the following types of questions:
   a. How do African American families discuss and react to European American, Mexican American, and Asian American people?
   b. What do Mexican American families think of African Americans and European Americans?

Racial Attitudes of Families

	FAMILY ATTITUDES ABOUT OTHER RACES					
Race of Family	Mexican American	African American	Puerto Rican American	Asian American	Native American	Other
Mexican American						
African American						
Puerto Rican American						
European American						
Asian American						
Native American						
Other						

(continued)

   c. What do Asian Americans think of European Americans and African Americans?

  3. After completion of the essays ask students to volunteer their reflections on their families' influence on their attitudes about race.

  4. If the class is racially heterogenous, the teacher should draw on the chalkboard the table on the previous page representing differing racial attitudes based on the race of the family. The number of actual racial categories will depend on the racial composition of the class.

  5. The teacher should fill in the table's blank boxes by soliciting suggestions from the class.

Teachers: Teachers should be aware of the potential complexity of the class discussion. First, not all families are racially homogenous. Second, there may be disputes over racial attitudes between family members. The teacher should adjust the lesson when these situations are raised.

Outcome: Students will gain an understanding of family influences on racial attitudes and the differing racial attitudes based on the racial composition of families.

[his father] has carried with him the impression that *los gringos* consider themselves better than nonwhite people and are inclined to use societal institutions to support that prejudice."[9]

The folk history of schools is often in conflict with official history. Official history of public schools creates an image of a helpful institution which experienced a period of racial segregation that was overcome by the civil rights movement. As a helpful institution, cultural minority groups and immigrants can look to it as a means of equality of opportunity. In contrast to this official image of the schools, the folk history of dominated groups creates a much more ambivalent image. For African Americans, the school is both a hope and a source of frustration because of the continual denial of equal educational opportunity. For Native Americans, the school was a means of destroying their culture. For Mexican Americans and Puerto Ricans, public schools are both a hope and a means for eradicating their cultures and language.

As indicated by Cassadore and Navarrette, this ambivalent attitude is a result of the folk history of families. And, this folk history is based on real events. Consider the educational history of Native Americans. In the nineteenth and early twentieth centuries, the U.S. government pursued a policy designed to strip Native Americans of their cultural heritage and replace it with European American culture. The stated method of the policy was to remove children from family and tribal influence at a young age so that traditions, customs, and language could not be passed on to them. Removed from their families, children were placed in boarding schools where they were not allowed, under the threat of severe punishment, to speak their native tongues, practice their religions, wear traditional clothing, or follow their native customs. Commissioner of Indian Affairs Thomas Morgan stated in 1889, "Children should be taken at as early an age as possible, before camp life has made an indelible stamp upon them."[10] Richard Pratt, founder of the first off-reservation boarding school, described his educational method as immersing "Indians in our civilization and when we get them under holding them there until they are thoroughly soaked."[11]

Puerto Ricans and Mexican Americans experienced similar treatment in public schools. Puerto Rico was annexed to the United States after Spain was defeated in 1898 in the Spanish–American War. It is important to note that Puerto Ricans never asked to become part of the United States. Similar to Native Americans, Puerto Ricans are a conquered people. Consequently, the U.S. government, in both Native American schools and Puerto Rican schools, mandated patriotic exercises to win the loyalty of the children to the conquerors. As part of an attempt to destroy Puerto Rican culture, the government mandated the use of textbooks reflecting the way of life in the United States. In addition, there was an attempt to replace the use of Spanish with English. It was this language policy that created the greatest resistance among Puerto Ricans. Eventually, the language policy was defeated.[12]

Mexican Americans faced not only attempts to destroy their culture and language but also discrimination, segregation, and the denial of educational opportunities. After the U.S. government captured the northern territories of Mexico and annexed Texas in 1848, there developed widespread discrimination against the conquered Mexican Americans. In 1855, the California Bureau of Instruction mandated, in an effort to end the use of Spanish in the schools, that instruction be conducted in English. In 1870, the Texas state legislature passed a law requiring that English be the language of instruction. In *The Decline of the Californios: A Social History of the Spanish-Speaking California*, Leonard Pitt writes regarding these requirements, "This linguistic purism went hand in hand with the nativist sentiments expressed in that year's legislature, including the suspension of the publication of state laws in Spanish."[13] After the immigration of Mexican farm workers in the late nineteenth and early twentieth centuries, one of the major goals of school systems was to deny an education to the children of Mexican workers. As one Texas farmer said, "Educating the Mexicans is educating them away from the job, away from the dirt."[14] When they did attend school, they attended segregated schools. In 1918, the Texas state legislature made it a criminal offense to use any language but English in the schools.

African Americans experienced a paradoxical situation with regard to schooling. Freed from slavery, the rush for an education was considered an essential step in the exercise of freedom. At incredible sacrifice, African Americans were able to overcome the legally enforced illiteracy of slavery. But, in their efforts, they often encountered public school systems which segregated and denied equality of opportunity. Similar to the experience of Mexican Americans, the public school was seen as an institution designed to serve white people. African Americans struggled to ensure that the schools also served their needs. Certainly, the civil rights movement of the 1950s and 1960s focused a great deal of its concern on the lack of equal educational opportunity. Therefore, from an African American frame of reference, the school is the hope, but as an institution it is viewed with suspicion and criticism.

In sum, the folk history of dominated groups creates an image of schools quite different from what might be found in official history. For Native Americans, Puerto Ricans, and Mexican Americans, the historical image of U.S. public schools is of an institution designed to destroy their cultures and relegate them to the menial rungs of society. While African Americans consider education important, the ability of public schools to provide an education to their children is viewed with a certain level of suspicion. The African American image of schools is full of hope tempered by the reality of the denial of equal educational opportunity.

GENDER

Gender perspective varies with ethnic identity, and with monocultural and bicultural perspectives. It involves both men and women. Some women of dominated groups feel that the issue of racial discrimination takes precedence over gender discrimination. On the other hand, some women worry that the macho image held by dominated males is self-destructive and destructive to women. For some members of dominated groups, there is a concern with strengthening the self-image of men. Men and women in immigrant families often face changes in gender roles when coming to the United States.

In recounting over 100 years of their lives, one of the Delany sisters, Bessie, comments, regarding their many years of participation in civil rights struggles for African Americans and women, "I was torn between two issues—colored and women's rights."[15] The lives of these two African American women spanned the period covering the enactment of Jim Crow laws in the South in the 1890s to the continued civil rights struggles of the 1990s. While the issue of gender was constantly present in their lives, they felt the race issue had a greater impact. Bessie recalls, "But it seemed to me that no matter how much I had to put up with as a woman, the bigger problem was being colored. People looked at me and the first thing they saw was *Negro,* not *woman.*"[16]

The complicated nature of women's rights among women of dominated cultures is illustrated in Mary Crow Dog's autobiography, *Lakota Woman.* Growing up on the Sioux reservation in South Dakota, her active support of the contemporary Native American movement brought her into contact with feminists in New York City. While she felt that the women's movement was mainly "a white middle class affair," and that contraception and abortion issues were of little interest to her because she believed Indian women needed to procreate "to make up for the genocide suffered by our people in the past," her contact with the movement changed her perceptions about Native American men. After contact with the feminist movement, she states, "I was no longer the shy Sioux maiden walking with downcast eyes in the footsteps of some man."[17]

Mary Crow Dog is concerned that many Native American men do not take responsibility for their actions, particularly regarding the fathering of children and the beating of women. She felt a disgust at Indian men telling women "Let's you and me make a little warrior" and then leaving to make little warriors somewhere else. That some Indian men abused women became a particular concern after returning to the reservation from New York City. Reflecting her changed perception of Indian life, she states, "Before New York I had taken certain things for granted, almost as a normal part of daily life. But . . . it no longer seemed quite so normal to me that so many Sioux men habitually beat their wives."[18]

The changes in Mary Crow Dog's perception of male and female roles are similar to the encounter stage of ethnic identity. In this case, the encounter is with the feminist movement outside of Native American life. Mary Crow Dog's sister Barb, who also experienced the same encounter with the women's movement, left her boyfriend after he beat her up with a two-by-four ripped from a fence. Commenting on the situation, Mary Crow Dog reminds her that Sioux women do not usually leave their men even after they have been beaten. Recognizing that she is not following the traditional female role in the tribe, Barb responds, "Indian women are stronger than the men because they have to put up with all that shit, but I've had it." Emphasizing their new perception of gender roles, Mary Crow Dog replies, "Barb, we've been away for too long. We don't see things the way we used to."[19]

For immigrant families, differences in gender roles between the United States and their former countries can be a source of family conflict. A 1994 *New York Times* interview with women of Asian descent found them torn between

What Did My Family Teach Me about Gender?

Grades: High School through College

Objective:

To understand the role of the family in shaping attitudes about gender.

Lesson:

1. Ask students to write a short essay about their families' attitudes about gender. This essay could include discussions of the following situations:
   a. The reactions of family members to gender issues.
   b. Differing treatment by parents of children based on gender.
   c. Differing expectations of family members, particularly mother and father, regarding male and female children.
   d. Family discussions or nondiscussions of gender issues. The fact that gender might never have been a topic of family discussion is important because it might reflect a denial or avoidance of gender issues in the United States.
2. After completion of the essays ask students to volunteer their reflections on their families' influence on their attitudes about gender.
3. List varying family attitudes about gender on the chalkboard.
4. Draw the following table on the chalkboard.

Family Attitudes about Gender

Gender of Family Member	ATTITUDES ABOUT GENDER ROLES	
	Female	Male
Female		
Male		

5. The teacher should fill in the table's blank boxes by soliciting suggestions from the class.

Teachers: This exercise could evoke emotional discussions regarding family life. The teacher must remain sensitive to the potential psychological impact of these discussions.

Outcome: Students will gain an understanding of family influences on gender attitudes.

the independence of U.S. society and feeling responsible for maintaining a traditional family. Helen Lee, a daughter of Korean immigrants, sees this tension as a product of biculturalism. She commented, "I was raised with one set of values and living in a world with another set."[20]

For many immigrant women, the United States provides an opportunity for self-assertion and a break with former servile roles. In Chapter 1, I discussed Bharati Mukherjee's immigrant novel *Jasmine* and how she praises American culture for providing people the freedom to make choices about who they want to be. There is also an important gender theme in the novel. Jasmine compares her life as a woman in rural India to that of cattle: ". . . we are brought up to be caring and have no minds of our own. Village girls are like cattle; whichever way you lead them, that is the way they will go."[21] Her marriage partner was selected when she was 13 years old. After her husband's death, she travels to the United States to burn up his clothes and herself in front of the college he planned to attend. Instead, she goes through a transition from living in an Indian community in New York City to being married to a banker named Bud in Iowa. As a woman, she becomes an American when she learns to make choices and realizes she can determine her own future. She does not like the immigrant Indian men she meets in the U.S. because they remind her of her former servile role.

Mukherjee makes a distinction between "hyphenated Americans" and a complete immigrant transformation. Jasmine and Bud adopt a Vietnamese refugee boy named Du. According to Mukherjee, Du remains a hyphenated American because his primary social orientation is toward the immigrant Vietnamese community in the United States. Jasmine leaves the role of hyphenated American when she leaves the Indian community in New York City.

Within the framework of Mukherjee's argument, many Asian women remain as hyphenated Americans because they continue to live within the confines of an immigrant community. Shirley Hune, associate dean of the graduate division of the University of California at Los Angeles, argues that racial discrimination often isolates Asian Americans. She states, "No matter how hard you try, you can't blend in as someone of Euro-American heritage."[22] The most obvious result of this racial discrimination and isolation is the long-standing existence of Chinatowns in major U.S. cities.

Amy Tan's novels focus on the transformation of Chinese women after their arrival in the United States and of their daughters after they leave the confines of San Francisco's Chinatown. In the Prologue to *The Joy Luck Club*, Amy Tan tells the story of a Chinese woman who sails to the United States accompanied by a swan, which symbolizes her good intentions. For the woman, the promise of America is freedom for her daughters from the tyranny of Chinese men. On the journey she says to the swan, "In America I will have a daughter just like me. But over there nobody will say her worth is measured by the loudness of her husband's belch. Over there nobody will look down on her."[23] But, as Amy Tan portrays, the daughter's liberation is at the cost of generational friction and loss of traditions. The mother stands with one foot in the past and one in the new American present. The daughters escape the bondage of the past.

In Tan's *The Kitchen God's Wife,* Pearl Louie becomes closer to her mother after hearing of her life in China. Pearl was born in the United States and left the Chinese community after marrying a European American. Her mother's first marriage in China was the result of a family arrangement. For her mother, the marriage was a living hell with a tyrannical husband who beat her and demanded absolute servitude. Her freedom comes after meeting a Chinese American man working for the U.S. military in China who finally rescues her from the serfdom of her marriage. Symbolically, her daughter, similar to Jasmine, becomes a liberated woman with a career and the ability to determine her own future.[24]

In France, immigrant Arab women are more likely than Arab men to adopt the gender roles of French society. Consequently, they are more likely to want to blend into French culture. A *New York Times* report states, "Many experts say Muslim girls, eager not to repeat the cloistered lives of their mothers, are usually more motivated to succeed than boys." As an example, the *Times* reporter interviewed an 18-year-old girl of Algerian extraction who felt free and ignored her parents' orders to date only Muslim boys. "I'm sure they suspect something, but what can they do?" she told the reporter. In the attempt to integrate Arabs into French society, Simone Veil, France's social affairs minister, calls Arab women the secret weapon because "they want to escape the inferior status assigned to them by many Arab and African cultures."[25]

Male roles are also problematic in dominated and immigrant groups. Afrocentric educators want to change male identity as a means of resolving the type of complaints made by Mary Crow Dog regarding male machismo. For these educators, the issue of race and gender go hand in hand. Originally, until court decisions required Afrocentric schools to serve both males and females, the schools were organized for males. It is believed that the black male is being destroyed by the tension between his male identity and the realities of a racist society. The title of Jawanza Kunjufu's book, *Countering the Conspiracy to Destroy Black Boys,* conveys the sense of urgency to save men from a life of drugs, crime, and self-loathing. I will discuss Kunjufu's educational program for changing the macho self-image of African American males in Chapter 11.

In contrast to Kunjufu's concern about the survival of black males who adopt a macho perspective of the world, Gus Lee worries about Asian American males surviving because of a lack of macho image. In *China Boy,* Lee's main character, Kai Ting, is a Chinese immigrant boy living in a rough-and-tumble area of San Francisco. His Chinese masculine identity, Kai Ting reflects, would lead him "to a remote mountain monastery in East Asia where I could read prayers and repeat chants until my mind and soul became instruments of the other world. I had a physique perfect for meditation."[26] Lee portrays the major problem for Kai Ting as the difference between the masculine attributes demanded by his father and those required by the male culture of the United States. For his immigrant father, Kai Ting thinks, the male culture of his new country "ran counter to the very principles of his original culture and violated the essence of his ancient, classical education and the immutable humanistic standards of Chinese society."[27]

Kai Ting bridges the gap between his Chinese male identity and that required of youth in the United States by learning to box at his local Y.M.C.A.

While learning to box, his physique is strengthened, and he loses his fear of the macho actions of U.S. youth. By the end of the book, he achieves his new masculine identity by beating up the neighborhood bully. After his victory, Kai Ting proudly reflects on his new male identity, "I saw myself as my mother might see me, cringing with her horror for the bloodied physical condition of her Only Son, the unmusical, nonscholarly, brutish sport which her offspring had adopted as a way of life."[28]

China Boy highlights the complex nature of gender as a filter in the cultural frame of reference. Some immigrant Asian males feel threatened by the macho image of men in the United States. On the other hand, some Asian women see a world that offers freedom from traditional servile roles. Some women in dominated groups see cultural domination as a more important issue than liberation from the macho actions of their men, but, at the same time, resist those macho actions because of their contact with a broader women's movement. Afrocentric educators see the problem for African American males as one of a macho image. All of these different factors should be considered when thinking about gender as one filter in a person's cultural perspective.

SOCIAL CLASS

Social class is an important filter. As jobs and income become more dependent on the level of educational attainment, peoples' perceptions of the quality of their education influences their perceptions of their ability to succeed economically. Increasingly in the United States, the quality of education varies with social class. Those children living in low-income neighborhoods tend to receive an education which is qualitatively below that received by children living in high-income neighborhoods. This situation tends to lock children into the social class of their parents. Also, despite family wealth, children of dominated groups still have to deal with the issue of racism.

I am defining social class according to family income. As represented in Table 6–1, the middle class is the 60 percent of families located between the upper class

TABLE 6–1   Social Class by Mean Household Income, 2000 Census

Social Class	Percentage or Quintile	Mean Household Income of Each Quintile in 2000— Adjusted Dollars
Upper	Highest 20%	$141,621
Upper-middle	Fourth 20%	65,727
Middle	Third 20%	42,359
Lower-middle	Second 20%	25,331
Lower	Lowest 20%	10,188

Source: Adapted from U.S. Bureau of the Census, "Money Income in the United States: 2000" (Washington, DC: U.S. Printing Office, September 2001), p. 8.

of the top 20 percent of family incomes and the lower class of the bottom 20 percent of family incomes. Most Americans think of themselves as middle class. However, the census material suggests the limitations of this self-concept.

In *The Work of Nations: Preparing Ourselves for 21st-Century Capitalism*, economist Robert Reich argues that in the future there will be a close relationship between the educational requirements of a job and the level of income.[29] In the future, many jobs (60–80 percent) will require only minimum levels of education. The use of computers has deskilled many jobs in production and service. For instance, a worker in a fast-food restaurant need only push a smiling hamburger symbol on a cash register and the amount of the purchase is immediately displayed. The worker then punches in the amount of money given by the customer and the machine displays the change. In factories and in offices, the majority of work is repetitive and requires minimum levels of education. In contrast, between 20 and 40 percent of the jobs, what Reich calls "symbolic-analytic services," require high levels of education and creative and independent thought. These are the jobs that receive the highest incomes.

Reich argues that the education of those performing symbolic-analytic services takes place in elite public school systems and private schools. In the college preparatory tracks of the best primary and secondary schools, Reich argues, students learn the critical thinking skills and methods of dealing with information that are necessary to succeed as symbolic analysts. In contrast, the majority of students in the United States receive either a traditional education or, in the poorest school districts, no education at all. This traditional education prepares students for tedious and routine occupations.

Reich believes that symbolic analysts are able to pass on their privileged positions and incomes to their children by living in protected suburban enclaves with elite public schools or by sending their children to elite private schools. From the perspective of these parents, it doesn't matter what the quality of education is in schools serving low-income families.

In *Savage Inequalities: Children in America's Schools*, Jonathan Kozol documents the extent of differences between school districts serving low-income families and those serving high-income families.[30] In school districts serving low-income families, he found a lack of textbooks, regular teachers, course offerings, counselors, science equipment, and educational technology. In addition, he found overcrowded classrooms, with students doing monotonous and tedious work, and unsanitary conditions. He found just the opposite conditions in school districts serving high-income families.

Private boarding schools play an important role in giving children from privileged families a perception that they are members of America's elite. Sociologist G. William Domhoff writes, "The linchpins in the upper-class educational system are the dozens of boarding schools . . . developed . . . with the rise of a nationwide upper class whose members desired to insulate themselves from an inner city that was becoming populated by lower-class immigrants."[31] The most important function of these schools is to create a web of social connections across the country. The most elite of these schools, according to Domhoff, include Saint Paul's, Saint Mark's, Saint George's, Groton, and Middlesex. While these are elite board-

LESSON 6.4

What Did My Family Teach Me about the Rich and Poor?

Grades: High School through College

Objective:

To understand the role of the family in shaping attitudes about social class.

Lesson:

1. Ask students to write a short essay about their families' attitudes about social class. This essay could include discussions of the following:
   a. Family beliefs about their own social class position.
   b. Attitudes of family members toward the rich or those in a higher social class than the family.
   c. Attitudes of family members toward the poor or those in a lower social class than the family.
   d. Family encounters with those in social classes different from that of the family.
   e. Family discussions or nondiscussions of social class issues. The fact that social class might never have been a topic of family discussion is important because it might reflect a denial or avoidance of social class issues in the United States.
2. After completion of the essays ask students to volunteer their reflections on their families' influence on their attitudes about the lifestyles and social attitudes for different social classes.
3. List varying family attitudes about social classes on the chalkboard.
4. Draw the following table on the chalkboard.

PARENTAL ATTITUDES ABOUT SOCIAL CLASSES

Parents' Social Class	Rich	Middle Class	Poor
Upper			
Upper-middle			
Middle			
Lower-middle			
Lower			

5. The teacher should fill in the table's blank boxes by soliciting suggestions from the class.

Teachers: Most students do not think of social class according to the five categories present in Table 6–1 of this chapter. For this reason, the table used in this lesson simply refers to rich, middle class, and poor.

Outcome: Students will gain an understanding of family influences on social class attitudes.

ing schools, local areas have elite private schools serving children whose families choose not to board them away from home.

For dominated groups, perceptions of privileged schooling are often tainted by awareness of racism. For example, Jake Lamar, who grew up in a wealthy African American family in New York City and attended elite private schools, recalls the following comment from a fellow student at the Fieldston School: "You don't sound like a black person." Lamar responded, "Who am I supposed to sound like . . . Uncle Remus?"[32] Reflecting his feeling of ambivalence about his identity in U.S. society, he titled his autobiography *Bourgeois Blues.* He found various forms of racism following him through Harvard to his position as a writer for *Time* magazine.

In contrast to Jake Lamar, Alex Kotlowitz recorded the following comment from a 10-year-old African American boy living in a low-income public housing project in Chicago: "If I grow up, I'd like to be a bus driver." Reflecting on the violence in the housing project, Kotlowitz commented, "*If*, not *when.* At the age of ten, Lafeyetee wasn't sure he'd make it to adulthood."[33]

In his study of two boys growing up in a public housing project, Kotlowitz captures differences in perceptions between social classes. The boys are playing on a commuter railroad track when they hear the approach of a train. The boys run in panic because they "had heard that the suburb-bound commuters, from behind the tinted train windows, would shoot at them. . . . One of the boys, certain that the commuters were crack shots, burst into tears as the train whisked by." On the other hand, Kotlowitz recorded, "Some of the commuters had heard similar rumors about the neighborhood children and worried that, like cardboard lions in a carnival shooting gallery, they might be the target of talented snipers."[34]

Social class also affects the perceptions of immigrants regarding their chances in the United States. For instance, well-paid Japanese corporate executives often choose Scarsdale as their place of residence in the New York metropolitan area because of its superior public school system. In contrast, poor Haitian immigrants crowd public school classrooms in New York City. Kozol recorded the problems faced by immigrant children in the Camden, New Jersey, school system. Camden is the fourth poorest city in the United States. With limited resources, Camden provides little hope, as compared to wealthier New Jersey school systems, for children who want to go on to college. Reflecting the overworked and depressed attitudes of the school system's staff, a young Cambodian girl, Chilly, told Kozol about her trip to the school counselor to find out about being a lawyer. The counselor, because of work pressures, limited the interview to 15 minutes. During that short time he told her, "No, you cannot be a lawyer. . . . Your English isn't good enough. . . . Look for something else. Look for an easier job." Chilly told Kozol, "This upset me very much because, when I came to America, they said, you know, 'This is the place of opportunity.' "[35]

CONCLUSION

Variations in cultural frames of reference highlight individualism and membership in a group. People's perspectives are influenced by the different lenses they wear in viewing the world. A European American woman could be bicultural, with a strong ethnic identity, with a historical perspective shaped primarily by official history, with a concern about discrimination against women, and with a social perspective shaped by membership in the lower class. A woman of Asian descent might share all these characteristics with the European woman except for ethnic identity. The two women might closely relate to each other on issues of poverty and women's rights, and on bicultural views of society and history, while, at the same time, be divided because of their differing ethnic identities.

How these variations affect perspective is exemplified by a discussion in one of my classes. Because he was black, an Ethiopian student found himself sharing similar experiences with other African Americans. But he found himself having difficulty interpreting these experiences because he lacked the same folk history as African Americans. For instance, one day he was driving on the New York Thruway accompanied by a white female. A white New York State Trooper pulled his car over and asked the white woman, "Are you O.K.?" When the woman replied yes, the trooper left. Since Ethiopia only experienced colonialism for a brief period in the twentieth century, the Ethiopian student never experienced racism. Consequently, he could not understand the actions of the trooper. On the other hand, other African Americans, whose perspectives were shaped by a folk history of racism, interpreted the incident to the Ethiopian as a racist act on the part of the trooper.

These variations in cultural frames of reference are a warning against stereotyping. An upper-class African American might be more influenced by her or his social class position than by ethnic identity. An immigrant Cambodian student might be more concerned with gender issues than her or his ethnic identity. A European American of Polish descent might be more concerned with her or his ethnic identity than gender and social class issues. One Native American might be more influenced by an official history that glosses over policies of genocide by the U.S. government, while another might be more influenced by a folk history of these genocides. One Mexican American could be at the pre-encounter stage of ethnic identity, while another Mexican American could be at the internalization stage.

In summary, people are individuals by the way they share common perspectives. It is in this manner that individualism is embedded in common social experiences and perspectives. Also, this chapter only dealt with five influences on cultural perspectives. Religion, political affiliation, literature, and many other influences might determine a person's cultural frame of reference. Consequently, it is often difficult to understand another person's cultural perspective. On the other hand, a consideration of the issues raised can provide some understanding of differences in cultural frames of reference.

PERSONAL FRAMES OF REFERENCE

You might want to consider the effect of history, gender, and social class on your own thinking.

1. How much has your cultural perspective been shaped by official history?
2. What is the influence of folk history on your thinking?
3. Do you think governments should manage historical images through public schools?
4. How much has your gender shaped your view of the world?
5. What has been the influence of your social class background on your cultural perspective?

Notes

1. Joel Spring, *Images of American Life: A History of Ideological Management in Schools, Movies, Radio, and Television* (Albany: State University of New York Press, 1993), p. 44.
2. Quoted in Ibid., p. 206.
3. Ibid., pp. 205–14.
4. Terrie Epstein, "Multiculturalism and the Politics of History: A Response to Thomas Sobol," *Teachers College Record* 95, no. 2 (Winter 1993), p. 273.
5. Ibid., p. 278.
6. Ibid., p. 280.
7. National Project on Asia in American Schools, *National Review of Asia in American Textbooks in 1993* (Ann Arbor, MI: Association for Asian Studies, 1993).
8. Mick Fedullo, *Light of the Feather: Pathways through Contemporary Indian America* (New York: William Morrow, 1992), p. 117.
9. Ruben Navarrette, Jr., *A Darker Shade of Crimson: Odyssey of a Harvard Chicano* (New York: Bantam, 1993), p. 7.
10. Quoted in Spring, *Deculturalization and the Struggle for Equality: A Brief History of the Education of Dominated Cultures in the United States,* 4th ed. (Burr Ridge, IL: McGraw-Hill, 2004), p. 30.
11. Ibid., p. 28.
12. Ibid., pp. 89–97.
13. Quoted in Spring, *Deculturalization,* p. 84.
14. Ibid., p. 85.
15. Sarah Delany and A. Elizabeth Delany, *Having Our Say: The Delany Sisters' First 100 Years* (New York: Kodansha International, 1993), p. 141.
16. Ibid.
17. Mary Crow Dog, *Lakota Woman* (New York: HarperCollins, 1990), p. 244.
18. Ibid., pp. 244–45.
19. Ibid., p. 245.
20. "Asian-American Women Struggling to Move Past Cultural Expectations," *The New York Times,* 23 January 1994, p. 14.
21. Bharati Mukherjee, *Jasmine* (New York: Fawcett Crest, 1989), p. 39.
22. "Asian-American Women," p. 14.
23. Amy Tan, *The Joy Luck Club* (New York: Ivy Books, 1989), p. 3.
24. Amy Tan, *The Kitchen God's Wife* (New York: Ivy Books, 1992).
25. Alan Riding, "France, Reversing Course, Fights Immigrants' Refusal to be French," *The New York Times,* 5 December 1993, p. 14.
26. Gus Lee, *China Boy* (New York: Dutton, 1991), p. 4.
27. Ibid.

28. Ibid., p. 319.
29. Robert Reich, *The Work of Nations: Preparing Ourselves for 21st-Century Capitalism* (New York: Alfred Knopf, 1991).
30. Jonathan Kozol, *Savage Inequalities: Children in America's Schools* (New York: Crown, 1991).
31. G. William Domhoff, *Who Rules America Now? A View for the '80s* (New York: Simon & Schuster, 1983), p. 25.
32. Jake Lamar, *Bourgeois Blues: An American Memoir* (New York: Plume Books, 1992), p. 94.
33. Alex Kotlowitz, *There Are No Children Here: The Story of Two Boys Growing Up in the Other America* (New York: Anchor Books, 1991), p. x.
34. Ibid., p. 7.
35. Kozol, *Savage Inequalities*, pp. 155–56.

CHAPTER 7

The Intersection of School Culture with Dominated and Immigrant Cultures

Many of the educational problems faced by dominated and immigrant groups are a result of the clash between their cultures and the culture of the public school. The cultural values of public schools were institutionalized during their formation in the early nineteenth century and during their adaptation to modern corporate culture in the early twentieth century. These cultural values are part of the structure of public schools today.

The basic values of public schools are equality of opportunity, inequality, individualism, the importance of property, and individual economic achievement. Often, these basic values clash with the needs of dominated and immigrant cultures. Similar to other U.S. government institutions formed in the early nineteenth century, public schools reflected white Anglo-Saxon Protestant traditions. In this regard, Arthur Schlesinger, Jr., is correct about the values underpinning U.S. institutions. As Carl Kaestle states in his classic study of the rise of public schooling, most public school advocates were native-born Anglo-American Protestants who called for "government action to provide schooling that would be more common, more equal, more dedicated to public policy, and therefore more effective in creating cultural and political values centering on Protestantism, republicanism, and capitalism."[1] During the early part of the twentieth century, when public schools took on the appearance they have today, these values were modified as schools adapted to the needs of the modern corporate state.[2]

One of the central concerns of early common-school advocates was reducing tensions between social classes by providing equality of opportunity to all children. It is important to understand that the concept of equality of opportunity in the nineteenth century and today is based on the idea of inequality. Equality of opportunity, according to supporters of common schools, meant giving everyone an equal education so that each person could have an "equal opportunity" to compete in the economic system. Family wealth as a contributor to economic success was to be replaced by individual merit. The advantage of family wealth was to be nullified by giving all children an equal education. But, in the end, this form of equality of opportunity would lead to a society where people were unequal based on their ability to compete. The ability to compete would be a function of a person's education. The ultimate goal of competition is the accumulation of property.[3]

There are several important things to note about this early concept of equality of opportunity. First, equality of opportunity is a function of schools. This idea is embedded in public schooling today. Second, inequality is considered a natural part of organized society. Today, as I will explain regarding the influence of corporate culture, this idea of inequality is a basic part of public schooling. Third, individual competition in school and in the economic system is a basic assumption of schools. And fourth, one of the primary purposes of public schools is the economic advancement of the individual and society.

With the development of the corporation in the early twentieth century, equality of opportunity became the primary goal of public schools. The structure of modern corporations requires individual specialization, competition, and cooperation. The need for specialization is directly related to equality of opportunity and inequality. Schooling is to provide everyone with an equal opportunity to be educated for a specialized task in the corporate structure. Corporate efficiency is to be achieved by eliminating the influence of family background. Everyone will have an equal opportunity to compete in the classroom and corporation. An individual's achievement in the classroom and workplace is, according to this concept of equality of opportunity, a reflection of individual merit and competition.[4]

It is important to understand, because of the consequences for dominated and immigrant cultures in public schools, that this concept of equality of opportunity is premised on inequality of outcomes in the school and corporation. Corporate efficiency is dependent on students achieving unequal educational outcomes that will match their unequal incomes, status, and jobs in society and the corporation.

That American schools are based on inequality becomes clear when one examines the institutional means for achieving equality of opportunity that was introduced under the influence of the corporate model. In the corporate model, schools separate students according to abilities and interests by using a combination of standardized tests, teacher and counselor judgments, and student choices. Standardized tests and teacher and counselor judgments are assumed to be free of any bias, and, therefore, are to provide equality of opportunity to all students.[5]

The structural mechanisms of inequality are ability grouping and tracking, which often divide students according to their social class background. Similar to the labor force in the modern corporation, students are separated according to ability in the classroom. Separate reading, math, science, and social studies groups are now a common part of the U.S. classroom. In addition, special education, gifted programs, and special language programs become another means of separation. Tracking is usually a phenomenon of secondary education when students are placed in specialized curricula ranging from vocational training to college preparation according to their future social destinations. These institutional forms of inequality are premised on the idea that the primary purpose of

TABLE 7–1   Five Basic Cultural Values of U.S. Public Schools

Equality of Opportunity	All students have an equal chance to compete for grades and other rewards. All graduates have an equal chance to compete for jobs.
Inequality	Competition for grades and jobs will result in unequal rewards. Some students will receive high grades and others low grades. Some graduates will earn high incomes and others will receive low incomes.
Individualism	The individual student competes with other students for grades. This is best exemplified by the assignment of grades according to a bell-shaped curve.
Individual Economic Achievement	Individual competition in school is preparation for individual competition with others for jobs and income.
Property	The ultimate goal of competition in school is later success in competing for high-paying jobs. Success at attaining a high-paying job results in the accumulation of property. In other words, the goal of schooling becomes increased wealth.

education is preparation for a workforce and that this will be achieved through individual competition for grades and, later, for the accumulation of property.

For the modern corporation, inequality and individual competition need to be balanced with cooperation. The modern corporate structure requires people who are able to work together to meet the goals of the corporation. This means educating individuals who do not rebel against inequalities in pay and status. In addition, cooperation needs to be balanced with competition. The modern corporate person must learn to cooperate and, at the same time, compete for jobs within the corporation and for increased profits for the whole corporation.

These corporate values were institutionalized into public schools in the form of extracurricular activities. In the 1920s, educators were quite explicit that they were introducing assembly programs, pep rallies for school spirit, clubs, student government, and athletics as a means of preparing students for the modern corporate world. The acceptance of athletics as a regular part of school activities, something never dreamt of by common-school advocates in the nineteenth century, directly reflected corporate values. Football and basketball, the most important of high school spectator sports, reflected the new corporate ideology of specialized roles, cooperation, and competition. Building school spirit through pep rallies, assemblies, and after-school athletic events was, according to educators in the 1920s, preparation for acquiring corporate spirit. Students were to transfer school spirit to their corporate workplace where they would then work for the good of the company. It is not accidental that corporate sales meetings often resemble high school pep rallies.[6]

The intersection of this school culture with the cultures of dominated and immigrant groups has resulted in inequality of opportunities and a confusion

Confucius Attends a U.S. Public School

Grades: Middle School through College

Objective:
To show the difference between the five basic cultural values of U.S. public schools as listed in Table 7–1 and other cultures.

Lesson:

1. Review with the class Table 7–1 regarding cultural values of U.S. schools.
2. Outline the following principles of Confucian education on the chalkboard. Confucius lived and taught circa 551–479 B.C.E.
   a. It is the responsibility of each person to promote harmony.
   b. Everyone should be concerned about the welfare of others.
   c. All people are of equal worth.
   (See: Paul Gordon Lauren, *The Evolution of International Human Rights: Visions Seen* (Philadelphia: University of Pennsylvania, 1998), p. 11. Confucius states in *The Analects*, "Men are close to one another by nature. They diverge as a result of practice." Another translation of this passage from *The Analects* is "By nature close together, through practice set apart." Also, Confucius stated: "In education there should be no class distinctions." See Confucius, *The Analects,* translated by D. C. Lau (New York: Penguin Books, 1979), p. 143; and Irene Bloom, "Mencian Confucianism and Human Rights," in *Confucianism and Human Rights,* ed. William Theodore De Bary and Tu Wei-ming (New York: Columbia University Press, 1998).
3. Divide the class into small groups of four or five.
4. Instruct each group to develop two short lesson plans for teaching an arithmetic lesson on addition with one plan reflecting the cultural values of U.S. schools and the other plan reflecting Confucian values.
5. Have each group present its two lesson plans to the class.
6. Engage in general class discussions over differences in cultural values in teaching and schooling.

Teachers: Because of limitations of time, you might want to restrict the number of presentations of lesson plans.

Outcome: Students will gain an understanding of the differences in cultural values in U.S. schools and the educational values of others.

over the goals of schooling. The mechanisms of inequality are used to ensure the continuation of the inequality of opportunities. As education becomes the chief means of acquiring employment, the structural mechanisms for creating inequality in schooling, such as grouping and tracking, are a means of ensuring that dominated and some immigrant cultures remain in the lowest paying jobs. The emphasis on education as a means of economic advancement is sometimes confusing for immigrant groups that prize learning as a good in and of itself. The mechanisms for building corporate cooperation sometimes result in a replication of the inequalities in the corporate structure, with students from elite families, as they prepare to be the corporate managers, running student governments, while students from dominated groups, as they prepare to do the grunt work in corporations, are playing on the football and basketball teams.

INEQUALITY AND SCHOOLING

Despite the premise that public schools could, without reference to a student's social class and race, scientifically and professionally establish inequality, there exist studies from the 1920s to Jeannie Oakes's *Keeping Track: How Schools Structure Inequality* that conclude that ability grouping, tracking, counseling practices, participation in school activities, discipline practices, special classes, and methods of instruction reflect the social class and race of the student. In other words, inequality as a cultural value embedded in U.S. public schools results in the reproduction of existing inequalities in society.[7] Again, it is important to note that the goal of inequality in schooling is to promote industrial efficiency by placing students into academic and vocational programs based on their individual abilities and not on their racial and social class backgrounds. But the professional and scientific means for structuring inequality, and the cultural values that shaped U.S. schools, reflect the cultural values of the dominant group in society. Consequently, standardized tests that are used for placement in ability groups, placement in curriculum tracks, and measurement of student progress reflect the values of the dominant culture and, therefore, discriminate against low-income, immigrant, and dominated groups. Teacher expectations and judgments, which affect placement in ability groups and tracks, also tend to discriminate against low-income, immigrant, and dominated groups. School counselors tend to replicate the inequalities in society by tracking low-income and dominated students into low-income careers.

Even discipline practices vary according to the social background of students. Schools serving upper-income families tend to allow more independence in schoolwork and school activities than schools serving low-income families, which tend to be more authoritarian. It is argued that these differences in discipline practices tend to parallel the needs of the labor market. Students from upper-income families who are given more time for independent decision making in their schoolwork are being prepared for professional and business jobs requiring similar forms of independence, while students experiencing authoritarian environments are being prepared for jobs requiring obedience. It has also been found that students from low-income families who are failing in school are most often counseled as discipline problems, whereas failing students from upper-income families tend to be counseled for learning problems. Even differences in methods of instruction are related to social class and the job market. Schools serving low-income families tend to rely on rote forms of learning as opposed to methods of instruction that require higher-order critical skills. The result, as it is in the other examples, is that children educated in schools serving low-income families learn intellectual skills appropriate for routine and monotonous work, while students from upper-income families are learning intellectual skills appropriate for high-paying professional and business jobs.[8]

One of the major contributors to inequality of educational opportunity is the existence of separate school districts that allow families to choose public schools based on family income. Many families choose housing according to the quality of schools in a particular district. Consequently, families with high incomes will choose expensive housing in districts providing the best school services. Low-income families are excluded from these districts because they cannot afford the rents or costs of buying a home. The result is what Jonathan Kozol calls *savage inequalities,* with some school districts providing a rich abundance of qualified teachers, supplies, and courses, while other districts lack regular teachers, complete sets of textbooks, equipment to maintain scientific laboratories, and advanced academic courses.[9]

RESISTANCE: THE INTERSECTION OF SCHOOL AND DOMINATED CULTURES

Inequality, as a cultural value embedded in the structure of U.S. schools, would obviously create problems for students from dominated cultures. In addition, anthropologist John Ogbu argues that there is a broader clash between the culture of dominated groups and the white Anglo-Saxon Protestant and corporate values embedded in the structure of schooling that results in the creation of a culture of resistance. This culture of resistance among students from dominated groups manifests itself in actions that are antischool, such as tardiness, absenteeism, failure to do homework, vandalism to school property, and disruption of classrooms. Afrocentric educator Jawanza Kunjufu also argues that many African American students believe that school achievement depends on "acting white." Consequently, according to Kunjufu, many African American students reject the culture of schools and accept failure in school studies.

Often, I encounter complaints by African American students in my multicultural education courses that resistance theory is a function of social class rather than just race. Many of my students grew up in suburban African American families where educational achievement was emphasized in the home and among peers. These students argue that resistance culture is more associated with African Americans from low-income families than from high-income families. Therefore, it is important to keep in mind in this discussion of resistance theory that it appears to be a function of class and culture.

Maori Go to School

Grades: Elementary School through College

Objective:
To show the difference between the five basic cultural values of U.S. Public Schools as listed in Table 7–1 and other cultures.

Lesson:

1. Review with the class Table 7–1 regarding the cultural values of U.S. schools.
2. Read the following description of the educational model used in the schooling of New Zealand's Maori people:
   "The first activity of the morning begins with a child standing to deliver a greeting that describes their tribal affiliation . . . [and history]. This allows children to discover and connect to one another, to their ancestors, and to the environment. This way of learning truly embraces the child, the family, and the community in a culturally appropriate way." (Kate Cherrington, "Building a Child-Centered Model: An Indigenous Model Must Look to the Future," in *Indigenous Educational Models for Contemporary Practice: In Our Mother's Voice*, ed. Maenette Kape'ahiokalani Padeken Ah Nee-Benham with Joanne Elizabeth Cooper (Mahawah, NJ: Lawrence Erlbaum Publishers, 2000), p. 34).
3. Ask the class to compare this description of Maori education with the opening activities in a U.S. elementary school.
4. List differences on the chalkboard.
5. Ask the class to describe differences in cultural values as reflected in differences in opening activities.
6. List differences in cultural values on the chalkboard.

Teachers: You could ask a group of students to demonstrate the differences in opening school activities before the rest of the class.

Outcome: Students will gain an understanding of the differences in cultural values in U.S. schools and the educational values of others.

African American culture contains strong values regarding the importance of education while maintaining a level of distrust of white people and dominant institutions. The African American experience in public schools has been a mixed bag of segregation and denial of equal educational opportunity, and educational achievement that protects political rights and provides economic advancement. For Native Americans, Puerto Ricans, and Mexican Americans schooling represents an ongoing battle over preservation of cultures and languages. Consequently, dominated groups have developed attitudes toward public schools that are combinations of hope, anger, frustration, and a sense of futility about the schools ever serving their needs.

Ogbu found these contradictory attitudes among African American students while doing research in the Stockton, California, school system. Black students verbalized a strong desire for education and believed that schooling was an important means of escaping poverty. Despite these attitudes about the value of education, Ogbu found these African American students behaving in ways that guaranteed their failure in school. They tended to lack a serious attitude about schoolwork, they were frequently tardy and absent, and they did not attempt to achieve in school.[10]

Referring to the work of Lois Weis[11] and the historical development of African American culture, Ogbu argues that "blacks developed high educational aspirations and initiated a long history of collective struggle for equal education *as a form of opposition* against white people who denied them access to education and equality of educational opportunity."[12] On the other hand, African Americans discovered that educational achievement did not result in the same economic opportunities as it did for whites. Therefore, according to Ogbu, there is no contradiction between the fact that black students verbally support the importance of education but reject the process of schooling that guarantees inequality.

In tracing the historical origins of resistance culture, Ogbu identifies two important causes for its development among African American youths. One cause is black youth observing their parents and other adult blacks struggling for economic advancement through education and mainstream jobs. Second, because of racial barriers to employment, Ogbu argues, "they have evolved a folk theory or folk theories of making it which do not necessarily emphasize strong academic pursuit."[13]

Combined with the contemporary and historical experience that education will not, in fact, provide a road to economic opportunities is the historical distrust of whites and their institutions. These combinations of factors become the cultural attitudes and knowledge, in Ogbu's words, "transmitted to and acquired by Black children . . . [it is] what they bring to school."[14] These beliefs, and the prejudice and discrimination they encounter in schools, result in some African American students developing oppositional attitudes toward schools and a belief that they will eventually fail at schoolwork.

Therefore, according to this argument, the intersection of African American culture and the culture of the school often results in students demonstrating low academic effort and antischool attitudes. Ogbu develops three scenarios for how this intersection of cultures is played out. In one scenario, black students equate academic work and required classroom behavior with "acting white." From this perspective, educational achievement is a subtractive process requiring students to give up their culture for the white culture of the school. In addition, there is peer pressure not to cross cultural boundaries and to remain within the resistance culture of other African American students. In the second scenario, African American students encounter outright hostility from the white-controlled institution and they have conflicts with white students. In the third scenario, the students' attitudes are shaped by folk history and, consequently, they lack the development of a strong academic tradition and orientation. All three of these scenarios result in antischool behaviors which, in turn, result in low academic achievement.

Obviously, Ogbu's framework has implications for other dominated cultures and social groups that feel that schools are not working in their interests. The inequality inherent in schooling can create a sense of futility among all students coming from low-income families. Attending schools with low financial support, being relegated to slow learning groups and nonacademic tracks, and witnessing a world where family members and friends have not advanced because of schooling can result in a disparaging attitude toward educational achievement. "Why bother" can become the attitude.

RESISTANCE: NATIVE AMERICANS

The attitude of "why bother" can quickly move to open hostility and anger when the school is perceived as reflecting the values of the dominant group. Native Americans might feel hostility because public schools reflect the values of those who took away their lands and tried to destroy their cultures. Education was used by the U.S. government to destroy the languages and cultures of Native Americans. These attempts at deculturalization left a legacy of resentment. As a Ponca Indian told a Senate subcommittee, "School is the enemy!"[15]

For Native Americans, resentment toward schools is compounded by present-day discrimination. In her study of the Ute Indians in Utah, Betty Jo Kramer concluded that Utes perceived schools as hostile to their children because of past history, "the racist attitudes of many non-Indians, and . . . the differing values and expectations held by Utes and the public schools." Because of these perceptions, Utes consider the school "a threatening rather than a beneficial force in the lives of Ute children."[16]

Inequality was cited by the Ute Indians as one of their basic cultural conflicts with white-controlled schools. Ute Indians complained that they did not understand why public schools honored students who made the honor roll and athletic teams that won the most games. Utes believe that the rewards should go to those "who tried the hardest" rather than those with the highest grades and scores. In art, Utes complained that prizes were based on judgments about the quality of the final product rather than "the intensity and satisfaction of the creative process."[17]

Just as with African Americans, the combination of historical experience, current racism, and cultural conflict can cause some Native American youth to consider the school a hostile environment. To do well in school, within this context, means "to act white." These perceptions can lead to a resistance culture which results in low academic performance. For those working outside Native American culture, this low academic performance might be considered negative. On the other hand, those Native Americans wanting to protect traditional cultural values might applaud the development of a resistance culture.

LATINOS/LATINAS: THE INTERSECTION OF SCHOOL, DOMINATED, AND IMMIGRANT CULTURES

One test of resistance theory is to compare Latino students from dominated Mexican American and Puerto Rican cultures with immigrant students from other Latin American countries. Marcelo Suarez-Orozco compared the research literature on Puerto Ricans and Mexican American students with the attitudes and academic success of immigrant students from Central America. Research findings suggest that many Puerto Rican and Mexican American students, as do many African Americans and Native Americans, view the school "as one further tool of the oppressor to maintain the inequality of the status quo."[18] During Suarez-Orozco's research, Mexican American parents constantly complained that schools were not teaching their children and, in one case, that the school system was giving their children the same textbooks year after year. Other studies showed a profound alienation of Mexican Americans from public schools because of negative school experiences and discrimination.

Therefore, a combination of a history of discrimination and segregation, current school practices, and a perception that education will not provide economic mobility creates a resistance culture among some Mexican American and Puerto Rican students. Doing well in school is believed to require "acting white or Anglo." And, as it does with African American and Native Americans, this resistance culture results in poor academic performance.

In contrast, recently arrived Latinos from Central America "'put all their chips' in the educational system, at times succeeding practically against all odds."[19] Teachers comment that they find these immigrant Latino students more desirable than students born of Latino ancestry in North America. One factor in this success is that immigrant families focus on the educational advancement of their children. Many immigrants told Suarez-Orozco that concern about the welfare of their children was a major reason for leaving their countries.

Success for these students was often achieved despite the fact that they attended schools that were overcrowded, lacked educational materials, and were staffed by prejudiced teachers. From the perspective of these Central American immigrants, these conditions were still far better than those they left. Suarez-Orozco found Central American immigrants pausing during interviews to compare the "here" with the "there." For Mexican Americans there was no "here" and "there," but only a world of "here" which was oppressive. Consequently, Central American immigrants could say that no matter how bad conditions were in the United States they were not as bad as what they left. In general, these immigrants believed the Anglo-American world to be "fairer than the Latin American."[20]

Therefore, Central American immigrant values embrace the cultural value of inequality embedded in U.S. public schools. They believe that success and upward mobility in the United States depend on schooling. Education is a chance to rise above others and one's past. Rather than perceiving the schools, as do dominated groups, as another means of keeping one at the bottom of the economic ladder, the schools are considered a means of climbing the ladder. Without a history of discrimination and segregation in U.S. public schools, and with a belief in the fairness of U.S. public schools, Central American immigrants tend not to develop a resistance culture similar to that of Puerto Rican and Mexican American students.

One important qualification needs to be made to the above comparison of dominated and immigrant cultures. That qualification is the age of the student when entering the United States. Suarez-Orozco found that younger immigrant students were affected by "teachers' hostilities, overcrowded schools, poor living conditions, lack of parental supervision (attributable to work schedules), and peer pressures."[21] The younger the students when entering the United States, the more likely they are to develop poor academic attitudes. The effect of prejudicial conditions in the United States on young children is also supported by studies that found that children who were born and spent their formative years in Puerto Rico did better in schools on the U.S. mainland than children of Puerto Rican descent born and raised on the mainland. The same differences in educational achievement were found between children born in Mexico and children of Mexican descent born in the United States.[22]

ASIANS: COMPARING DOMINATED AND IMMIGRANT CULTURES

Asian American students are often perceived as having high academic motivation and a culture that is compatible with the culture of U.S. public schools. But, as Yongsook Lee argues, when Asians are a dominated group they have difficulty in school. Lee reaches this conclusion in comparing the academic success of Korean students in Japan with Korean students in the United States. In Japan, Koreans are a dominated culture and, consequently, do not do as well academically as Japanese students. In contrast, in the United States students of Korean descent do as well in school as students of Japanese descent.[23]

Before exploring the comparison between Koreans in Japan and the United States, it is important to consider the cultural values that Lee identifies as the reasons for the success of Chinese, Japanese, and Korean students in U.S. schools. Lee argues that all three cultures are influenced by Confucian values regarding education and the family. Historically, all three cultures relied upon education for achieving middle- and high-level positions in government. For over 1,000 years, both Japan and Korea used national examinations as a means of access to these positions. In addition, the Confucian tradition gives high status to the educated person. In Lee's words, "Formal education developed as the principal mechanism of social mobility."[24]

Consequently, there is a close compatibility between the competition and inequality of U.S. schools and the cultural perspective of these Asian American students. In other words, both sets of cultural values consider education as a means of social mobility where some win and some lose. Unlike dominated groups in the United States that consider the inequality of schooling as a means of keeping them down, Asian Americans consider inequality as a means of their economic and social advancement.

This valuing of educational competition and mobility is given support by family values. Within the Confucian tradition, individuals sacrifice their own good for the harmony and closeness of the family. Children are expected to be obedient to their parents into adulthood. While expecting obedience, parents are permissive in their child rearing and allow their children to participate in much of adult life. This combination of obedience and love results, according to Lee, "in the establishment of an unconditional basic trust and a strong bond between parents (especially mothers) and children."[25]

Chinese, Japanese, and Korean parents are also willing to sacrifice their own comfort for the good of their children. This is particularly true with regard to education. The startling proof of this willingness to sacrifice is evidenced in a research study which found in interviews with parents in two Chicago-area schools that 92 percent of Korean parents as compared to 25 percent of Anglo parents would be willing to sell their only home to finance their child's college education.[26]

Within the context of these family values, academic achievement is not a personal matter but is related to the honor of the parents. Children are told that they have a responsibility to do well in school because of their obligation to the family. In addition, within the Confucian tradition, the teacher is an extension of the parent. Teachers are given a great deal of respect and status. Students are expected to obey and respect their teachers in the same way that they respect their parents.[27]

Therefore, the combination of valuing schooling as a means of social mobility, expecting sacrifice and obedience for the good of the family, sacrificing for the good of one's children, and valuing scholars and teachers seems to explain much of the success of Japanese, Chinese, and Korean students in U.S. schools. Also, Lee argues, "The quiet, industrious, disciplined and orderly behavior emphasized by Korean culture is also rewarded at school, because American teachers tend to interpret these behaviors as traits of a good student."[28]

Similar to other people of color, Asians do encounter prejudice and discrimination in U.S. society. But these encounters are against a background of belief by many Asians in the superiority of their own cultural traditions. In addition, Lee found for Koreans, similar to other immigrants, that discrimination and prejudice are considered just obstacles to overcome on the way to better lives. They are not considered obstacles that will result in condemnation to the lowest economic rungs of society.

In contrast, Koreans in Japan suffer the same fate as dominated groups in the United States. In Lee's words, most Japanese "despise Koreans."[29] Korea became a colony of Japan in 1910. Large-scale immigration of Koreans into Japan started in 1922 when Japanese industrialists recruited them for their expanding economy. The resentment of Japanese toward these Korean laborers was expressed in the 1923 massacre of between 4,500 and 20,000 Koreans. During World War II, the government forced 2 million Koreans to come to Japan as laborers and military conscripts. Japanese colonial control of Korea ended with the conclusion of World War II.

Today, Koreans in Japan are discriminated against in employment, and they are not eligible for pensions, insurance, and public housing. They cannot be hired by national and local governments, public schools, and universities. Naturalization has provided legal citizenship, but not social equality. Applications for jobs, schools, or membership in any group require a copy of one's family registration.

Korean school graduates face barriers at every level of employment. In school, Koreans experience overt and covert discrimination. Many private schools will not admit Koreans. Some public schools will only admit Koreans if they take a pledge "not to disturb school order."[30] In one prefecture in Japan, it was found that 14 out of 35 high schools would not admit Koreans. Japanese textbooks present a negative image of Korean history and culture.

As a result of this domination, students of Korean descent in Japan do not do as well in school as their Japanese counterparts. Lee concludes that the comparison between Koreans in Japan and in the United States has important implications for dominated groups "such as American blacks, because they show that a minority group can have very different achievement patterns in different host societies."[31]

ALIENATION: THE INTERSECTION OF SCHOOL AND FAMILY VALUES

"My homecoming was a bitter disappointment to me . . . [there was] no happy gathering of family and friends, as I had so fondly dreamed there might be . . . they gave me to understand very plainly that they did not approve of me," wrote Thomas Alford after returning from Hampton Institute to his Shawnee tribe.[32] The goal of boarding schools for Native Americans was to destroy Native American cultural values and replace them with European American values. Alford's statement exemplifies the feeling of alienation from their families and cultures that haunts Native American and some other students from dominated and immigrant cultures who are successful in school.

This feeling of alienation takes three different forms. One form, as in the case of Native Americans, is where the school teaches cultural values that are in conflict with the cultural values of the home. Since boarding schools were specifically organized to change the cultural values of Native American children, and eventually those of the tribe, student success in these schools meant alienation from tribal values. Another form of alienation takes place between successful students and their peers. If success in school for dominated groups, as Ogbu argues, requires acting "white" or "Anglo," then successful students from dominated groups feel an alienation from their peers. The third form of alienation results from a student acquiring a body of knowledge and values that are not held by other family members. Unlike the situation with Native American boarding schools, this form of alienation is not the result of the family rejecting the cultural values of the successful student. The family supports the success of the student, but the student feels alienated as she or he gains a greater knowledge of the world.

The first form of alienation, in which there is a basic conflict between the values acquired by the student and family values, is exemplified by the history of Native American education. Michael Coleman, in his study of the experience of Native American students, found boarding school pupils reacting in several ways to the imposition of alien values. One reaction was simply to run away and return to the tribe. This involved a complete rejection of any attempts to alienate the student from tribal values. The second reaction, according to Coleman, was resistance to the imposition of cultural values. Just as Ogbu described for African American students, Coleman recounts seemingly endless stories of pranks by Indian students as examples of resistance. These pranks ranged from making insulting drawings of teachers and other students to placing wasps in teachers' desks.[33]

Another reaction was acceptance of the goals of the boarding schools and attempts to be academically successful. Of course, success meant alienation from tribal values. Besides the example of Shawnee Thomas Alford, Coleman describes heart-wrenching scenes of successful students proudly returning to their tribes and experiencing rejection. When Helen Sekaquaptewa returned to her Hopi tribe after 13 years at school, she wrote, "I didn't feel at ease in the home of my parents now."[34] After his schooling, Don Talayesva enraged fellow Hopi by breaking tribal taboos against relationships with clan relatives and by aiding white anthropologists. Many returning students alienated fellow tribal members because of their sense of superiority and desire to change tribal values. Qoyawayma's mother responded to her attempts to "uplift" the tribe after returning from school, "What shall I do with my daughter, who is now my mother?"[35]

Alienation from one's peer group is a common complaint by students from dominated cultures. Ruben Navarrette felt alienation from other Chicano students as he progressed through school. By secondary school, his academic success alienated him from other Chicano students. His feeling of loneliness resulted in fantasies about reestablishing relationships with his peer group. Interestingly, when he finally did go to Harvard he established close relationships with other Chicano students who had followed similar paths of academic success.[36]

In *To Be Popular or Smart: The Black Peer Group,* Jawanza Kunjufu recalls how academic success during college alienated him from his black peer group. This experience caused him to ask the provocative question: "Why do some Black youth consider being smart synonymous with being White?"[37] In response to Kunjufu's comments, a black student in my multicultural class argued that this is no longer the case on campuses with black or African studies departments. These departments give African American students the feeling that educational achievement no longer requires acting "white." Richard Rodriquez's *Hunger of Memory* captures the alienation from the family that occurs when a student's academic knowledge exceeds that of his or her parents and the parents support the continued education of the child. This is a sad story for parents who want the best for their children. As the family sacrifices for the education of their children, their children grow apart from them. Growing up in a Chicano family, Rodriquez's alienation is intensified by the learning of English.

During his elementary and secondary school years, Rodriquez feels the growing gap between himself and his family. By the time he is working on his doctoral dissertation, the educational differences are a source of embarrassment. Coming from a poor family, his higher education is financed by scholarships. "The scholarship boy," he writes, "cannot afford to admire his parents. He permits himself embarrassment at their lack of education."[38] The scholarship boy's allegiance, he argues, is transferred from his parents to his teacher. The growing alienation of the scholarship boy was felt by his mother who complained "that the family wasn't close anymore, like some others. . . . Why weren't we close, 'more in the Mexican style'?"[39] When Rodriquez departed home for college as a scholarship boy he reflected, "My departure would only make physically apparent the separation that had occurred long before."[40]

The alienation experienced by Rodriquez highlights the dissonance that occurs when there is a basic conflict between family values and school values. This conflict of cultural values can be a reflection of race or ethnic identity. It can also be a reflection of social class. The poor boy or girl becomes the scholarship student. The intersection of conflicting school and family values can result in students either rejecting schooling, forming a culture of resistance, or alienating themselves from their families and peer groups.

CULTURAL CONFLICTS

One source of alienation is the conflict between the values of the home and the cultural value of inequality embedded in U.S. public schools. Inequality requires competition where one student proves he or she is better than another student. This competition fosters individualism where students rely on their own resources to prove that they are better than other students. Inequality requires examinations that separate students according to their performance on the test. Academic competition reflects the values of the marketplace, where people compete to see who can accumulate the most property.

For many groups, individual academic competition does not cause a conflict between family and school values. Those families fostering white Anglo-Saxon Protestant values do not feel a conflict with the competitive goals of public schools. White Anglo-Saxon Protestant values emphasize individualism, individual competition, and inequality. As I discussed earlier in this chapter, Chinese, Japanese, and Koreans have long traditions of individual academic competition centered around the taking of examinations. These Asian American families feel little conflict between their values and the competitive values of schools.

On the other hand, there are many cultures that stress cooperation over competition. The most notable among these in the United States are Native American and Hispanic cultures. To understand how cooperation contrasts with competition in schools, consider the following example. Imagine a school where the goal is to maximize the learning of all students, and not to separate and grade students according to competitive tests. In this cooperative school, students would not see themselves in competition with each other for the highest grade. Instead, students would be concerned about how well everyone learned the material. Students would help each other. The purpose of examinations in this cooperative school would be to determine what the student needed to learn. Students would not be graded on their examinations. In fact, the atmosphere of the examination would be one where students freely talked to each other about the questions and decided in what areas they lacked knowledge and skills.

Many educators refer to the difference between cooperative and individual learning as field dependent and field independent, respectively. One of many recommendations for dealing with these differences is to provide field dependent learners with cooperative learning situations. On the other hand, field independent learners perform better in situations of individual competition. Some educators, such as Sonia Nieto, argue that classroom instruction should be adjusted to meet the needs of both the field dependent and field independent student.[41] But one wonders if adjustment in classroom teaching methods is enough when the entire educational system is geared for individual economic competition.

Traditional Native American values stress the sharing of wealth and cooperative activity. It can be argued that many Native American children today would find cooperative learning more beneficial than individual competition. In my discussion of the Ute, I noted that families were upset that high grades by students and high scores by athletic teams were honored rather than student effort. In part, this reaction of the Ute parents reflects a rejection of individual competition for grades.

The cultural values of students of Latino background emphasize cooperation over competition. Angela Carrasquillo writes, "The Latino emphasis on interdependence and cooperation can be antithetical to the mainstream culture's preference for competition and individual achievement."[42] Carrasquillo recognizes that since competition and individualism are so ingrained in the U.S. public school system, she does not see adjustment of methods of instruction as the solution for the cultural conflict between the student in the school. What she proposes is that the Latino student become bicultural and learn to function in the world of the school while maintaining the values of the home. In her words, "A suggestion for ameliorating cultural conflict may be an understanding by Hispanic children and youth that the traits of the primary culture that are not needed may be dropped, with the result that there can be two modes of functioning. Thus, it is possible to gain white cultural traits without totally losing Hispanic ones."[43]

CONCLUSION

Embedded in the structure of U.S. schools are the values of inequality, competition, individualism, accumulation of property, corporate cooperation, and loyalty to the institution one serves. These values were explicitly made part of U.S. schools by their founders in the early nineteenth century and by the influence of modern corporations in the twentieth century. These values support an economic system in which there is inequality in the distribution of wealth and status, individual economic competition for the accumulation of property, and cooperation and loyalty to the corporation.

Inequality in schools can result in the reproduction of the social structure of society, which assures that dominated and some immigrant cultures remain at the bottom of the economic ladder. Resistance is one reaction to this situation. Resistance results in the development of antischool behaviors, which in the context of the modern economic system is self-defeating. Resistance ensures that students remain at the bottom of the economic pile. The differences in response between immigrant and dominated groups to inequality in schooling highlight the effect of years of discrimination and prejudice. This is best exemplified in the studies of the differences in attitudes toward school by Koreans in the United States and Japan, and between students of Latino ancestry born in the United States and those who immigrate into the United States. The intersection of school values and family values can also result in student alienation from peers and home. Cultural conflict can also occur between values of cooperation and competition.

Resistance, alienation, and competition versus cooperation highlight the fact that embedded in U.S. schools are cultural values different from those of many other cultures. Consequently, it is important to understand that this model of schooling teaches a particular set of values related to the economic and social organization of U.S. society. One of the important consequences of the global spread of this type of schooling might be the teaching of cultural values that support the role of modern corporations.

PERSONAL FRAMES OF REFERENCE

Two important issues in this chapter regarding schools are inequality and cultural differences. In reflecting on these issues, you might want to consider the following questions:

1. Did you benefit or were you disadvantaged by the inequalities in education in the United States or other countries?

2. Were there educational inequalities in the schools you attended?
3. How did the schools you attended compare to other schools within the United States or other countries?
4. Do you believe that schools should sort students for the labor market? If not, how should this occur in society?
5. Was there a clash between the culture of your home and the culture of the schools you attended?
6. What was your experience in the cultural life of the schools you attended?

Notes

1. Carl F. Kaestle, *Pillars of the Republic: Common Schools and American Society, 1780–1860* (New York: Hill and Wang, 1983), p. 103.
2. See Joel Spring, *Education and the Rise of the Corporate State* (Boston: Beacon Press, 1972), p. 3.
3. Joel Spring, *The American School: 1642–2000,* Fifth edition (New York: McGraw-Hill, 2000), pp. 103–130.
4. Ibid., pp. 188–212.
5. Ibid., pp. 248–80.
6. Ibid., pp. 213–34.
7. There is a vast array of literature on inequality in schooling in the United States. One summary of this work is Caroline Persell, *Education and Inequality* (New York: Free Press, 1979). An important early study of the role of education in maintaining social inequalities is A. B. Hollingshead, *Elmstown's Youth* (New York: John Wiley, 1949). An important statistical study on the relationship between family background and schooling on social inequality is Christopher Jencks, *Inequality* (New York: Harper and Row, 1972). A study of the role of teacher expectations in promoting inequality is Robert Rosenthal and Lenore Jacobson, *Pygmalion in the Classroom: Teacher Expectation and Pupils' Intellectual Development* (New York: Irvington, 1988). And, of course, the most important recent study is Jeannie Oakes, *Keeping Track: How Schools Structure Inequality* (New Haven: Yale University Press, 1985).
8. Samuel Bowles and Herbert Gintis, *Schooling in Capitalist America* (New York: Basic Books, 1976).
9. Jonathan Kozol, *Savage Inequalities: Children in America's Schools* (New York: Crown, 1991).
10. John Ogbu, "Racial Stratification and Education: The Case of Stockton, California," *IRCD Bulletin* 12, no. 3 (1979), pp. 1–26 and see also his *Minority Education and Caste.*
11. For his discussion of resistance culture among African American students, Ogbu, in part, relies on Lois Weis, *Between Two Worlds: Black Students in an Urban Community College* (Boston: Routledge and Kegan Paul, 1985).
12. John Ogbu, "Class Stratification, Racial Stratification, and Schooling," in *Class, Culture, & Gender in American Education* (Albany: State University of New York Press, 1988), p. 171.
13. Ibid., p. 173.
14. Ibid.
15. Quoted in Betty Jo Kramer, "Education and American Indians: The Experience of the Ute Indian Tribe," in *Minority Status and Schooling: A Comparative Study of*

Immigrant and Involuntary Minorities, ed. Margaret A. Gibson and John U. Ogbu (New York: Garland Publishing, 1991), p. 300.

16. Ibid., p. 287.
17. Ibid., p. 297.
18. Marcelo M. Suarez-Orozco, "Immigrant Adaptation to Schooling: A Hispanic Case," in *Minority Status and Schooling,* p. 42.
19. Ibid., p. 45.
20. Ibid., pp. 46–47.
21. Ibid., p. 56.
22. Sonia Nieto, *Affirming Diversity: The Sociopolitical Context of Multicultural Education* (White Plains, NY: Longman Inc., 1992), p. 28.
23. Yongsook Lee, "Koreans in Japan and the United States," in *Minority Status and Schooling,* pp. 131–67.
24. Ibid., p. 148.
25. Ibid.
26. Ibid., pp. 157–58.
27. Ibid., p. 149.
28. Ibid., p. 160.
29. Ibid., p. 143.
30. Ibid., p. 144.
31. Ibid., p. 162.
32. Michael C. Coleman, *American Indian Children at School 1850–1930* (Jackson: University Press of Mississippi, 1993), p. 178.
33. Ibid., pp. 146–77.
34. Ibid., p. 179.
35. Ibid., p. 181.
36. Ruben Navarrette, Jr., *A Darker Shade of Crimson: Odyssey of a Harvard Chicano* (New York: Bantam Books, 1993).
37. Jawanza Kunjufu, *To Be Popular or Smart: The Black Peer Group* (Chicago: African American Images, 1986).
38. Richard Rodriquez, *Hunger of Memory: The Education of Richard Rodriquez* (New York: Bantam Books, 1982), p. 49.
39. Ibid., p. 57.
40. Ibid.
41. Nieto, *Affirming Diversity,* pp. 111–12.
42. Angel L. Carrasquillo, *Hispanic Children & Youth in the United States: A Resource Guide* (New York: Garland Publishing, 1991), p. 57.
43. Ibid.

PART THREE

Perspectives on Teaching Multicultural Education

CHAPTER 8

Teaching about Racism

The strange twists and turns of racial concepts in the United States were high-lighted when DNA tests offered proof that Thomas Jefferson fathered children with his slave Sally Hemings. The first question, in what would unfold as a maze of racial identities, was the race of Sally Hemings. Her grandfather Hemings, a British sea captain, was white according to the racial codes of the day, while her unnamed grandmother was a slave and black. Given the mul-tiracial heritage, Sally Hemings's mother might be considered white or black by current standards. However, the racial codes of the day made her black be-cause any African ancestry created a black identity. This was called the "one-drop" rule. One drop of African blood resulted in being considered black. In addition, the status of slavery was passed on through the mother. Therefore, Sally Hemings's mother was born with the status of black and slave rather than white and free.

Complicating the issue was that Sally Hemings's father, John Wayles, was white. Therefore, according to the popular language of the nineteenth century, Sally Hemings was three-fourths white and one-fourth black. Despite this pre-ponderant white ancestry, the one-drop rule and slave code meant that Sally was nonetheless born with the status of black and slave. In addition, her fa-ther's other daughter, Martha Wayles, born of a white wife, was Sally's half-sister. It was this half-sister who married Thomas Jefferson. Jefferson had two sets of children. Martha Wayles's children were born with the status of white and free. Sally's children by Thomas Jefferson were seven-eighths white and one-eighth black. But, again, according to the one-drop rule of the nineteenth century, these children were classified as black and slaves. Therefore, Jeffer-son's children were related but divided by social concepts of race and slavery.

In a letter to *The New York Times,* the great-great-great-great granddaughter of Jefferson and Hemings, Dorothy Jefferson Westerinen, describes how her branch of the Jefferson family eventually passed into white society. "We've never," she wrote, "experienced the life that might have been ours had circum-stances been different."[1] In addition, she cautioned those who deny common racial ties. "Racial prejudice must be revealed as the travesty that it is," she states. "We all come from a long line of ancestors and cannot say that we are from unmixed backgrounds. Our common heritage cannot be denied."[2]

Westerinen's comments suggest that anyone with U.S. ancestry dating back to the early nineteenth century must consider the possibility of sharing both African and European roots. Commenting on the descendants of Hemings and Jefferson, Annette Gordon-Reed, professor at the New York Law School, stated, "I think the moral of this story is that the thing this shows very clearly is that we're not two separate people, black and white; we are a people who share a common culture, a common land, and it turns out a common blood line, and this is something that we haven't wanted to deal with openly."[3]

Even more revealing are the generations of white historians who denied the relationship between Jefferson and Hemings. While evidence seemed to indicate the relationship, historians dismissed it arguing that Jefferson's character would not allow him to impose his will on a female slave. It is important to note that Sally Hemings was a slave and not necessarily a willing mistress. She was Jefferson's property and, therefore, unable to stop his sexual advances. *The New York Times* culled from standard historical works previous attempts to dismiss Jefferson's actions. Truly, one could call this the "whitewashing" of history. The following are two examples of the seven major biographies of Jefferson that denied his relationship to Hemings:

> Dumas Malone, *Jefferson the President, First Term, 1801–1805* (Little, Brown and Company, 1970). "[The charges of a sexual relationship with Sally Hemings] are distinctly out of character, being virtually unthinkable in a man of Jefferson's moral standards and habitual conduct."

> Merrill D. Peterson, *Thomas Jefferson and the New Nation* (Oxford University Press, 1970). "Unless Jefferson was capable of slipping badly out of character in hidden moments at Monticello, it is difficult to imagine him caught up in a miscegenous relationship. Such a mixture of the races, such a ruthless exploitation of the master-slave relationship, revolted his whole being."[4]

THE CONCEPT OF RACE

As revealed in the discussion of Thomas Jefferson's children, the concept of *race* is socially and historically constructed, and its meaning is full of ambiguity. Discussions of racial issues are often emotionally charged and, in the context of racism in the United States, cause a crisis in white identity. Consequently, I will link my discussion of race and racism to the guilt and anger expressed by some white students when they are confronted with issues of racism. One method of dealing with these emotional issues, as I will explain later in this chapter, is to develop in white students a self-identity that is antiracist. The development of a white antiracist identity might reduce the anger and hostility some black people feel toward whites. In addition, I will describe educational programs and methods designed to end racism. The antiracist programs described in this chapter would be welcomed by global corporations wanting to utilize a cooperative multiracial workforce and to enter new world markets. In the concluding section, I will discuss the issue of racism in the context of the global economy.

Often, concepts of race are the product of the justification of the economic exploitation of one group by another group. Consequently, racism divides a society both socially and economically. For instance, in the United States the major, but not the only, racial division is between blacks and whites. Indicative of the continuing divisiveness of racism in the United States is the title of Andrew Hacker's 1992 book, *Two Nations: Black and White, Separate, Hostile, Unequal*.[5]

Of course, racism is not limited to the United States but occurs throughout the world. While in most cases racism involves whites against people of color, there are situations where people of color claim their racial superiority over whites. As I will demonstrate, this racial division began as an economic division between enslaved and free labor and continues today in economic differences between blacks and whites in income and economic opportunities.

Concepts of race and culture are connected in traditional European thought. Early Romans viewed others as inferior in both race and culture. For Romans, those who lived by Roman law and within the limits of the Roman Empire were human. Those who lived outside Roman rule were less than human. Those outside the empire were considered irrational barbarians or natural slaves. Cicero, as quoted by Anthony Pagden, wrote that Roman conquest of barbarians "is justified precisely because servitude in such men is established for their welfare."[6] This concept of barbarian and natural slave appeared often in European justifications of empire. Similar to Cicero, Fox Morcillo, writing in the sixteenth century, conceptualized Native Americans as natural slaves who should be pressed into servitude for their own good. Justifying enslavement of Native Americans, Morcillo wrote, "They should be civilized by good customs and education and led to a more human way of life."[7]

Arrogantly, Romans, and later Europeans and Americans, justified Western expansionism as necessary for civilizing inferior races and cultures. For early Romans, the goal of *Imperium romanum*, the geographical authority of the Roman people, was the entire world. The ultimate destiny of the Roman Empire, its leaders believed, was "to civilize" the world's peoples. The word "civil" meant a form of law and the verb "to civilize" meant to bring a people under the control of the law. In other words, to bring people under Roman law was to civilize them.

The advent of Christianity turned Roman concepts of empire and civilizing into "white love." White love is a term I borrowed from Vicente Rafael. In his study of the U.S. conquest of the Philippines, he used "white love" to describe the desire to save the "savage" and "heathen" by conversion to Christianity, replacement of native languages with English, and changing native cultures.[8] In other words, Christianity combined with the legacy of Rome to convince Westerners that it was their destiny to civilize and convert the world. For early Christians, barbarian was synonymous with *paganus*. Pagans were both non-Christian and without civilization. *Imperium romanum* and Christianity were considered geographically the same. Consequently, pagans or non-Christians

Is the Death Penalty a Racist Law?

Grades: High School through College

Objectives:

1. To understand how laws might promote racism.
2. To teach how laws must be analyzed from the standpoint of their racial impact.

Lesson:

1. Present the class with the following case:

As reported on Page A12 of the 12 January 2003 issue of *The New York Times,* a Maryland state-sponsored study found that "blacks who kill whites are significantly more likely to face the death penalty in Maryland than are blacks who kill blacks . . . the race of the defendant was essentially irrelevant."

The article study included the following diagrams under the Headline "Victims Race Pivotal for Death Penalty:"

TABLE 1 Death Penalty—Eligible Cases

Defendant	Victim	
	Black	White
Black	48%	23%
White	2	22

Note: Of the 1,311 death penalty–eligible cases in Maryland from 1978 to 1999, half involved black victims.

TABLE 2 Death Penalty Sentences

Defendant	Victim	
	Black	White
Black	18%	50%
White	1	30

Note: Of the 76 death penalty sentences over the same period, 80 percent involved white cases.

2. Discuss the case with the class to ensure that there is a clear understanding of the report.
3. Divide the class into small groups of four or five to discuss and answer the following questions:
   a. Is the intent of the law racist? What research must be done to find out the answer to this question?
   b. Are the results of the law racist?

(continued)

4. Each group reports its answers to the rest of the class followed by a general class discussion of the case.

Teachers: Teachers should emphasize that there are no correct answers to these questions without further research. However, teachers should emphasize the importance of examining the racial intent and consequences of laws.

Outcome: Students will understand the importance of examining the racial consequence of laws.

were considered less than human.[9] White love served as a justification and a rationalization for imperialism. Under the banner of saving a population from backward or savage cultures and pagan and heathen religions, many Europeans, and later Americans, could feel they were doing good as they conquered Native American, African, and Asian nations.

To understand racism in the United States, it is important to note that the majority of the white population until the late nineteenth century was of English ancestry. As Arthur Schlesinger, Jr., rightly points out, government institutions in the United States, including public schools, were created and shaped primarily by white Anglo-Saxon (English) Protestants,[10] often referred to in literature as the WASPS. Consequently, those racist practices embedded in U.S. institutions had, in most cases, their origins in English attitudes regarding race.

English colonists to North America believed in the superiority of English culture over other world cultures. This sense of superiority resulted in two differing attitudes toward other cultures. One attitude was that other cultures, such as Irish, Native American, and African, could be "civilized" and their cultures changed to be like English culture. The other attitude was that these groups were separate races that were inherently inferior and could never be civilized. Highlighting the socially constructed nature of the concept of race, the English from the sixteenth century through the eighteenth thought of the Irish as a separate and inferior race of people.[11] As the English declared groups racially inferior, they took away their lands and, in the case of Africans, turned them into slave labor. Racism and economic exploitation go hand in hand.

Many of the Founding Fathers of the United States acted according to racial ideas. For instance, Benjamin Franklin worried that the "purely white people" were very small in number when compared to the populations of Asia and Africa. Consequently, he believed that the European invasion of North America provided the opportunity for the expansion of the white race. He asked, "Why increase the Sons of Africa, by Planting them in America, where we have so fair an opportunity, by excluding all Blacks and Tawnys, of increasing the lovely white . . . ?"[12]

The Founding Fathers' desire to ensure white political and economic dominance in the United States was contained in the Naturalization Act of 1790, which excluded from citizenship all nonwhite immigrants and Native Americans. Native Americans were classified as domestic foreigners and could not seek citizenship because they were not white.[13] Most Native Americans were denied U.S. citizenship until 1924, when Congress passed the Indian Citizenship Act.[14]

Reflecting the continuing racial attitudes of the majority of members of the U.S. government, the Naturalization Act of 1790 remained in effect until 1952.[15] During its more than 150 years of existence, the Naturalization Act of 1790 was used by members of federal and state governments to try to keep the population primarily white. The law denied U.S. citizenship to immigrants from Africa and Asia, as well as Native Americans. Of course, children born in the United States were citizens. The law was used to deny Asian immigrants the right to own property. In the 1920s, laws were passed in California, Washington, Arizona, Oregon, Idaho, Nebraska, Texas, Kansas, Louisiana, Montana, New Mexico, Minnesota, and Missouri denying the right to own land to individuals who were ineligible for U.S. citizenship. The purpose of these laws was to deny land ownership to Asians, who, because of the Naturalization Act of 1790, were ineligible for citizenship.[16]

U.S. Supreme Court interpretations of the Naturalization Act of 1790 made it clear that race was primarily being defined according to skin color. In the early 1920s, a group of Asian Indians claimed that they were eligible for citizenship because they were Caucasian. Previous rulings of the U.S. Supreme Court declared that the reference to "white person" in the Naturalization Act of 1790 was synonymous with Caucasian. This 1922 interpretation of the law was used to deny citizenship to Japanese immigrants. When a group of Asian Indians argued in 1923 in *U.S.* v. *Bhagat Singh Thind* that they were Caucasian and therefore eligible for citizenship, the Supreme Court stated that, while the Asian Indian was a Caucasian, he or she could not be considered a "white person." As the Supreme Court understood the term "white person," it meant an immigrant from Europe. The Supreme Court stated, "It may be true that the blond Scandinavian and the brown Hindu have a common ancestor in the dim reaches of antiquity, but the average man knows perfectly well that there are unmistakable and profound differences between them today."[17] The Court argued that "the intention of the Founding Fathers was to 'confer the privilege of citizenship upon the class of persons they knew as white.'"[18]

Consequently, the legacy of the Founding Fathers is a society that defines race primarily according to skin color. Racism is often thought of as "whites" oppressing "people of color." Of course, there are many problems with this definition. If one parent is black and another white, are their children considered black or white? Can one white-skinned child of this marriage be considered white while one dark-skinned child is considered black? Jake Lamar recalls how the confusion over skin color sparked the development of his racial consciousness at the age of three. Jake was sitting at the kitchen table when his Uncle Frank commented about "how obnoxious white people were." Jake responded, "But Mommy's white." His Uncle replied that his mother was not white but was "just light-skinned." Jake then said that he thought his father, brother, and himself were black while his sister and mother were white. His mother then explained that they had many white ancestors which caused the variation in skin color, but they were still "all Negroes." Thinking back on this incident, Jake Lamar reflected, "Black and white then meant something beyond pigmentation . . . so my first encounter with racial awareness was at once enlightening and confusing, and shot through with ambiguity."[19]

While the social and historical construction of the meaning of race is full of ambiguity, the United States still remains a society divided by race. Just as racial concepts were used to justify economic exploitation, racial divisions continue to reflect economic differences. The major racial division in the United States is between black and white, which also reflects major economic differences. According to the 1990 census, the average white family income was $36,915 while the average black family income was $21,423. But, even more indicative of economic differences based on race were the differences in the economic value of education. On the average, black men earned 20 percent less than white men when they had the same level of education. For instance, a black man without a high school education earned on the average 20.3 percent less than a white man without a high school education. A black man with a high school diploma earned on the average 23.6 percent less than a white man with a high school diploma. A black man with 4 years of college earned 20.2 percent less than a white man with a similar education, and a black man with more than 5 years of college earned 22.9 percent less than a white man with a similar education. Therefore, despite similar educational opportunities there are still sharp economic differences along racial lines. In 1990, the average unemployment rate for whites was 4.1 percent, while for blacks it was 11.3 percent. There are also major racial divisions in the labor force with blacks being overrepresented in many occupations and underrepresented in others.[20]

Andrew Hacker attempts to determine the economic value white students place on being white by presenting them with a fictional account of a white person being visited by representatives of an unnamed institution. The white person is informed that a terrible mistake was made and that the person should have been born black. Consequently, the person was now going to be given a black skin and facial features, but his or her memory and ideas would remain the same. Since this was a mistake, the person would be offered financial compensation for being made black. The white students were then asked to name what they felt should be the compensation for becoming black. Their answer was $1 million yearly for the rest of the person's life.[21]

RACISM

Racism refers to acts of oppression of one racial group toward another. Often, racism is defined as prejudice plus power. This definition of racism distinguishes between simple feelings of hostility and prejudice toward another racial group and the ability to turn those feelings into some form of oppression. For instance, a black person might have prejudicial feelings toward white people but have little opportunity to express those prejudicial feelings in some form of economic or political oppression. On the other hand, prejudicial feelings that white people might have toward blacks can turn into racism when they become the basis for discrimination in education, housing, and the job market. Within this framework, racism becomes the act of social, political, and economic oppression of another group.

When discussions of racism occur in my multicultural education classes, white students complain of a sense of hostility from black students and, consequently, accuse black students of racism. Black students respond that their feelings represent prejudice and not racism because they lack the power to discriminate against whites. The troubling aspect of this response is the implication that if these black students had the power they would be racist. One black student pointed out that there are situations where blacks can commit racist acts against whites. The black student used the example of recent killings of white passengers by a black man on a commuter railroad. The evidence seemed to indicate that the killer was motivated by extreme hatred of whites, which the newspapers labeled "black rage." This was a racist act, the black student argued, because the gun represented power.

Andrew Hacker argues that racism in the United States occurs in three forms. One form involves individual acts of discrimination that cause harm to a particular racial group. For instance, Hacker uses the example of a white taxi driver refusing to stop for black passengers because of a fear of robbery. The taxi driver knows that there are wealthy black citizens and also white criminals. But the racial image overwhelms the other images in the taxi driver's mind and the black person is passed up by the taxi. Since the taxi driver does have the power to provide transportation, this becomes a racist act. The second form of racism is institutional, when the structure of an organization discriminates against a racial group. For instance, public schools exhibit institutional racism when people of color are placed disproportionately in vocational tracks and special education classes, and when they are forced to attend school districts spending significantly less on the education of each student than districts serving white students. The third form of racism is the articulation of scientific theories of racial superiority. Hacker cites psychologist Arthur Jensen and Nobel Prize winner William Shockley as examples of this form of racism. Hacker argues that despite the difficulty of providing a biological definition of race and the impossibility of separating environmental influences from genetic factors, these men constantly sift scientific evidence to try to prove that there is such a thing as racial superiority.[22]

Some scholars of racism consider that the definition "prejudice plus power equals racism" is too simplistic. They argue that the definition overlooks divisions caused by social class and gender.[23] For instance, some upper-class blacks can be identified who might have worked with whites to ensure the continuing oppression of black people. This charge has often been brought against Booker T. Washington.[24] In addition, white women have less opportunity, because they lack power, than white men to commit racist acts, and white women can, along with black women, complain of sexism in politics and the job market.

Racist attitudes also seem to vary with social class. For instance, poor whites often express extreme hostility toward blacks. Ironically, poor whites are in the same economic boat as most black people and, consequently, have more to gain by working cooperatively with people of color for economic justice than engaging in racist acts. Writer Lloyd Van Brunt, who grew up as a poor white, wrote, "Unlike blacks and other racial minorities, poor and mostly rural whites have few defenders, no articulate cause . . . they have been made to feel deeply ashamed of themselves—as I was."[25] Called "rednecks" and "crackers" in the South, "woodchucks" in New England, and "lunch pails" in the industrial Midwest, poor whites tend to be the most bigoted members of the white population. It is this group, Brunt argues, that "join the Klan or become skinheads who tattoo themselves with swastikas."[26] Consequently, poor whites are despised by most people of color. Even in prisons, where Van Brunt taught creative writing courses, poor whites were detested by other prisoners. One black prisoner told Van Brunt, "We're talkin' white trash here, my man." Van Brunt reflected, " 'White trash.' That said it all."[27]

Therefore, in discussing race and racism it is important to understand that both concepts are socially constructed and ambiguous, and that they take on different meanings in the context of issues of gender and social class. Also, discussions of these concepts can often make whites feel guilty, and this guilt can quickly turn into hostility and resentment.

TEACHING ABOUT WHITE GUILT

Educator and African American activist Beverly Tatum worries about the loss of white allies in the struggle against racism and the hostility she feels from white college students when teaching about racism. Reflecting on her teaching experiences, she writes, "White students . . . often struggle with strong feelings of guilt when they become aware of the pervasiveness of racism. . . . These feelings are uncomfortable and can lead white students to resist learning about race and racism."[28] Part of the problem, she argues, is that seeing oneself as the oppressor creates a negative self-image, which results in a withdrawal from a discussion of the problem. What needs to be done, she maintains, is to counter the guilt by providing white students with a positive self-image of whites fighting against racism. This creates a self-image for whites of being allies with blacks in the struggle against racism.

Similar to Tatum, I frequently encounter white student resistance to discussions of racism. One of the first times I taught multicultural education to an all-white class, a student blurted out, "Why do blacks get all the benefits?" Another student jumped into the discussion, "Yeah, my brother took the firemen's test. Blacks get special treatment on the test. Isn't that reverse racism?" "My family never owned slaves," interjected another student. "Why should I feel guilty?" Another student exclaimed, "My great-grandparents came over on a boat and worked hard. Blacks can do the same." I realized, as Tatum does, that before I could begin a meaningful discussion of racism that I would have to do something about the anger and resentment resulting from students feeling that they were personally being blamed and criticized for one of the major problems in U.S. society.

I also realized the value of Tatum's approach when discussing the issue of racism in a class composed of black and white students. White students claimed that when they tried to bridge the gap between blacks and whites on campus they encountered a wall of hostility from black students. White students said that they felt resentment from black students when taking courses focusing on African American issues and when they tried to join in the struggle against racism. A black student affirmed the impressions of the white students and stated that black students did feel hostility and resentment toward white students.

Using Tatum's model, I would argue that an important reason for the hostility of black students toward white students and the feelings of resentment

The Strange Transformation of Malcolm X

Grades: Middle School through College

Objective:
To understand historical changes in images of crusaders for racial justice.

Lesson:

1. Have the class read Malcolm X's *The Autobiography of Malcolm X* or explain the book to the class.
2. Read the following statement by Professor Marable Manning quoted by Emily Eakin in "Malcolm X Trove to Schomburg Center" in *The New York Times*, 8 January 2003, p. E6.: "There has been a dramatic transformation in how Malcolm is viewed. In 1965, when he was assassinated, he was seen as an anathema by many, a fiery demagogue. Now he's on a postage stamp."
3. Ask the class to suggest the causes for the public transformation of Malcolm X's image. Are warriors for racial justice first dismissed by many whites and then later embraced because of the triumph of racial justice?
4. List class responses on the board.

Teachers: Teachers should be actively involved in suggesting reasons for the transformation of Malcolm X's public image.

Outcome: Students will gain an understanding of how unpopular causes during one historical period become models of justice in later eras.

among white students during discussions of racism is the lack of a positive white identity, which is antiracist. Without a sense that historically and currently there are many whites who struggle against racism, black students stereotype all whites as being racist and, consequently, feel hostility and resentment. In turn, white students resent discussions of racism because they are made to feel personally guilty.

Tatum begins her discussion of racism with the issue of white identity. She asks students to think of the names of famous white racists. Students quickly respond with names of Southern politicians and Klan leaders. She then asks them to name nationally known white people who could be identified as antiracist activists. This question is often greeted with silence. Slowly participants name civil rights activists such as Viola Liuzzo, James Reeb, and Michael Schwerner. But even these names are known by very few whites. When Tatum adds the qualifier "still living" to her question, the responses are even slower.

Of course, the point of the questions is to make both white and black students aware that there are positive white role models for antiracist activities and that these role models are not part of their own mental constructs. For instance, most history texts do not highlight the role of white activists in countering racism in the United States. Abolitionists are often referred to in public school history texts, but the names of individual white abolitionists are not given as much prominence as black activists such as Frederick Douglas, W.E.B. DuBois, and Martin Luther King, Jr. Consequently, students can leave public schools without a full realization that whites played an important role in ending slavery and fighting for equal rights for all people.

Besides providing positive models of white antiracist activities, Tatum argues that students can be taken through several stages of identity development. Relying on the work of Janet Helms,[29] Tatum identifies six stages of white racial identity development. In the first stage, *contact,* white persons are unaware of their own racial identity and see themselves as normal. They also fail to see institutional forms of racism and the existence of white privilege. In the second stage, *disintegration,* white persons begin to feel guilt, anger, and withdrawal as they become aware of racism and white privilege. This is the condition encountered among white students in many classes dealing with racism. In the next stage, *reintegration,* guilt and anger are transformed into hostility toward people of color.

The next three stages of white identity development progress from white hostility to an active antiracist self-identity. In the fourth stage, *pseudo-independence,* white students abandon feelings of racial superiority and believe that they must do something to end racism. At this stage, they actively seek out people of color. In the fifth stage, *immersion/emersion,* the student grapples with the problem of what it means to be white. "Students at this stage," Tatum writes, "actively seek white role models who might provide examples for nonoppressive ways of being white. Such examples might be found in the form of biographies or autobiographies of white individuals who engaged in a similar process."[30] In the final stage, *autonomy,* the student has internalized a positive white racial identity and becomes actively antiracist.

Most antiracist education neglects this important issue of white identity. On the other hand, Tatum neglects the issue of social class. Her audience appears to be white middle-class students. What about poor rural whites? Is their racial hostility the product of lacking a positive white identity? In part, this might explain their continued racism. But, on the other hand, their racism might be fed by poverty and their own encounters with prejudice.

AN ANTI-BIAS CURRICULUM

One of the most popular antiracist curricula for preschool children is the National Association for the Education of Young Children's* *Anti-Bias Curriculum: Tools for Empowering Young Children.*[31] This curriculum and related methods of instruction are designed to reduce prejudice among young children regarding race, language, gender, and physical ability differences. The premise of the method is that at an early age children become aware of the connection between power and skin color, language, and physical disabilities. Cited as examples are a 2½-year-old Asian child who refuses to hold the hand of a black classmate because "it's dirty," and a 4-year-old boy who takes over the driving of a pretend bus because "girls can't be bus drivers."[32]

According to the *Anti-Bias Curriculum*, research findings show that young children classify differences among people and are influenced by bias toward others. By age 2, children are aware of gender differences and begin to apply color names to skin colors. Between ages 3 and 5, children try to figure out who they are by examining the differences in gender and skin color. By 4 or 5 years old, children engage in socially determined gender roles, and they give racial reasons for the selection of friends.[33] Based on these research findings, the advocates of the curriculum believe that prejudice can be reduced if there is conscious intervention to curb the development of biased concepts and activities.

To achieve this goal, it is recommended that an antibias environment in the classroom be created by displaying in the classroom images of children from a variety of cultural and racial backgrounds. These images should reflect a numerical balance between groups and accurately depict people's daily lives. There should be a fair balance of images of males and females depicted in a variety of occupational roles. There should be images of people with disabilities doing work and involved in a variety of family roles. Books should be selected for the classroom that reflect a diversity of racial and cultural backgrounds and of gender roles.[34]

Play equipment, art materials, and other classroom materials should be selected to enhance racial understanding and ensure diversity in gender play. Paints, crayons, magic markers, and paper should be available that can represent a variety of skin colors. The curriculum recommends that a teacher occasionally comment on the use of different colors for skin: "You are using a

*For a catalogue of publications write to this address: National Association for the Education of Young Children, 1834 Connecticut Avenue, N.W., Washington, DC 20009.

beautiful chocolate brown—it matches your skin"; "You are using a beautiful peach color, which is just like your skin."[35] It is recommended that dramatic play be used to show nonstereotypic gender roles and families from a variety of racial and ethnic backgrounds.

With regard to activities specifically dealing with racial differences, the curriculum recommends making a book titled "We All Look Special." The book should include color photos of the children and staff with each child describing herself or himself according to skin color, hair, and eyes. The curriculum recommends getting paint chips from a local store to match with the children's skin colors. A small amount of hair can be cut from each child and placed on an index card. Each child can then be asked to identify each swatch of hair. All of these activities are designed to make the children feel comfortable with themselves and others.[36]

One of the interesting recommendations is the use of "persona" dolls. These are a collection of classroom dolls, each of which is given his or her own life story. The dolls are supposed to enhance a child's connection to the story and cause children to participate in solving problems in the stories. In the classroom described in the curriculum, there are 16 dolls representing a variety of racial and cultural groups. In addition, one of the dolls is deaf and another has cerebral palsy. Stories are created for each doll that reflect differences in family life, cultural background, race, and differing abilities. Each doll is introduced to the child with a simple introductory story followed by stories reflecting children's everyday lives. The teacher should relate these stories specifically to antibias themes. These themes can emerge from the children's daily lives, current events in the world, information the teacher wants the children to know, and history.

The creator of the dolls, Louise Derman-Sparks, uses them to create positive antiracist and antibias identities. She writes, "I do want to give them a sense of the great many people like themselves who have reflected a spirit of justice and freedom. I use historical stories about the Montgomery Bus Boycott, Harriet Tubman, Frederick Douglas, Helen Keller."[37]

The *Anti-Bias Curriculum* provides many other activities dealing with prejudice reduction among young children. One important aspect of the program is the preparation of the teacher through consciousness-raising activities with a support group. It is recommended that, as part of consciousness raising, teachers define for the group their own racial/ethnic identities and how they learned their racial/ethnic identities and gender roles. Teachers are to share with the group how they agreed or disagreed with their parents regarding issues of race and gender and how they developed their own ideas. Then teachers are asked to list what they think are acceptable and unacceptable behaviors of boys and girls, and what they want other people to know about their racial/ethnic identities. These lists are shared and discussed with the group. Teachers are then asked to discuss their feelings regarding people with disabilities. These consciousness-raising sessions provide the teachers with an opportunity to deal with their own stereotypes regarding racial, ethnic, and gender differences, and regarding people with disabilities.[38]

In a broader context, the Anti-Bias Curriculum does approach the issue of racism and sexism from a psychological standpoint and not from an economic and political perspective. My comment should not be taken as a criticism of a very fine effort to reduce prejudice. I merely want to point out that this type of program would be readily supported by international corporations because such programs could be used to reduce friction in a multicultural workforce without threatening corporate leaders with issues involving inequalities in income and political power.

THE TEACHING TOLERANCE PROJECT

After a group of teenage skinheads attacked and beat to death an Ethiopian man on a street in Portland, Oregon, in 1988, the members of the Southern Poverty Law Center decided it was time to do something about teaching tolerance. Dedicated to pursuing legal issues involving racial incidents and denial of civil rights, the law center sued, on behalf of the victim's family, the two men who were responsible for teaching violent racism to the Portland skinheads. These two teachers, Tom Metzger, the head of the White Aryan Resistance, and his son, became symbols of racist teachings in the United States. In a broad sense, the Teaching Tolerance Project is designed to provide information about teaching methods and materials that will counter the type of racist teachings represented by Metzger and his son.[39]

Similar to the Anti-Bias Curriculum, the Teaching Tolerance Project primarily defines racism as a function of psychological attitudes in contrast to an emphasis on racism as a function of economic exploitation. On the inside cover of its magazine, *Teaching Tolerance,* tolerance is defined as "the capacity for or the practice of recognizing and respecting the beliefs or practices of others."[40] Within the context of this definition, the project members "primarily celebrate and recognize the beliefs and practices of racial and ethnic groups such as African Americans, Latinos, and Asian Americans."[41]

The primary purpose of the Teaching Tolerance Project is to provide resources and materials to schools to promote "interracial and intercultural understanding between whites and nonwhites."[42] While this is the primary focus of the project, there have been decisions to include material dealing with cultural tolerance, homelessness, and poverty.

One of the project's leaders, Joseph Hawkins, realizes that discussions of racism and the history of white treatment of African Americans will heighten tension between the two groups. But building tolerance, he argues, depends on the exposure of this ugly side of U.S. history to all groups. Of course, there is the possibility a history of racism will inflame the anger of people of color and build a greater wall of division between whites and blacks. After all, why would African Americans want to be tolerant of whites after exposure to the brutal history of race relations in the United States? Writing in *Multicultural Education,* Hawkins responds to this argument: "In the short run, hurt feelings or even increased tensions may result from studying the history of 'others' but those of us in this thing (multiculturalism) for the long run see a light at the end of the tunnel (or at least we dream one). One day we will get past the hurt feelings and the tensions."[43] It is this belief in the power of education to end racial tensions and heighten interracial tolerance that underpins the Teaching Tolerance Project.

In 1992, the Southern Poverty Law Center sponsored the publication and distribution of 150,000 free copies of the biannual *Teaching Tolerance* magazine to every public and private school in the United States.* The purpose of the magazine is to share ideas on how to teach tolerance and to provide a guide to teaching resources. The magazine staff does not claim to have a magical formula for teaching tolerance but sees its role as being a conduit of information.

The Teaching Tolerance website, www.tolerance.org, describes the organization:[44]

> Founded in 1991 by the Southern Poverty Law Center, Teaching Tolerance supports the efforts of K-12 teachers and other educators to promote respect for differences and appreciation of diversity.
>
> 1. Teaching Tolerance serves as a clearinghouse of information about anti-bias programs and activities being implemented in schools across the country. The ideas presented on this website and in our semiannual magazine, *Teaching Tolerance,* represent some of the most innovative, useful initiatives we've found to date.
> 2. Teaching Tolerance also produces and distributes free, high-quality anti-bias materials. We recognize that budgetary and time constraints often limit the ability of educators to create original anti-bias curricula. We develop resources that speak to various academic subject areas and grade levels, because tolerance education is the responsibility of every teacher.
> 3. Online, Teaching Tolerance shares space with another Center program, Tolerance.org, a Web-based initiative that encourages people from all walks of life to "fight hate and promote tolerance." Schools are not islands unto themselves, but rather exist within the larger community.

LA ESCUELA FRATNEY

One of the schools featured in *Teaching Tolerance* and in George Wood's book, *Schools That Work,*[45] is the Fratney Elementary School in Milwaukee, Wisconsin.† Carol Heller and Joseph Hawkins of the Teaching Tolerance Project laud the Fratney School because it makes the battle against "racism, sexism, and homophobia . . . a full-time commitment."[46] The school is a two-way bilingual school where students are taught in both English and Spanish. It has a multicultural curriculum with an explicit antiracist component and it uses cooperative learning methods.

---

*To obtain a free copy of *Teaching Tolerance* write to this address: *Teaching Tolerance*, 400 Washington Ave., Montgomery, AL 36104.
†Two books have been written by the staff, students, and parents: *La Escuela Fratney: Year Three* and *Growing with La Escuela Fratney: Year Two*. For copies, write to this address: La Escuela Fratney, 3255 N. Fratney St., Milwaukee, WI 53212.

For example, in his-fifth grade classroom at Fratney Elementary School, Bob Peterson asks for examples of racial stereotypes. Students respond with "All white people are prejudiced"; "All whites are rich snobs"; "All blacks sell dope."[47] The class goes on to talk about how stereotypes lead to prejudice and racial discrimination.

The teaching of history at Fratney involves both instruction in areas such as black history and Mexican American history and the examination of history from differing cultural frames of reference. One of the interesting projects is to ask students to envision a world where no one race or culture is superior.

Antiracism, bilingualism, history, and vocabulary lessons are combined in single lessons. For instance, George Wood describes a class lesson that involves the teacher reading to the students *Follow the Drinking Gourd.* The story, which deals with slaves escaping through the underground railroad, provides an opportunity to discuss African American history and the effect of racism. The teacher holds up a large sheet of paper on which are pasted pictures from the story. Students are asked to name the pictures in either English or Spanish. The names given to the pictures become the vocabulary list.[48]

These lessons are part of a series of six themes around which the curriculum of the school is organized. Each theme takes 6 weeks with all six themes taking up the school year. The themes are as follows:

1. Our Roots in the School and Community
2. The Native American Experience
3. The African American Experience
4. The Hispanic Experience
5. The Asian American/Pacific American Experience
6. We Are a Multicultural Nation[49]

The Fratney school demonstrates how an antiracist and multicultural agenda can infuse the curriculum of an entire school. The following discussion demonstrates how educators can remove the racial bias from an apparently racially neutral subject such as mathematics.

RACISM AND MATHEMATICS INSTRUCTION

William Tate, a professor of mathematics instruction at the University of Wisconsin, believes that even a subject as seemingly neutral as mathematics can reflect a racial bias.[50] As he points out, the 1991 professional standards of the National Council of Teachers of Mathematics recommends that all mathematics teachers know the following:

1. How students' linguistic, ethnic, racial, gender, and socioeconomic backgrounds influence their learning of mathematics.
2. The role of mathematics in society and culture, the contribution of various cultures to the advancement of mathematics, and the relationship of school mathematics to other subjects and realistic applications.[51]

Tate argues that most school mathematics are taught from the context of white experiences. For example, he observed a student teacher giving a second-grade class the following problem: "Joe has five pumpkin pies. Karen has six pumpkin pies. How many pumpkin pies do Karen and Joe have all together?" The teacher thought the problem was appropriate because Thanksgiving was only a few weeks away. The white students busied themselves with the problem, while an African American student looked uninterested. Tate asked the teacher if most families ate pumpkin pie for Thanksgiving. When she responded "probably," he then asked to question the children. They discovered, he wrote, "that pumpkin pie was indeed a Thanksgiving ritual in the homes of the white children. For the African American child, however, sweet potato pie was the dessert of the day. Thus the background discussion to the problem was 'foreign' to this student."[52]

In another example, he refers to a situation where African American students at an urban middle school responded "strangely" to a districtwide mathematics test which asked whether paying $1.50 each way to ride a bus between home and work was a better deal than buying a weekly pass for $16. The test constructors assumed that the correct answer would be paying a daily fare based on riding to work five times a week. When school officials questioned the students, the students responded that they would choose the pass because they could loan it to other family members and use it on weekends. In Tate's words, "For these students, choosing the weekly pass is economically appropriate and mathematically logical."[53]

Therefore, Tate argues, a mathematics curriculum can be racist if it is centered in a white experience to which African American students cannot relate. It denies to African American students an equal chance to learn mathematics. "I submit," Tate argues, "that failing to provide African American students with curriculum, instruction, and assessment that are centered on their experiences, culture, and traditions is a major obstacle to providing them with . . . mathematical experience."[54]

In addition, Tate maintains that mathematical problems can help students to bring about political changes. In this sense, "empowerment" through mathematics becomes part of African American liberation from an oppressive white culture. For instance, one group of African American students found that the disproportionate number of liquor stores in their neighborhood was a function of local legislation. The students developed a formula with mathematically based incentives to get liquor stores to locate away from their neighborhood. In this situation, mathematics becomes an instrument for social change. For African American students, mathematics can become another tool for ending racial oppression.

CONCLUSION: RACISM AND THE GLOBAL MARKET

Racism is a divisive and complex factor in the development of a global economy. Global corporations have an interest in ending racism as they enter new markets around the world. For instance, with China and other Asian countries as major markets, U.S. companies cannot afford to have employees acting according to the racist attitudes held by many whites towards Asians throughout U.S. history.[55] Many whites resisted Asian immigration in the nineteenth and twentieth centuries, warning of the "yellow peril." World War II fanned the flames of anti-Asian feelings.[56] In asking my classes to construct a family tree reflecting the evolution of feelings within the family toward other cultures and races, white students were surprised at the anti-Asian attitudes of their parents. Many parents linked these anti-Asian feelings to the anti-Japanese propaganda of World War II. For similar reasons, racist attitudes cannot be tolerated as global corporations expand into African and South American markets.

Also, racism is a destructive element in the global workplace. As global corporations rely upon a racially diverse workforce to keep wages down, they must be concerned about racial tensions. The ironic twist in this concern is that global corporations can be accused of being racist because they tend to rely on people of color as a source of cheap labor. But to accuse global corporations of racism is a little simplistic because Japanese corporations have built plants in the United States to take advantage of the cheap, as compared to Japan, labor force.

Issues of social class as related to racism are avoided by global corporations. As economic writer David Reiff argues, global corporations are interested in ending racism and gender bias, but not the privileges of social class. Reiff writes, "Were women and blacks represented proportionately at the top of corporate America, this would not change the nature of class distinctions one iota—which is precisely why capitalism is in no sense seriously opposed to the multicultural project."[57] For the world business elite, discussions of social class represent a direct threat to their power and position. On a world scale, the business elite are identified more by their employment than by their race and nation. Reiff writes, "A financial broker from New York would feel more commonality with a broker from Tokyo than he or she would with someone from Harlem or the South Bronx."[58] I would add to Rieff's statement that the New York broker, whether black or white, would also feel closer to the Tokyo broker than to poor rural whites.

Earlier discussions of "white trash" versus "the power elite" highlight the importance of considering race with social class. After all, some members of the black community now occupy positions within the power elite. The largest number of low-income families are white. Who has the privileged position when a poor white meets a black member of the power elite? The poor white might exhibit racism toward blacks while the black elite might display prejudice toward low-income whites.

In keeping with the world business elite's focus on racism, but not social class issues, most antiracist education programs concentrate on reducing prejudice and not on promoting economic justice for all people. The exceptions are approaches similar to those proposed for mathematics education by William Tate. In other words, reducing prejudice does not necessarily result in ending economic injustices. Simple prejudice reduction programs can result in all races participating equally in a system that maintains economic inequalities.

Emotions often make it difficult to deal with personal attitudes about race. But it is important to understand that racial attitudes do not fall out of the sky.

They do have an origin. One of the things you might want to do is construct a family tree of attitudes about other cultures and races. This might provide a means for understanding how these attitudes developed within your family. Remember that not all attitudes are negative. For instance, I have met many whites who admire the humor, music, and lifestyle of African Americans. Also, you might consider the effect of media on your attitudes about other races. For instance, African American Henry Louis Gates, Jr., recalls the influence of television shows in his childhood on his images of whites: "These shows for us were about property, the property that white people could own and that we couldn't. About a level of comfort and ease at which we could only wonder."[59]

PERSONAL FRAMES OF REFERENCE

1. How did you develop your attitudes about race and people of other races?
2. Do you know any white antiracists?
3. Imagine that the Elmtown School District has hired Janet Helms, Beverly Tatum, Cristina Igoa (Chapter 5), William Cross (Chapter 5), and John Ogbu (Chapter 7) as consultants. What might they recommend to improve academic achievement and reduce racial tensions as presented in the following discussion of education in Elmtown?

Education in Elmtown   Since the 1920s, the Elmtown School District served a primarily working-class population. Most of the working population had been employed in a local auto plant that closed down in 1996. Until the 1960s, the population was mostly white. Beginning in the 1960s, the auto plant began to hire black workers. By the 1980s, the community was racially split with a black working-class population living on the northside and a white working-class population living on the southside. In the 1990s, a poor white population began moving into areas between the two districts. The black and white working-class kids referred to these newcomers as "white trash." In addition, the State Department moved a small population of Afghan war refugees into the community in the early 1990s.

In 1998, the school district was concerned with the following problems:

1. For the first time in the school district's history, a fight broke out in the cafeteria between a group of black students and newly arrived poor white students. Prior to this fight, there had been few major tensions between white and black students.
2. Academic achievement was low among Afghan students. Elementary school teachers complained about the lack of cooperation from Afghan students.
3. Parents of Afghan students were complaining about the sexual mores of U.S. teenagers. They wanted the school board to provide special protection for their female children.
4. Academic achievement among black students remained low. Administrators complained that the integrated social relationships during elementary

school disappeared in high school. These administrators feared that this would heighten racial tensions.

5. Middle school teachers complained that recently arrived poor white students seemed withdrawn in class. Recently, a group of girls left the middle school without permission during class hours. An administrator found them crying near a trailer park close to school. Apparently, both black and white students had been making fun of their clothes and sticking notes on their lockers reading "White Trash Here."

Notes

1. Dorothy Jefferson Westerinen, "To the Editor," *The New York Times,* 9 November 1998, p. A24.
2. Ibid.
3. "The Content of Jefferson's Character Is Revealed at Last, Or Is It?" *The New York Times,* 8 November 1998, p. 7.
4. Ibid.
5. Andrew Hacker, *Two Nations: Black and White, Separate, Hostile, Unequal* (New York: Scribner's, 1992).
6. Anthony Pagden, *Lords of All the World: Ideologies of Empire in Spain, Britain and France c.1500–c.1800* (New Haven: Yale University Press, 1995), p. 20.
7. Ibid., p. 99.
8. Vicente L. Rafael, "White Love: Surveillance and Nationalist Resistance in the U.S. Colonization of the Philippines," in *Cultures of United States Imperialism,* ed. Amy Kaplan and Donald Pease (Durham: Duke University, 1993), pp. 185–218.
9. Pagden, pp. 24–25.
10. Arthur M. Schlesinger, Jr., *The Disuniting of America* (Knoxville, TN: Whittle Direct Books, 1991), p. 8.
11. For a discussion of the evolution of English concepts of race beginning with the Irish see Ronald Takaki, *A Different Mirror: A History of Multicultural America* (Boston: Little, Brown and Company, 1993), pp. 24–51, 139–66.
12. Ibid., p. 79.
13. Ibid., pp. 79–80.
14. Francis Paul Prucha, ed., *Documents of United States Indian Policy,* 2nd ed. (Lincoln: University of Nebraska Press, 1990), p. 218.
15. Takaki, *A Different Mirror,* p. 400.
16. Ronald Takaki, *Strangers from a Different Shore: A History of Asian Americans* (New York: Penguin Books, 1989), pp. 203–5.
17. Ibid., p. 299.
18. Ibid.
19. Jake Lamar, *Bourgeois Blues: An American Memoir* (New York: Plume Books, 1992), pp. 34–35.
20. Hacker, *Two Nations,* pp. 94–95, 103, 111.
21. Ibid., pp. 31–32.
22. Ibid., pp. 17–30.
23. See Barry Toryna, *Racism and Education* (Philadelphia: Open University Press, 1993), pp. 9–15.
24. For instance, see W.E.B. DuBois's comments on Booker T. Washington in *The Souls of Black Folk* (New York: Signet Classic, 1969), pp. 79–95.

25. Lloyd Van Brunt, "About Men: Whites Without Money," *The New York Times Magazine,* 27 March 1994, p. 38.
26. Ibid.
27. Ibid.
28. Beverly Tatum, *Why Are All the Black Kids Sitting Together in the Cafeteria? And Other Conversations on Race* (New York: Basic Books, 1999).
29. J. E. Helms, *Black and White Racial Identity: Theory, Research, and Practice* (Westport, CT: Greenwood Press, 1990).
30. Tatum, *Teaching White Students,* p. 15.
31. Louise Derman-Sparks and the A.B.C. Task Force, *Anti-Bias Curriculum: Tools for Empowering Young Children* (Washington, DC: National Association for the Education of Young Children, 1989).
32. Ibid., p. ix.
33. Ibid., pp. 1–3.
34. Ibid., pp. 11–16.
35. Ibid., p. 25.
36. Ibid., pp. 31–38.
37. Ibid., p. 19.
38. Ibid., pp. 111–15.
39. Carol Heller and Joseph Hawkins, "Teaching Tolerance: Notes from the Front Line," *Teachers College Record* (Spring 1994), p. 2.
40. For instance see *Teaching Tolerance* (Fall 1993), p. 4.
41. Heller and Hawkins, *Teaching Tolerance: Notes,* p. 8.
42. Ibid.
43. Joseph Hawkins, "To the Editor," *Multicultural Education* (Spring 1994), p. 4.
44. More information on Teaching Tolerance can be found at http://www.tolerance.org.
45. George H. Wood, *Schools That Work: America's Most Innovative Public Education Programs* (New York: Plume, 1993).
46. Heller and Hawkins, *Teaching Tolerance: Notes,* p. 17.
47. Priscilla Ahlgren, "La Escuela Fratney: Reflections on a Bilingual, Antibias, Multicultural Elementary School," *Teaching Tolerance* (Fall 1993), p. 28.
48. Wood, *Schools That Work,* p. 21.
49. Ibid., pp. 20–21.
50. William F. Tate, "Race, Retrenchment, and the Reform of School Mathematics," *Phi Delta Kappan* (February 1994), pp. 477–84.
51. For these standards Tate cites: *Professional Standards for Teaching Mathematics* (Reston, VA: National Council of Teachers of Mathematics, 1991).
52. Tate, *Reform of School Mathematics,* p. 480.
53. Ibid.
54. Ibid.
55. See David Rieff, "Multiculturalism's Silent Partner: It's the Newly Globalized Consumer Economy, Stupid," *Harper's,* July 1993, pp. 62–78.
56. Takaki, *Strangers from a Different Shore.*
57. Reiff, *Silent Partner,* p. 67.
58. Ibid., p. 66.
59. Henry Louis Gates, Jr., *Colored People: A Memoir* (New York: Alfred A. Knopf, 1994), p. 21.

CHAPTER 9

Teaching about Sexism

Revealing how little changed in classroom practices in the twentieth century, a poster distributed by the National Education Association in 1944 depicts the findings of research of the 1990s on sexism in the classroom.[1] In the poster, a boy and a girl of elementary school age are standing around a world globe. A female teacher crouches between the two children so that her head is below that of the boy and about even with the head of the girl. The teacher's face is turned away from the passive-looking girl and her complete attention is given to the animated face of the boy. Ignored by the teacher, the girl stares blankly at the globe with her arms dangling empty by her sides. In contrast, the boy clutches a notebook in one hand while a finger of the other hand points to a place on the globe. Both smiling, the teacher and the boy stare directly into each other's eyes.[2]

Besides portraying current research findings that females are often ignored in classroom instruction, the poster portrays the female as both the liberator and nurturer of males, and as submitting to male domination. The female teacher helps the boy understand his future power as symbolized by the world globe. She liberates his power through her attention and nurturing. The passive female student symbolizes the subservient role of women in the boy's future.

I will begin this chapter by first examining different concepts of women and women teachers in European American culture. Then I will discuss the findings of current research on gender discrimination in schools and in standardized testing. The chapter will conclude with descriptions of programs to eliminate sexism in schools and examine the issue of sexism in the global economy.

REPUBLICAN MOTHERHOOD

The seemingly contradictory qualities of women as liberators and nurturers of men as symbolized in the 1944 National Education Association poster can be traced back to the American Revolution. The concept of "republican motherhood," the term coined by historian Mary Norton, emerged after the American

Gender in Advertising

Grades: Middle School through College

Objective:
To understand public images of gender roles.

Lesson:
Depending on the availability of magazines, have students work individually or in small groups.

1. Have students cut out advertisements depicting men and women.
2. Have students analyze the advertisements regarding:
    a. Gender stereotypes.
    b. Career models for males and females.
    c. Social and economic independence of males and females.
    d. Overall characteristics of the differences and similarities of males and females.
3. Have students present their analysis to the class.
4. List on the chalkboard conclusions about the depiction of gender roles in advertising.

Teachers: Teachers should participate in this assignment by doing their own analysis of the depiction of gender roles in ads.

Outcome: Students will gain an understanding of the public images of gender differences and similarities.

Revolution when there was concern about educating citizens to meet the needs of the new republic. What, it was wondered, would be the public role of women within this experimental form of government? The answer was that women would have the major responsibility for nurturing future republican male leaders. In defining the role of women, Norton writes, "They [male citizens of the new republic] located woman's public role in her domestic responsibilities, in her obligation to create a supportive home life for her husband, and particularly in her duty to raise republican sons who would love their country and preserve its virtuous character."[3]

Denied the political power to participate directly in the new republican government, women took on the role of molding future male republican leaders. But in this subservient role of political teacher were the seeds of future female emancipation. Similar to concepts of racism in European American culture, the origins of both female domination and female emancipation can be found in English culture. For instance, the origins of republican government in the United States are often traced to the writings of John Locke, who, in the late seventeenth century, wrote *Some Thoughts Concerning Education and An Essay Concerning Human Understanding*. Locke provided a theoretical justification for the American Revolution by arguing that government existed by social contract and that, if the government violated its part of the contract, then a new social contract and government should be formed.

Within this concept of the social contract, women were made politically subservient to men. Locke argued that men are rulers of the family and that they have final power over family disputes. The concept of the father as ruler of the family including women and children is reflected in his educational writings. "Be sure then to establish the authority of a father," Locke wrote, "as soon as he [the child] is capable of submission, and can understand in whose power he is."[4] In the family, Locke argued, the father functions as a temporary government before the child grows up and submits to the government of the state. The English colonial family operated under the same premises, and, in addition, Calvinist religious thought placed a woman's access to God in the hands of the husband. The colonial family operated under the following premise: "He for God only, she for God in him."[5] This meant that women were to bow to the God in men, and men were to assume the spiritual care of women. In legal matters, the married woman was at the mercy of her husband—she was without rights to own property, make contracts, and sue for damages.

While republican motherhood was structured under this umbrella of subservience to the husband and the government, there developed a strong argument for the education of women. This struggle for education eventually contributed to the political emancipation of women. One source of the argument for women's education was that republican mothers needed to be educated in order to nurture republican male citizens. In other words, the public role of women in the new republic required their education. The other source was from women themselves.

In 1821, Emma Willard opened the Troy Female Seminary after telling the New York State Legislature, in the language of republican motherhood, "Who knows how great and good a race of men may yet arise from the forming hands of mothers, enlightened by the bounty of that beloved country,—to defend her liberties, to plan her future improvements and to raise her to unparalleled glory?"[6] Willard justified the education of women as being necessary for the development of republican mothers and, most important, as teachers for schools. After the Revolution, many schools began to seek female teachers. This was not only because they were inexpensive, since they were usually paid less than men, but also because they were believed to be morally purer than men. Willard encouraged women to be self-supporting and educated. She provided " 'instruction on credit' for any woman who would agree to become a teacher, the debt to be repaid from her later earnings."[7] Willard maintained a placement bureau at the seminary to help women find employment as teachers. Willard's activities reflected an important career opportunity that was opening for women—public schoolteachers.

Some men supported the education of women and the hiring of female schoolteachers because they believed that women would make the best moral models for schoolchildren. But the belief in the moral superiority of women often led men to argue that women required an education that was different from that given men. Unlike Mary Wollstonecraft, these men wanted women to be educated for moral purity. In addition, some men argued that women should not be subjected to the rigors of the type of education received by men. A widely read book in the late nineteenth century, Edward Clark's *Sex in Education*, warned that the rigors of education would divert women's blood from their reproductive organs to their brains, thus causing many physical problems including constipation. Clark argued that women should attend separate schools with an easier curriculum and less study than required of men.[8]

What aided increased educational opportunities for women in the early twentieth century was the expansion of white-collar jobs such as secretaries, typists, and clerks. A high school education, particularly a commercial education, became an established route to this sex-segregated labor market.[9] But, it should be recognized that this form of vocational education severely limited the occupational prospects for women. Women were not being educated to be managers, doctors, lawyers, engineers, and scientists. In fact, a college education for women was often thought of as a means of getting a career as a schoolteacher.

Despite these limitations on the education of some women, there did develop a cadre of women who continued the struggle for equal political rights, which culminated in 1920 in the passage of the Nineteenth Amendment giving women the right to vote. For women, it had been a long struggle from the role of republican mothers in the eighteenth century to political equals in the twentieth century.

While education contributed to the exercise of reason, which contributed to the increased political power of women and the right to vote, the educational system still treated women as second-class citizens. Sexism continued to pervade the educational system. Boys were tracked into curricula that would potentially lead to higher-paying jobs, women were discriminated against in science, mathematics, and vocational courses, and more money was channeled to men's athletic programs. In 1972, women scored another victory with the passage of Title IX, which made it illegal for schools to discriminate in vocational training, vocational counseling, athletics, financial aid, and college admission practices.

Despite these victories, current research indicates that women are still receiving an unequal education. The 1944 National Education Association poster of the teacher attending to the active boy and ignoring the passive girl is still the standard practice in many classrooms. Frequently, women are still being prepared for republican motherhood and not Wollstonecraft's vision of reasoning political equals. Unequal educational opportunities for girls still contribute to unequal opportunities in the labor market.

THE GLASS CEILING OF THE CLASSROOM

While equality of educational opportunities has increased for women, there still exists a level of classroom discrimination that denies full participation of women in the educational system. The term "glass ceiling" is most often used to describe the problems women face in climbing the corporate ladder. As Cindy Skrzycki has documented, women, while gaining promotions in corporations, seem to encounter an invisible barrier, or glass ceiling, that keeps them from reaching the top corporate positions of president or chairman of the board.[10]

After more than 20 years of research on gender issues in the classroom, Myra and David Sadker have made visible the structure of the classroom's glass ceiling. When they began their work in the late 1960s, the glass ceiling was so invisible that Myra Sadker's and Nancy Frazier's *Sexism in School and Society*,[11] published in 1973, was primarily purchased by patrons of pornography stores rather than educators. This was discovered in the second year of its publication when the publisher reported that many purchasers were returning the book and demanding their money back. Upon investigation, it was found that pornography stores stocked the book on their shelves thinking that it had a sexy content related to schools. In addition, most educators were unaware of the existence of sexism in education. Reflecting back on this incident in their 1994 book, *Failing at Fairness: How America's Schools Cheat Girls*, the Sadkers state, "In thirty years we have journeyed from Betty Friedan's 'problem that has no name' to a realization that sexism affects every part of our lives . . . from the preaching in our religious institutions to the teaching in our schools."[12]

Before discussing the elements that create the glass ceiling for women in education, I will summarize the Sadkers' findings regarding the nature of the ceiling. The Sadkers found that girls were equal to or ahead of boys in most measures of academic achievement and psychological health during the early years of schooling, but by the end of high school and college, girls have fallen behind boys on these measurements. Why? On entrance examinations to college, girls score lower than boys, particularly in science and mathematics.

Why? Boys receive more state and national scholarships. Why? Women score lower than men on all entrance examinations to professional schools. Why?[13]

With regard to psychological health, girls suffer a greater decline than boys in self-esteem from elementary school to high school. Of course, an important general question about the following statistics is why both boys and girls decline in feelings of self-esteem. As a measure of self-esteem, the Sadkers rely on responses to the statement, "I'm happy the way I am."[14] They report that in elementary school 60 percent of girls and 67 percent of boys responded positively to the statement. By high school, these positive responses declined to 29 percent for girls and 46 percent for boys. In other words, the decline in self-esteem for girls was 31 percentage points as compared to 20 percentage points for boys. Why is there less self-esteem and a greater decline in self-esteem among girls as compared to boys?

The answer provides insight into one of the elements in the glass ceiling of the educational system. As a method of getting an answer to the question, the Sadkers create a scenario similar to that used by Andrew Hacker where white students were asked what they thought the economic compensation should be for being required to become black. In this case, the Sadkers asked students how their lives would be different if they suddenly were transformed into a member of the opposite sex. In general, girls responded with feelings that it wouldn't be so bad and that it would open up opportunities to participate in sports and politics. In addition, girls felt they would have more freedom and respect. With regard to self-esteem, girls expressed little regret about the consequences of the sex change. In contrast, boys expressed horror at the idea and many said they would commit suicide. They saw themselves becoming second-class citizens, being denied access to athletics and outdoor activities, and being racked with physical problems. With regard to self-esteem, and in contrast to girls, boys expressed nothing but regret about the consequences of the sex change.[15]

Contributing to the lack of self-esteem among girls, the Sadkers argue, are modes of classroom interaction, the representation of women in textbooks and other educational materials, and the discriminatory content of standardized tests. In one of their workshops with classroom teachers, the Sadkers illustrate classroom sex bias by asking four of the participants—two men and two women—to act like students in a middle school social studies classroom. The lesson is about the American Revolution and it begins with an examination of homework. Acting as the teacher, David Sadker perfunctorily tells one woman that two of her answers are wrong and comments to the group on the neatness of the other woman's homework. He tells one of the men that two of his answers are wrong and, unlike his response to the woman with wrong answers, he urges the man to try harder and suggests ways of improving his answers. David then states to the other man that he failed to do his homework assignment. In contrast to the woman with the neat paper, this man illustrates what the Sadkers call the "bad boy role."[16]

David Sadker then continues the lesson by discussing battles and leaders. All of the Revolutionary leaders are, of course, male. During the course of the lesson he calls on the males 20 times each, while only calling on one woman twice and completely ignoring the other woman. The one woman that is called on misses her questions because she is given only half a second to respond. When questioning the men, David Sadker spends time giving hints and probing. At the end of this demonstration lesson, the Sadkers report, one woman commented that she felt like she was back in school. She often had the right answer but was never called on by the teacher.

What this workshop demonstration illustrates, based on the Sadkers' findings on classroom interaction, is that boys receive more and better instruction. Boys are more often called upon by the teacher, and boys interact more with the teacher than girls. In a typical classroom situation, if both boys and girls have their hands raised to answer a question, the teacher is most likely to call on a boy. A teacher will spend more time responding to a boy's question than to a girl's question. In other words, girls do not receive equal educational opportunity in the classroom.

In addition, women are not as well represented as men in textbooks. The Sadkers found that, in 1989 elementary school language arts textbooks, there were from two to three times as many pictures of men as women. In one elementary history text, they found four times more pictures of men than of women. In one 1992 world history textbook of 631 pages, they found only 7 pages with material related to women. Two of those pages were devoted to a fifth-grade female student who made a peace trip to the former Soviet Union.[17]

It is most likely that the treatment received by girls in the classroom and in textbooks contributes to their low self-esteem and to their decline, as compared to boys, in performance on standardized tests from elementary school to high school. It would seem logical that, if less instructional time is spent with girls than boys, boys would more rapidly advance academically. In addition, without equal representation in textbooks, girls might value themselves less and have less incentive to achieve. Instructional time and representation in textbooks contribute to the glass ceiling of the classroom.

The glass ceiling of the classroom and content bias may contribute to the significant gender gap in scores on standardized college entrance examinations and entrance examinations to professional schools. For instance, on the widely used Scholastic Aptitude Test (SAT), males score 50 points higher on the math section and up to 12 points higher on the verbal section.[18] It is important to understand that discrimination in standardized testing involves the denial of economic rewards. These economic rewards are in the form of scholarships and career opportunities.

The content bias and economic value of standardized tests were recognized in a 1989 ruling by a federal judge in New York. The judge ruled that the awarding of New York State scholarships using the SAT discriminated against female students. The case was brought to court by the Girls' Clubs of America and the National Organization for Women. The court argued that the scholarships were to be awarded on the basis of academic achievement in high school and that the SAT was not constructed to test achievement but to determine college performance. The court's decision states, "The evidence is clear that females score significantly below males on the SAT while they perform equally or slightly better in high schools."[19]

In this court case, academic achievement was defined according to grades received in high school courses. Interestingly, the Sadkers argue that this apparent paradox between girls' high grades and low standardized test scores is a result of grade inflation. This grade inflation results from female passivity and their willingness to follow classroom rules. Often, teachers formally and informally incorporate evaluations of student behavior in their academic grading practices. For girls, good behavior can result in good grades.[20]

But the issue of grade inflation still results in the puzzle of lower performance by girls on tests like the SAT. One possible answer is that the content of standardized tests is biased. The Sadkers suggest that this is one possible reason for the differences in scores between males and females. Boys are more familiar with organized sports, financial issues, science, wars, and dates. Consequently, test items referring to these areas tend to favor boys. As an example, the Sadkers describe a gifted high school girl who lost her concentration on the Preliminary SAT when she encountered an analogy question comparing a "football and a gridiron."[21] The analogy baffled her because she had little knowledge of football.

One possible solution to teacher bias in classroom interaction, the Sadkers suggest, is to have an observer code classroom interactions so that the teacher becomes aware of any possible bias. If the teacher is unconsciously favoring boys, then this observation provides the opportunity for teachers to change their behavior. One teacher told the Sadkers that she distributes two chips to all students. When a student wants to comment or ask a question he or she has to give up one chip. Before the class is over, all students must use their two chips. This guarantees equal participation of all students and assures that classroom interaction is not dominated by only a few students.[22]

In addition, the Sadkers recommend that teachers consciously search for books portraying strong female characters in a variety of occupational and social roles. They point to the work of the National Women's History Project, which, since the 1970s, has published materials emphasizing women's roles in history. In addition, the Sadkers recommend the use of workshops to heighten teachers' awareness of their own possible sexist behavior and to understand how to find nonsexist educational material for the classroom.[23]

SINGLE-SEX SCHOOLS AND CLASSROOMS

Based on the Sadkers' findings, breaking through the glass ceiling of the classroom requires changing patterns of interaction in the classroom, building female self-esteem, and portraying more women in a greater variety of activities in textbooks and other educational materials. One possible solution is single-sex education. This would eliminate the problem of female students having to compete with male students for teachers' attention. In a classroom of only girls, the teacher would not tend to push girls aside and focus instructional efforts on

Women: The New Traditionalists

Grades: Middle School through College

Objective:
To clarify student opinions regarding the social and economic roles of women.

Lesson:

1. Distribute or read the following text from Joel Spring's *Educating the Consumer-Citizen: A History of the Marriage of Schools, Advertising, and Media:*

   "The 1950s housewife was reborn in the 1990s as *Good Housekeeping* magazine's 'The New Traditionalist' which was described as a 'reaffirmation of family values unmatched in recent history.' The ad language supporting the concept emphasized the ever present word 'choice.' Regarding the issue of work versus staying home, Carl Casselman, creative director of Jordan, McGrath, Case & Taylor said, 'We're saying they have a choice.' Supposedly the Yankelovich market research firm discovered the New Traditionalist and described it as a combination of family values of the 1940s and 1950s, and personal choice values of the 1960s and 1970s. In ads, personal choice meant consumer choice."

2. Divide the class by gender.
3. Have the male and female groups list their opinions about the concept of the New Traditionalist.
4. Have each group list their opinions on the chalkboard.
5. Ask the class whether they believe men could also be included in the concept of the New Traditionalist.
6. List class responses on the chalkboard.

Teachers: This is a very open-ended exercise. It is difficult to predict how students will respond to the concept of the New Traditionalist. Therefore, the teacher must work hard to elicit as many responses as possible. Also, the discussion of the New Traditionalist should create a broader dialogue about gender roles in modern society.

Outcome: Students will consider attitudes about gender roles in contemporary society.

boys. In an all-girls school or classroom, female students might receive the equal educational opportunity denied to them in a coed classroom.

Writing in favor of all-girls schools, Susan Estrich, professor of law and political science at the University of Southern California, notes that 60 percent of the National Merit Scholarship finalists are boys. Echoing the Sadkers' findings, she reports from a 1992 study of the American Association of University Women, "that even though girls get better grades (except in math), they get less from schools."[24] While she does not dismiss efforts to equalize opportunities for girls in coed schools, she argues that currently single-sex education is working. For instance, in all-girls schools, 80 percent of girls take 4 years of math and science, while in coed schools the average is 2 years of math and science. In *Fortune* 1,000 companies, one-third of the female board members are graduates of women's colleges, even though graduates of women's colleges represent only 4 percent of all female college graduates. In addition, graduates of women's colleges earn 43 percent of the math and 50 percent of the engineering doctorates earned by all women, and they outnumber all other females in *Who's Who*.[25]

Estrich does see the possibility of offering single-sex classes with a coed institution. She cites the example of the Illinois Math and Science Academy, which experimented with a girls-only calculus-based physics class. Instead of sitting meekly at their desks while boys commanded all the attention, girls actively ask and answer questions. In an all-girls algebra class in Ventura, California, the teacher reports spending time building self-confidence along with teaching math. For Estrich, at least at this point in time, all-girls schools are a means for ending sexism in education.[26]

Of course, for an all-girls school or classroom to completely overcome the problems of sexism, it would require the maintenance of the same educational expectations as there are for boys and the use of textbooks and other educational materials that provide strong female role models. As I discussed previously in this chapter, one of the problems with segregated female education in the nineteenth century was the belief that women did not have the physical and mental stamina to undergo the same academic demands as men. Consequently, to avoid sexism, there should be no watering down of the curriculum in female schools and classrooms. In addition, sex-segregated education would have to avoid the pitfalls of tracking women into a sex segregated-labor market. One of the problems in the development of the high school in the early twentieth century was that it tended to track women into certain occupations. For an all-girls school or classroom to avoid this form of discrimination, there would have to be an emphasis on opening up all career opportunities for women.

There are many critics of proposals for all-female schools. One University of Michigan researcher, Valerie Lee, found that many all-girls classrooms still contained high levels of sexist behavior on the part of the teacher. In one case, a history teacher assigned a research paper and told students that she would provide "major hand-holding" to help the students. Lee argued that the offer of major hand-holding would not occur in a boys school. In addition, she found "male bashing" taking place in some all-female schools.

Lee also found boys in all-male schools engaging in serious sexist comments about women.[27] In other words, all-female schools do not do anything about the sexist attitudes of men. In fact, all-male schools might reinforce male sexist behavior. For instance, in a 1994 court case involving a suit by Shannon Faulkner to gain entrance to the all-male military college, The Citadel, one of the witnesses, a 1991 graduate of the school, reported that the word 'woman' was used on campus in a derogatory manner "every day, every minute, every hour [it was] a part of the life there."[28]

Therefore, there is the possibility that single-sex education might result in greater academic achievement for women while doing nothing about sexist attitudes among men. The academic gains made by women might mean little in a world dominated by sexist males. Also, the courts may not approve of single-sex public schools, because of a decision regarding all-boys African American schools in Detroit. The court argued that the all-boys schools were a violation of the 1954 *Brown* decision which declared as unconstitutional "separate but equal" schools that were racially segregated. In the Detroit case, separate but equal all-boys schools were declared unconstitutional.[29]

CONSCIOUSNESS RAISING ACCORDING TO THE METHODS OF PAULO FREIRE

One of the best examples I have encountered of applying the techniques of Brazilian educator Paulo Freire to U.S. schools was in a REACH project from 1987 to 1989 designed to raise consciousness regarding sexism of a group of third- and fourth-grade girls and a group of fourth- and fifth-grade girls.[30] The leaders of the groups were four women: two European Americans, one African American, and one Latina. The project followed the basic Freireian principles and, consequently, provides both a model of raising the consciousness of girls regarding sexism and a model for the application of Freireian techniques.

One of the basic principles of Freire's method is that teachers often impose their own subjective interpretation of reality on students. Consequently, it is important for teachers continually to examine their own feelings and assumptions. In this project, the teachers continually met to discuss their methods, the questions they were asking students, and how their own subjective realities were being engaged in instruction. Through this constant dialogue and reflection, the teachers in the project were able continually to refine their understanding of the students and themselves. In addition, the teachers engaged in a similar dialogue with the students. Rather than assuming that students feel and see the world in a particular way, teachers continually carried on dialogues with students.

The major role of teachers in the Freireian method is to create generative themes and engage students in a dialogue about the meaning of the themes. The development of these generative themes takes place in the dialogue among the teachers who try to identify key problems in the students' lives. In this project, the problems centered on issues of sexism. These generative themes were presented to students in a variety of ways. One method used for presenting generative themes about sexism was in the form of role-playing situations. For instance, one situation presented for role playing was as follows: "You are waiting in line to have your turn to shoot a basket during gym. A boy comes over and says, 'Give me that ball; I'll shoot. You can't do it.' You give him the ball."[31] The group of girls in the project discussed the question and agreed that if the girl gave up the ball she would never learn to play. They suggested as alternatives that the girl say no, invite the boy to help her to learn to play better, or have other girls intervene to protect her right to take a turn.

In another role-playing situation, a girl received a science prize but dismisses her achievement to an envious friend. The teachers believed that this role-playing situation reflected the generative theme of the core dilemma faced by women between achievement and maintaining friendships. The dialogue about this theme was lengthy with the discussions ranging from rejection of the prize to creating a situation where a lot of people could earn prizes. The final solution of restructuring the competitive situation so that there are more winners represents an important aspect of the Freireian method. In their dialogue, the students progressed from just accepting the competitive situation as self-evident to an understanding that the system can be challenged.[32]

One of the other generative themes focused on the tendency for women to hide their successes. As with other generative themes, the purpose was to create a dialogue about things that are often taken for granted. Often, Freire argues, people exist in a culture of silence and never question important aspects of their lives. The purpose of the dialogue is to raise to consciousness things that are taken for granted as an inevitable part of life. From the standpoint of the teachers in the project, the hiding of success is something women take for granted.

In the dialogue with students, the norm of behavior that was stated by the girls was, "You should be smart, but not too smart."[33] One student said this was accomplished in class by raising your hand when the teacher was not looking and lowering it when she looked. This method allowed the female student to indicate that she knew the answer but, by not being called on, avoided the situation where she would stand out in class. Other girls discussed how bad they felt when they failed at a class lesson. The girls were asked to role play by responding assertively to situations of both accomplishment and failure. One example, which a girl could use regarding ridicule for having difficulty in math, was as follows: "I feel insulted when you say I should give up on math because it's not fair. I could just work harder and I could try to do it."[34]

This REACH project is full of rich examples that can be used for consciousness raising. It is also suggestive of techniques that can be used with boys and in coeducational situations. The important thing is for the teacher to explore his or her own attitudes regarding sexism and identify generative themes that express sexist behavior in the classroom. The themes can be presented as role-playing situations or in some form of visual example. In conducting a dialogue with the students, it is important that the teachers do not impose their own interpretations on the students. For the dialogue to be effective, the students must be given the opportunity to express their real feelings.

CONCLUSION

While corporations and public schools in the United States might be criticized for the existence of glass ceilings, sexism is more prevalent in other cultures. For example, in Japan, women face greater segregation and have fewer job opportunities than in the United States. Of course, this discrimination against women is reflected in the international operations of Japanese corporations. In 1994, the Labor Ministry of the Japanese government surveyed 1,000 companies and found that half were cutting back in the employment of women so that they could hire more men. The reason given for this gender discrimination was that males remained with companies for longer periods of time than women and males did not make demands for child care leaves. In May 1994, the largest insurance company in Japan, Nippon Life Insurance Company, announced that it was reducing the number of women hired for career positions by 15 percent. Immediately after the announcement by Nippon Insurance Company, the Mitsubishi Corporation and two other companies made similar announcements.[35]

Besides blatant discrimination against women, it could be that the glass ceiling is caused by a hierarchical bureaucracy, which embodies characteristics most often associated with males. This is the argument of sociologist Rosabeth Kanter. She argues that corporations consider the ideal manager to be one who is rational and objective. In the nineteenth and twentieth centuries, these characteristics have most often been ascribed to males. Kanter states the following: This "masculine ethic" elevates the traits assumed to belong to men with educational advantages to necessities for effective organizations: a tough-minded approach to problems; no emotional considerations in the interests of task accomplishment; and a cognitive superiority in problem solving and decision making.[36]

In other words, Kanter argues, organizational forms specify certain characteristics for leadership, and if these characteristics are associated by society with a particular gender, then sex bias is built into the organizational model. According to Kanter, it was assumed in the nineteenth and twentieth centuries that women are governed by emotions and are prone to "petty" concerns with interpersonal relationships and responsibilities. In terms of the managerial requirements of a hierarchical bureaucracy, this means that women do not make good managers and that their role in this type of organization is to be supportive of male leaders.

In the context of consciousness raising, Kanter's arguments can lead to two possible conclusions. One is that women should be socialized to fit into the structure of existing corporations. In the example of consciousness raising in project REACH, girls were learning how to be more assertive and to compete with boys. This could be considered part of a process of preparing them to compete in the international corporate structure. The other possible conclusion is that the consciousness of women should be raised so that they can change the hierarchical and competitive structure of corporations. In other words: Should the socialization of women be changed to meet the needs of the existing corporate structure or should the corporate structure be changed to fit the socialization patterns of women?

PERSONAL FRAMES OF REFERENCE

One method for understanding your own attitudes about gender differences is to consider some of the questions and issues raised by Myra and David Sadker.

1. How would you feel if you were suddenly transformed into the opposite gender?
2. What do you think are the advantages of being female?
3. What do you think are the advantages of being male?
4. How did your gender affect your educational experiences?
5. Were males and females treated differently in your family?
6. Were males and females treated differently in your classrooms and schools?
7. Have you witnessed gender discrimination in education or the workplace?

Notes

1. Felcia Briscoe found this poster while doing research for me on the images of women during World War II. I used the poster as a book cover for *Images of American Life: A History of Ideological Management in Schools, Movies, Radio, and Television* (Albany: State University of New York Press, 1993).
2. An important set of case studies related to gender issues in schools is Judith Kleinfeld and Suzanne Yerian, eds., *Gender Tales: Tensions in the Schools* (New York: St. Martin's Press, 1995).
3. Mary Beth Norton, *Liberty's Daughters: The Revolutionary Experience of American Women, 1750–1800* (Boston: Little, Brown, 1980), pp. 297–98.
4. I quote this in Joel Spring, *Wheels in the Head: Educational Philosophies of Authority, Freedom, and Culture from Socrates to Paulo Freire* (New York: McGraw-Hill, 1994), p. 117. In this book, I provide a more general discussion of Locke's theories of the state, family, and education.
5. Quoted in Joel Spring, *The American School: 1642–2000,* Fifth Edition (New York: McGraw-Hill, 2000), p. 28.
6. Ibid., p. 100.
7. Ibid.
8. Myra Sadker and David Sadker, *Failing at Fairness: How America's Schools Cheat Girls* (New York: Scribner's, 1994), p. 30.
9. See John L. Rury, *Education and Women's Work: Female Schooling and the Division of Labor in Urban America, 1870–1930* (Albany: State University of New York Press, 1991).
10. Cindy Skrzycki, "Efforts Fail to Advance Women's Jobs: 'Glass Ceiling' Intact Despite New Benefits," *Washington Post,* 20 February 1990, *Executive News Service,* Compuserve.
11. Nancy Frazier and Myra Sadker, *Sexism in School and Society* (New York: Harper & Row, 1973).
12. Sadker and Sadker, *Failing at Fairness,* p. ix.
13. Ibid., pp. 13–14.
14. Ibid., p. 78.
15. Ibid., pp. 83–90.
16. Ibid., pp. 10–11.

17. Ibid., p. 72.
18. Ibid., p. 140.
19. Mark Walsh, "Judge Finds Bias in Scholarships," *Education Week* 8, no. 21 (15 February 1989), pp. 1, 20.
20. Sadker and Sadker, *Failing at Fairness,* pp. 157–59.
21. Ibid., p. 153.
22. Ibid., p. 269.
23. Ibid., pp. 265–74.
24. Susan Estrich, "For Girls' Schools and Women's Colleges, Separate Is Better," *The New York Times Magazine,* 22 May 1994, p. 39.
25. Ibid.
26. Ibid.
27. Ibid., p. 241.
28. Catherine Manegold, " 'Save the Males' Becomes Battle Cry in Citadel's Defense Against Woman," *The New York Times,* 25 May 1994, p. A4.
29. Estrich, "Separate is Better," p. 39.
30. I am using for this example a report of the project made by Lee Anne Bell, "Changing Our Ideas About Ourselves: Group Consciousness Raising with Elementary School Girls as a Means to Empowerment," in *Empowerment through Multicultural Education,* ed. Christine E. Sleeter (Albany: State University of New York Press, 1991), pp. 229–49.
31. Ibid., p. 237.
32. Ibid., pp. 237–38.
33. Ibid., p. 241.
34. Ibid., p. 243.
35. David Sanger, "Job-Seeking Women in Japan Finding More Discrimination," *The New York Times,* 27 May 1994, p. A9.
36. Rosabeth Kanter, "Women and the Structure of Organization: Exploration in Theory and Behavior," in *Another Voice,* eds. Marcia Millman and Rosabeth Kanter (Garden City, NY: Doubleday Anchor, 1975), p. 43.

CHAPTER 10

Teaching
and Language Diversity

It is the first public school in the United States dedicated to teaching fluency in English and Mandarin Chinese. Opened in the fall of 1998, kindergarten students at New York City's P.S. 184, also known as the Shuang Wen Academy, are greeted with tags written in bold Chinese characters and English and attached to students' tables, the classroom door, the clock, and the closet. The tags on the tables present student names in Chinese characters and English. Unlike some other programs that use bilingual instruction until the student has mastered English, this program is focused on teaching Mandarin Chinese and culture for its own sake. "We're different from a traditional bilingual program, where children are taught in their mother tongue just long enough to get them fluent in English," said Ling-Ling Chou, the head of the school. "Here we teach in both languages, and we want them to master both languages."[1]

The hope is that the Shuang Wen Academy will be able to ease the transition of Chinese immigrants to U.S. society. Larry Lee, a social worker, observed, "When I grew up I saw a lot of kids who rebelled against being Chinese and who rejected what they were. With this school, my hope is that these kids can be comfortable with who they are and also comfortable being American."[2]

The primary goal of affirming Chinese culture and language, in contrast to using bilingual education to teach English, is confirmed by the fact that only a quarter of the students speak Mandarin Chinese, the main language of China and Taiwan, while many speak Cantonese, the predominant language of New York's Chinatown. To compensate for student deficiency in speaking Mandarin, the students are grouped so that at least one student at each table speaks Mandarin. One parent praised the school's efforts, "We took her out of her culture, but we don't want her to lose it. And Shuang Wen, we think, will help her be more comfortable in the culture she was born in."[3]

The Shuang Wen school illustrates a belief in a link between language, culture, and power. In the United States, this link is reflected in the historic struggle over what should be the dominant language of public schools. Currently, the conflict over language is caused by the intersection of immigrant, dominated, and dominant cultures. One response to this conflict has been the development of bilingual education programs to serve the needs of children from non-English-speaking families.

In the context of a global economy, international corporations are concerned with problems of cross-cultural communications. International advertising requires an understanding of the cultural context of language. Corporate managers must be able to communicate to colleagues speaking different languages. To a certain extent, the power of international corporations requires sending clear messages across cultural lines. In addition, because of the importance of English in the international market, there is a worldwide growth in the study of English.

My discussion of language diversity will use the example of the relationship between American Sign Language, deaf culture, and the development of the deaf pride and power movement. This example will highlight the linkages between language, culture, and power. Then I will discuss the problem of cross-cultural communications by using the example of international advertising and communications between Japanese and North Americans. Against the background of this discussion of language and culture, I will describe the struggle over the language of the U.S. public school, and the arguments for and against bilingual education. And, as an example of the communication issues facing immigrants, I will discuss the language problems of Asian Americans.

LANGUAGE, CULTURE, AND POWER

> I found out that who I am.
> I am Deaf and Jewish girl.
> I learned a lot about deaf culture and deaf's language.
> Before Deaf Studies I was negative that I am deaf.[4]

A student at the Lexington School for the Deaf wrote the above statement in her journal under the heading "Who am I?" Her first identity was being deaf and her second was being Jewish. Deaf culture represents one aspect of the relationship between language and culture. Once suppressed as being "unbecoming, imbecilic, virtually bestial," American Sign Language (ASL) is now part of the glue that holds deaf culture together.[5] Not only do deaf people have their own language, but they have their own social clubs, athletic leagues, theater companies, university, periodicals, and international Olympics. And, in Leah Cohen's words, "Cultural transmission, formally and informally, has been carried out by schools for the deaf."[6]

The struggle for the acceptance and use of ASL is similar to the problems experienced by other language minorities in the United States. Historically, schools such as the Lexington School for the Deaf banned the use of sign language. Students were disciplined when found signing to each other. This parallels, as I will explain later, the punishment of students from Spanish-speaking families in public schools in the nineteenth century for communicating to each other in Spanish. Instead of teaching ASL, deaf schools taught oralism. Oralism, or learning to speak English, was considered the vehicle for integrating deaf people into mainstream society.

Oralism is also a means of alienating the child from deaf culture which traditionally was considered a low-status culture. "Wanting their deaf children to have access to the same privileged circles," Cohen writes about upper-income families, "they have tended to favor oralism as the method that will best keep their children out of contact with the deaf community and on a par with hearing people."[7] In fact, oralism originated from the desire of wealthy Spanish families in the mid 1500s to protect their deaf children. At the time, deaf people were barred from Holy Communion and from inheriting their family fortunes. Oralism allowed them to mask their physical disability.

The Lexington School, founded in 1864, was the first oral school for the deaf in the United States. By the 1880s, the school was holding public demonstrations of its students' abilities to read lips and respond orally. By the end of the nineteenth century, most schools for the deaf emphasized oralism with the use of sign language either being banned or used only with students who failed to achieve oralism. As oralism triumphed, signing became a badge of shame. In some schools, a red flag of shame was flown outside the classroom if a deaf student was found signing.[8]

The actions at the Lexington School in the nineteenth century reflected a broader debate about oralism versus signing. In the 1860s and the 1870s, Edward Miner Gallaudet advocated the teaching of signing as a means of communicating between deaf people and learning English. Gallaudet wrote, "It is only by employing signs that [the deaf] can gain the pleasure and profit that comes from conversation in the social circle, that they can enjoy freedom of intercommunication as shall make it possible for them to forget they are deaf."[9] During the same period, Alexander Graham Bell advocated oralism. Bell worried about the development of a separate deaf community and went so far as to advocate the prevention of intermarriage of the deaf and the sterilization of congenitally deaf children. But despite the differences between Gallaudet and Bell, Timothy Reagan writes, "Central to both the manualist and oralist perspectives is the late nineteenth- and early twentieth-century American concern with the commitment for cultural and linguistic assimilation."[10] In other words, the goal was to avoid the development of a separate culture among the hearing impaired.

The fact that not all deaf students could achieve oralism indicates that it is not the appropriate method of communication within the deaf community. This does not mean that oralism is not useful. Similar to arguments regarding the value for children from non-English-speaking families learning to speak English, oralism does help deaf people to get jobs, shop, and perform other daily tasks.

While signing is the appropriate means of communication in deaf culture, learning signing and oralism provides the deaf person with the ability to communicate in two languages. In other words, the deaf person becomes bilingual. As I will discuss later, it is easier for persons to learn another language if they first understand the structure of their own language. For instance, it is easier for a child from an English-speaking home to learn another language if she or he first learns to read and write in English. The same thing appears to be true for deaf people. Learning ASL is a bridge for learning English. In this situation, a bilingual classroom is one that uses both ASL and English.

With regard to culture and power, ASL becomes a language that binds the deaf community together, while oralism can destroy the deaf community by integrating the deaf into hearing society. Consequently, the deaf power and pride movement seeks to maintain both ASL and deaf culture. In 1988, "Deaf Power" was a slogan in the uprising at Gallaudet University when the deaf student body demanded the hiring of the first deaf president. The "Deaf President Now" movement was replayed in 1994 when students at the Lexington School went on strike demanding a deaf person be appointed as Chief Executive Officer of the school. *The New York Times* reported that students marched in front of the school signing, "We want a deaf C.E.O." Reflecting the issue of power, a teacher told reporters, "We don't have to depend on hearing people." Students claimed that many hearing administrators treated them in a paternalistic manner and that they wanted a role model at the highest levels of the administration.[11]

One of the cultural aspects of ASL is its function as a shared means of communication. It is important to understand, as I will explain in the next section, that communication involves shared cultural understandings. Within the deaf community, ASL is a means of cultural communication that involves an understanding of subtle nuances of body language and references to shared understandings. A hearing person can learn to sign but that person will have difficulty effectively communicating with deaf people because they do not share the same cultural background. An interpreter of sign language must learn to communicate between hearing and deaf cultures.

CROSS-CULTURAL COMMUNICATIONS

Cross-cultural communications is an important issue in the global marketing of products. When Coca-Cola was marketed in China in 1979, it was discovered that Chinese characters turned the literal meaning of Coca-Cola into "Bite the Wax Tadpole." A literal Spanish translation of a Frank Perdue chicken ad came out as, "It takes a sexually excited man to make a chick affectionate."[12]

Differences in cultures require a different emphasis in the marketing of products. Procter & Gamble found it difficult to market its Pampers diapers in Japan until it was discovered that, because of the importance of gender differences in Japan, separate diapers had to be made for boys and girls. The result was the introduction of pink diapers for girls and blue diapers for boys. Eventually, the company distributed the same gender-specific diapers in the United States. A perfume ad intimating a strong bouquet works in New York but not in Italy where an emphasis must be placed on a single exquisite smell.[13] Marlboro ads depicting an American cowboy are effective in most countries except Argentina where their cowboy, the gaucho, is considered a lower-class worker.[14]

The problems encountered in advertising global products highlight the fact that the meaning of a message is determined by the receiver. When an individual transmits a message the person has a particular meaning in mind. But when the message is received, the receiver imposes his or her own meaning on the message. It could be that both the transmitter and the receiver attach the same meaning to a message, but, even when both are members of the same culture and speak the same language, there can be differences in the meaning given to a message. When the transmitter and the receiver are from different cultures and grow up speaking different languages, there are often different meanings to the same message.

Therefore, there are often misinterpretations of messages that are sent between cultures. Sometimes these misinterpretations are a result of differences in cultural values. For instance, cultures might have different attitudes about the role of emotions and behaviors in communications. They might have different expectations regarding appropriate responses to a particular message or the proper form of response to a message.

Clarity in cross-cultural communications is very important for global corporations and governments. For corporations, a failure in communications can cause a loss of money, while for governments it could result in war. Consequently, more and more attention is being paid to the meaning of a message in a particular cultural context. Indicative of this concern is the creation of new series of books such as the Sage Publications series on *Communicating Effectively in Multicultural Contexts*. As an example of the problems in cross-cultural communications, I will discuss one of their first books in the series, *Bridging Japanese/North American Differences* by William Gudykunst and Tsukasas Nishida.[15]

COMMUNICATING BETWEEN JAPAN AND THE UNITED STATES

One of the major cultural differences affecting communication between Japanese and North Americans is the cultural frame of reference regarding the relationship of the individual to the group. The United States is considered an individualistic culture where a person sees herself or himself as a separate and unique individual, and whose self-definition does not include others. An individualistic culture places emphasis on individual goals.

Japan, on the other hand, is a collectivist culture where a person defines herself or himself in relation to others. The concept of *Wa* in Japan refers to harmony of the group where the self is merged into the group to form a grand harmony. The concept of *Enryo* refers to reserve or restraint resulting from conformity to the group. *Enryo* is a response to group pressure to conform.

The differences between individualistic and collective cultures are paralleled by differences in low- and high-context communications. A low-context communication, which is typical of North Americans, has most of its information in the explicit code of the message. In contrast, a high-context communication, which is typical of Japanese, has most of its information either in the physical context of the message or internalized in the transmitter and receiver.

For example, the United States is a low-context and individualistic culture that emphasizes direct communication. Common phrases in the United States that reflect this cultural style of communication are the following: "Say what you mean!" "Don't beat around the bush!" "Get to the point!"

As a high-context and collectivist culture, Japanese often use indirect forms of communications filled with qualifiers such as "perhaps," "probably," and "somewhat." The Japanese are self-effacing and strive to maintain the harmony of the group in their communications. Communications are not taken at face value and the receiver must infer the meaning behind them.

For instance, a boss in the United States might enter a room that is cold and say directly, "Aren't you cold? Please close the window." In Japan, the boss might simply say, "It's cold in here," and expect the listeners to infer that she or he wants the window closed.[16]

In their study of the cultural differences in communication, William Gudykunst and Tsukasas Nishida provide the following example of the confusion caused among North Americans by the indirect and low-context form of Japanese communication. In this particular case, the Japanese businessman is telling the foreign businessman that he does not want to buy his product.

> Foreign Businessman: Therefore, our products meet your requirements 100 percent. How soon do you think you can place an order?
> Japanese Businessman: Did you see the sumo wrestling last night?
> F.B.: Well . . . yes, I did. But back to our discussion, when would it be convenient . . . ?
> J.B.: What did you think of Jessie Takaiyama [a Hawaiian sumo wrestler]? Wasn't he terrific?[17]

One of the distinct differences in communication style is silence. People in collective cultures do not have to work hard to be accepted by others. They see themselves as part of a group or groups. Consequently, they spend less time trying to sell themselves. In Japanese culture, silence is accepted behavior in the company of others. Japanese believe that an indication of good manners is not talking too much. In contrast, North Americans talk more and try to control the conversation.

Congruent with being a high-context culture, Japanese like to avoid uncertainty. In conversation, they want to know the context of others to avoid uncertainty in the communication. It is considered proper to clearly identify who you are when first meeting. The more context a person can give about himself the more comfortable the listener feels. This concern about certainty in relationships often results in North Americans referring to Japanese as regimented, rigid, and closely ordered.

William Gudykunst's and Tsukasas Nishida's description of communication differences between Japan and North America highlights another aspect of the relationship between language and culture. To understand the message being transmitted between cultures requires understanding cultural differences. In addition, as exemplified by deaf culture, language becomes an important means of maintaining a culture. In the United States, the historic struggle over the language of the school and the development of bilingual education reflects the relationships among language, culture, power, and cross-cultural communications.

LANGUAGE AND CULTURE IN THE UNITED STATES

"There is a mood spreading against immigrants who do not come from Europe, who are not white, and this wave is about to scourge the United States," Pedro Aviles, director of the Latino Civic Rights Task Force, told reporters for the United

Press News Service after the Maryland state legislature passed bills on 28 March 1994 making English the official state language. "All this [the English-only legislation] has a discriminatory, racial trait," Aviles reiterated.[18] According to Aviles, the legislation would eliminate the requirement that schools provide bilingual education and end the practice of the Department of Motor Vehicles giving driving tests in other languages. From Aviles's perspective, the legislation would make it more difficult for students from non-English-speaking homes to succeed in school and, consequently, deny them equal opportunity to succeed in U.S. society.

Aviles's concerns about language reflect a long history of struggle over language issues in the United States. In the eighteenth century, Benjamin Franklin expressed his concern about the expansion of the German population in Pennsylvania by campaigning for English-only schools. In 1753, William Smith, an enthusiastic supporter of English-only schools for German children, believed that language was the key to transforming the German population into an English culture. He proclaimed: "By a common education of English and German youth at the same schools, acquaintance and connections will be formed, and deeply impressed upon them in their cheerful and open moments. The English language and a conformity of manners will be acquired."[19]

After the Revolutionary War, the U.S. government took a similar attitude toward Native Americans. In the early nineteenth century, the U.S. government sponsored missionaries to educate Native American tribes in the use of English. The most revealing document about language and the cultural transformation of Native American culture was the Indian Peace Commission report of 1868. This report stated that differences in language were the major source of continuing friction between whites and Indians. The report emphasized the teaching of English as a major step in reducing hostilities and "civilizing" Native Americans. Regarding the importance of language for the cultural transformation of Native Americans, the report states: "Through sameness of language is produced sameness of sentiment and thought; and thus in process of time the differences producing trouble . . . [will be] gradually obliterated."[20]

As a result of this belief in the link between culture and language, schools serving Native Americans under the control of the U.S. government forbade the use of Native American languages and taught only English. This policy did not change, as I will explain later, until the second half of the twentieth century.

The U.S. government and state governments instituted similar policies after the defeat of Mexico in 1848 and the conquest of Puerto Rico in 1898. In the Treaty of Guadalupe Hidalgo of 1848, Mexico surrendered to the United States territory from Texas to California. The Mexican population in these conquered territories were given U.S. citizenship. Throughout the conquered territories, English-only restrictions were imposed in public schools. In 1855, the California Bureau of Instruction mandated that teaching be conducted in English. In 1870, Texas passed a school law requiring English as the language of instruction in public schools.

To escape anti-Mexican feelings, and to preserve their culture and language, many Mexican American parents sent their children to Catholic schools. Bilingual education, teaching in Spanish and English, was used in many parochial schools to improve the ability of students to read and write in Spanish and English. These programs also emphasized the cultural traditions of Mexico and Spain.

In the early twentieth century, large numbers of Mexicans came to the United States as agricultural workers. In most cases, education was either denied to the children of these immigrants or was provided in segregated schools. In general, the policy of the schools was to discourage the use of Spanish by punishing students for using Spanish and to use only English in instruction. As historian Gilbert Gonzalez argues, the purpose of public schooling was to strip away the culture and language of Mexican American children while preparing them to enter the same occupations as their parents. In his words, the schools attempted to "Americanize the child in a controlled linguistic and cultural environment, and . . . to train Mexicans for occupations considered open to, and appropriate for, them."[21]

Puerto Ricans experienced the same language policies as those imposed on Native Americans and Mexican Americans. Puerto Rico was captured by the United States in the Spanish–American War. In the treaty at the conclusion of the war, Spain ceded Puerto Rico, Guam, and the Philippines to the United States. Upon taking over Puerto Rico, one of the first concerns of the U.S. government was winning the loyalty of the Puerto Rican population. One of the key parts of this policy was replacing the use of Spanish with English in the public schools. Throughout the first part of the twentieth century, the language issue was a major source of friction between the Puerto Rican population and U.S. authorities.[22]

Given this history of attempts by the U.S. government to impose English on Native Americans, Mexican Americans, and Puerto Ricans, it is not surprising that language became a major issue in the great civil rights movement of the 1950s and 1960s. Leaders of all three cultural groups believed that maintenance of their languages was essential for the retention of their cultural traditions. After years of protest, politicians began to respond to pressure from these groups. In the 1960s, Senator Ralph Yarborough of Texas created a special Senate subcommittee to hold hearings on the language issue. The hearings primarily sought the testimony of representatives of the Mexican American and Puerto Rican communities.[23]

As a result of these hearings, Yarborough supported the passage of the Bilingual Education Act of 1968. The legislation recognized the link between culture and language by supporting bilingual programs that imparted knowledge and pride to Mexican Americans, Puerto Ricans, and Native Americans. The goal of the legislation was to teach students to be fluent in English and their native languages. Native Americans received added support in their efforts to preserve their languages and cultures with the passage of the Native American Languages Act of 1990. This legislation committed the federal government to "preserve, protect, and promote the rights and freedom of Native Americans to use, practice, and develop Native American languages."[24]

BILINGUAL EDUCATION

Given the history of language policies in the United States, it is not surprising that some members of the Maryland state legislature, as I discussed in the previous section, would support English-only legislation. Since the passage of the Bilingual Education Act in 1968, there has been a steady stream of criticism of bilingualism and, echoing sentiments of previous generations of English speakers, demands for English-only in schools and in state governments.

Part of the debate is about the different forms of bilingual education. *Maintenance* and *two-way* bilingual education are most useful in supporting cultural traditions and, consequently, are the most controversial. *Maintenance* bilingual education teaches subject matter in both the language of the student's home and in English. The goal is to make the student literate in both languages. In contrast, *transitional* bilingual education programs use the student's language in the classroom until the student masters English. Once the student masters English, only English is used in the classroom and there is no attempt to improve the student's literacy in their home language. In this case, *transitional* literally means to only use the student's native language in transition to learning English. *Maintenance* literally means maintaining the use of the student's home language throughout her or his education.

Two-way bilingual education refers to a classroom situation where both English-speaking and non-English-speaking students learn to be bilingual. For instance, a classroom might be made up of English-speaking students and Spanish-speaking students. Lessons in all subjects are conducted in both Spanish and English. In this situation, all students become literate in both English and Spanish.

Critics of bilingualism, including supporters of the English-only movement, favor submersion and English as a Second Language (ESL) programs. In *submersion* programs, the student is put into a totally English-speaking classroom. There is no attempt to maintain the native languages. In *ESL* programs, students attend special classes to learn English. Again, there is no attempt to preserve their native languages.

In 1983, the critics of bilingual programs rallied around the newly created organization, U.S. English. Republican administrations in the 1980s appointed representatives to the National Advisory and Coordinating Council on Bilingual Education who favored submersion of non-English-speaking students in the English language, rather than teaching in a bilingual context. The founding of U.S. English and the actions of the Republican administrations prompted Gene T. Chavez, the president of the Association of Bilingual Education, to warn, "Those who think this country can only tolerate one language" were motivated more by political concerns than by educational concerns. The incoming president of the organization, Jose Gonzalez, attacked the federal government for entering an "unholy alliance" with U.S. English and other right-wing groups to oppose bilingual education.[25]

While the majority of criticism of bilingual education comes from groups wanting to maintain the dominance of the English language and traditional European American culture, there are liberal opponents who criticize bilingual education for not providing the student with the language tools necessary to compete in the mainstream economy. Rosalie Pedalino Porter, director of Bilingual and English as a Second Language programs in Newton, Massachusetts, and author of *Forked Tongue: The Politics of Bilingual Education*, writes, "The critical question is whether education policies that further the cultural identity of minority groups at the same time enable minority children to acquire the knowledge and skills to attain social and economic equality."[26] She worries that bilingual programs that are bicultural will result in language minorities being segregated into communities with little power. Similar to arguments in the nineteenth and twentieth centuries, she advocates language programs that would assure assimilation rather than promoting ethnic identities.

As in the past, the current debate over language programs reflects the link between language and culture. Those advocating the maintenance of non-English languages are, in most cases, interested in preserving the cultural traditions of their communities. This is particularly true of many members of the Native American, Mexican American, and Puerto Rican communities. Those opposing bilingual education, in most cases, favor the assimilation of these cultures into the dominant European American culture. Some opponents argue that assimilation and the preservation of English are necessary for national unity. Other opponents argue that language minorities should be assimilated with an emphasis being placed on learning English so that these language minorities can compete in the U.S. economy.

RESEARCH AND CORPORATE SUPPORT FOR BILINGUAL EDUCATION

Today, research tends to support bilingual education as the best method for teaching English to non-English-speaking students. In addition, since U.S. corporations expanded into international markets in the late nineteenth century, business has pressured public schools to teach more foreign languages. The push for instruction in foreign languages continued through the Cold War as the United States competed with the former Soviet Union for world domination.[27] Today, even more than in the past, global corporations are seeking bilingual and multilingual employees.

Recent research suggests that *two-way* bilingual education programs are the best way of instructing English-speaking students in a foreign language and non-English-speaking students in English. A study involving five urban school districts with students speaking more than 100 languages other than English concluded that "students in the two-way bilingual programs showed the greatest educational gains, while those in traditional *ESL* pullout programs—where students are offered no instruction in their native language—fared the worst."[28]

To understand the argument that *maintenance* and *two-way* bilingual education programs are the best methods for learning another language, consider the following hypothetical situation. Imagine that you are 5 years old and live in an English-speaking family that has recently immigrated to Russia. Also, assume that you have not learned to read and write in English; in other words, you speak English but you are illiterate in English. Now, imagine that you are placed in a public school where all the teachers and students speak only Russian. Your task is to learn to speak Russian and to learn how to read and write in Russian. In addition, you must learn the normal school subjects including history, science, and arithmetic.

In this situation, advocates of bilingual education argue that it will be easier for you to learn Russian if you become literate in English.[29] There is a commonsense aspect to this argument. I am sure that readers will agree, on reflection, that it would probably be easier for them to learn to read and write in Russian if they knew how to read and write in English. In addition, bilingual educators argue that, in order for you to transfer your knowledge and skills to the learning of Russian, there should be continuous instruction in English. In other words, instruction in English and Russian should occur simultaneously.

There is another aspect to this argument for bilingual education. Imagine yourself struggling to learn Russian, while classroom instruction in history, science, and arithmetic was being given in Russian. You would probably fail most tests in these subjects, since they would be given in Russian, and, as the school year progressed, you would probably fall further and further behind your Russian-speaking classmates. If the school has ability grouping, then you would probably be placed in the lowest ability group. If the school has special education classes, you might be placed in one of these classes. In other words, the odds would be against you achieving in school.

Now imagine that your classroom is bilingual with history, science, and arithmetic being taught in both English and Russian. Under these conditions you would not only have an easier time learning Russian, but you would also be able to keep up with other students in academic subjects. In other words, your chances of academic success would be greatly improved if this Russian school had a *maintenance* bilingual education program.

Now imagine that this Russian school offers a *two-way* bilingual education program. Of course, this requires that there be a sufficient number of students sharing your language background to make it possible to operate the program. Your class would be composed of English-speaking and Russian-speaking students and the class would be taught in English and Russian. All students would be taught to read, write, and converse in Russian and English.

In this *two-way* bilingual program it will be easier for you to learn Russian and to achieve academically. In addition, it will be easier for Russian-speaking students to learn English. From a purely academic viewpoint, a *two-way* bilingual program will produce better-educated students because they will all know two languages. From the standpoint of an international corporation, the graduate of a *two-way* bilingual program will be more employable because of knowledge of two languages.

Also, in our imaginary situation, a *maintenance* or *two-way* bilingual program will help you to become bicultural. It will help you to function in Russian culture *and* help you to preserve your cultural traditions. In addition, the preservation of your language and culture in the classroom will provide you with a positive self-image.

If you consider the above imaginary scenario in the context of the United States, you can understand why *maintenance* and *two-way* bilingual education programs would be beneficial to non-English-speaking students. One example of an effective bilingual school is the Fratney Elementary School in Milwaukee, Wisconsin. This school has an antiracist program that is also bilingual. The school uses team-teaching with two teachers teaching two classes. One day, half of the students receive instruction in English from one teacher, while the other half study in Spanish with the other teacher. On the following day the students switch teachers and languages. Teachers believe that their *two-way* bilingual program is "the school's most powerful tool in its quest to celebrate cultural differences."[30]

Jim Cummins, a leading advocate of bilingual education, uses the example of the preschool program of the Carpenteria School District in California to prove the importance of maintaining the child's home language. In describing the above imaginary scenario, I argued that you would fall further behind your classmates in all academic subjects if the subjects were taught in Russian. The Carpenteria preschool is taught in Spanish to children from Spanish-speaking homes. As a result, children, because they can comprehend what is happening in the preschool program, are better prepared for kindergarten than other Spanish-speaking children who attend a preschool taught in English. In addition, they are better prepared to learn English. In comparing the two preschool programs, an evaluation report concluded, "Although project participants [the Spanish language preschool students] were exposed to less *total* English, they, because of their enhanced first language skill and concept knowledge were better able to comprehend the English they were exposed to."[31]

PROBLEMS IN BILINGUAL EDUCATION PROGRAMS

Without adequate funding and trained teachers, bilingual education can become another form of segregation. This is what Flora Ida Ortiz concluded in her 6-year study of classrooms for Hispanic students in several southern California school districts. She found that bilingual classes were often held in portable classrooms that were some distance from the main building. Books and technology were scarce in the classrooms. Many of the bilingual teachers were on emergency and special credentials and they could not speak Spanish. The bilingual teachers were considered low-status teachers by the rest of the school staff. "In all cases," Ortiz states, "the quality [of classrooms and teachers] is less for Hispanic children."[32]

Since many of the teachers do not speak Spanish, Ortiz reports, they rely on Spanish-speaking teacher aides. Consequently, many bilingual teachers turn over instruction to their aides. Because of their low status and uncomfortable teaching environments, bilingual teachers have higher levels of absenteeism and tardiness than other teachers. This also contributes to greater reliance on aides. Ortiz writes, "The non-bilingual teacher tends to relinquish the bilingual children to the aide. The aide teaches all the classes in Spanish and some of those in English."[33]

Untrained in educational methods, the aides primarily conduct drill lessons. Little is done to promote critical-thinking skills. Consequently, bilingual students tend to spend most of their time doing worksheets, drill exercises, and filling in blanks. These bilingual students receive a segregated and inferior education as a result of their separate classrooms, lack of instructional materials, inferior and poorly trained teachers, and lack of instruction to challenge their critical thinking. As Ortiz points out, the intention of bilingual education was to help these Hispanic students, but the final result, because of poor funding and bias on the part of the school administration, is to assure their academic failure.

LANGUAGE ISSUES AMONG ASIAN AMERICANS

While there are problems in bilingual programs caused by lack of funding and qualified teachers, many educators still believe that it is the best method for helping non-English-speaking students learn English. For instance, Henry Trueba, Li Rong Lilly Cheng, and Kenji Ima in *Myth or Reality: Adaptive Strategies of Asian Americans in California* advocate bilingual education for Asian Americans who are having difficulty learning English.[34]

Language problems are one of the major reasons why some Asian American students drop out of school and why Asians are found disproportionately in scientific and technical occupations. Trueba, Cheng, and Ima argue that many Asian immigrants are never able to enter mainstream classrooms because they never learn English.[35] Consequently, many Asian Americans drop out of school before graduation. These Asian American dropouts often go unnoticed because of the academic success of other Asian American students.

According to their study, Asian immigrants who received no prior training in English before coming to the United States are most at risk for dropping out of school. The importance of prior training in English for academic success is highlighted by the argument "that the higher academic performance of Asians in contrast with Hispanics is consistent with the fact that 31 percent of Asians had training in English prior to their arrival . . . in contrast with only 3 percent for Hispanics."[36]

In addition, certain Asian immigrants come from areas with oral traditions and they have little exposure to written materials in their own language. This is particularly true of children from Pacific Islands, Laotian rural groups, and Montagnards from Vietnam. This lack of exposure to a written language is a major obstacle to learning English. These students, it is argued, have difficulty differentiating between the written language forms of the classroom and oral language forms.[37]

Trueba, Cheng, and Ima provide a case study of a 15-year-old immigrant from Taipei, Shia-chi, who experiences limited success in U.S. schools. She was a below-average student in Taipei, and she had studied English for 3 years. When she arrived in the United States, she could not read, write, or communicate in English. She lives with her aunt who runs a restaurant in Santa Monica, California. She has difficulty understanding what is happening in her classes and she has a difficult time in her *ESL* class. Most of her friends are Chinese, and consequently, she speaks her native language in most of her social activities. After 2 years in the United States, she still speaks limited English and is doing poorly in her schoolwork.[38]

But even Asian American students who are successful in school continue to have language problems. At both the undergraduate and graduate levels in college, Asian Americans are predominantly in engineering, physical sciences, mathematics, and computer sciences. "Asian students," the authors write, "pursue occupations they perceive as having higher status and ones in which communicative language skills are less required."[39] Choosing fields requiring little communicative skills limits Asian American choices in the job market.

Trueba, Cheng, and Ima argue that bilingual education programs for non-English-speaking Asian American students are essential for helping both failing and successful students. Echoing the sentiments of bilingual educators, they believe that the study of the students' language aids in the learning of English. For instance, in the case of Shia-chi, she would be more academically successful if she attended a bilingual program as opposed to an *ESL* class. Bilingual education programs would make it possible for Asian American college students to choose from a greater variety of career opportunities. From the perspective of Trueba, Cheng, and Ima, there is a need for more bilingual programs for non-English-speaking Asian Americans.

THE LANGUAGE OF THE CORPORATION

At this stage of research, bilingual education is the most promising method for helping non-English-speaking students learn English. Because of the link between culture and language, bilingual programs are most often bicultural. Consequently, bilingual programs are a political battleground with those wanting to maintain the cultural traditions of language minorities supporting bilingual programs and those wanting to maintain the dominated European American culture of the United States opposing bilingual programs.

In the context of a global economy with mass migrations of workers, *ESL* programs are the most widely used method for teaching English. As explained by Naomi Silverman, acquisitions editor for education and English as a second language college textbooks at St. Martin's Press, immigrants to English-speaking countries often take *ESL* classes in their native countries. Once arriving in the United States, many immigrants either begin or continue in *ESL* programs in adult-training programs, public schools, and colleges.

In addition, English is one of the major, if not the major language, of international business. This has resulted in the growth of *ESL* programs in non-English-speaking countries. This growth in international corporate use of English is highlighted in the following interview with Naomi Silverman. In the interview, Naomi Silverman is referring specifically to the college and adult market for *ESL* texts.

AUTHOR: What is your estimate for the annual purchase of *ESL* texts in colleges including 2-year colleges and intensive language programs?

NAOMI SILVERMAN: It is difficult to make these estimates because publishers do not want other companies to know their sales figures. There are approximately 3,000 teachers of *ESL* in 2-year schools, colleges, and intensive English programs in the United States. On the average, an ESL instructor might teach 50 to 100 students per year. If we take the lowest figure, this means the number of student buyers of textbooks for these courses is a minimum of 150,000 per year.

A: What is your estimate for college and adult *ESL* texts in the international market?

N.S.: I have been told by sales experts who are opening up markets for U.S.-published *ESL* texts that the average sale per book in the Asian market is between 5,000 and 10,000 copies with best-selling texts reaching sales of 50,000 copies. This is just the Asian market. The world market is rapidly growing—literally as we speak—international corporations are expanding across the globe into regions formerly closed to them. This is increasing the need for English-speaking workers at all levels of corporate operations. This is particularly true since the fall of the former Soviet Union has opened this region to international capitalism.

A: In other words, the international market is larger than the U.S. market for *ESL* texts?

N.S.: Yes.

A: Has the international market for *ESL* texts increased or decreased over the last decade? Why?

N.S.: It has increased because of the number of immigrants planning to come to the United States or other English-speaking countries. Also, the growth of the international economy—global economy—is resulting in English becoming the international language of business. English may not be the only international language, but it is certainly one of the major languages.

A: Do you perceive any philosophical differences between *ESL* and bilingual teachers?

N.S.: The boundaries between the two are getting fuzzier. Historically, bilingual methods were supported by dominated groups who wanted their native languages and cultures affirmed. Traditionally, *ESL* methods were supported by those advocating assimilation and the extinguishing of native languages. But over the last decade there has been a crossover of language and learning theories. There is a growing segment of *ESL* writers and teachers who incorporate the values, goals, and methodologies that, in the past, were the characteristics of the bilingual education movement.[40]

Reflecting Silverman's remarks on the demand for learning English in Asia, John Foggin, a retired U.S. Army sergeant who moved to Vietnam in 1994 and opened a cafe in a remote hamlet in the Mekong Delta, commented that many Vietnamese came to his cafe to learn English. Even in this rural area of Vietnam, as Foggin states, "Everyone is trying to learn English these days, and a lot of the local kids come to our cafe to practice and improve pronunciation. They all want jobs with the American companies starting up in Vietnam, and for that you have to speak English."[41]

The interview with Naomi Silverman highlights the growing effect of the worldwide movement of labor and the global marketplace on the language of the world. Given these conditions, more and more of the world's people will become bilingual with their second language being English or possibly German or Japanese. It is possible that the movement toward a bilingual world will result in an expansion of bilingual programs on a world scale. As Naomi Silverman suggests, many of those teaching *ESL* are incorporating bilingual methods. In addition, bilingualism provides the opportunity for people to be bicultural. Biculturalism would allow workers to function within the culture of international business while maintaining their own native cultural traditions.

CONCLUSION: THE MULTICULTURAL AND LANGUAGE DEBATE

There is considerable debate over bilingual education and its linkages to multicultural education. Table 10–1 shows the relationship between the different forms of multicultural education discussed in Chapters 1 and 2, and language issues.

As indicated in Table 10–1, those people supporting cultural unity through instruction in white Anglo-Saxon values and E. D. Hirsch's cultural literacy programs are usually opposed to bilingual education and advocate instruction

TABLE 10–1   Multicultural Education and Language Issues

	Dominant Culture As White Anglo-Saxon Values	E. D. Hirsch and Cultural Literacy	Diversity	Empowerment through Multicultural Education	Ethnocentric Education: Dominated Cultures
Culture of the Home/ Ancestry	Not considered	Not considered	Utilized in instruction	Utilized in instruction	Focus of instruction
Tolerance of Other Cultures	Western culture considered superior to other cultures	Western culture considered superior to other cultures	Goal is building tolerance of other cultures	Cultures are examined from a critical perspective	Tolerance is not a goal—possible development of biculturalism
Cultural Instruction	Values and literature of fundamental institutions of U.S. society dominant	E. D. Hirsch's cultural terms and ideas for understanding the culture of literate elite	Exposure and instruction about the values, customs, religions, and manners of a wide variety of cultures	Critical dialogue about culture	Focus on learning the culture and history of the students' ancestry, e.g., Native American and Afrocentric
Language of Instruction	English-only	English-only	Possibly bilingual—maintenance or transitional	Possibly bilingual—maintenance or transitional	Possibly bidialectical or maintenance bilingual

in English. Of course, this does not exclude foreign language instruction in separate classes, such as French and Spanish classes. It means that the language used for instruction in all non-language subjects, such as math and science, should be in English. On the other hand, those advocating pluralism, empowerment, and ethnocentric forms of multicultural education tend to support some form of bilingual education.

In Chapters 1 and 2, I also discussed cultural education programs related to economic success as illustrated by black attendance at elite boarding schools and the proposals of Lisa Delpit. These proposals also contain a language dimension as indicated in Table 10–2.

Low-income minority students placed in elite boarding schools experienced total immersion in a new culture and a new dialect of English. They felt alienated from their home conditions and peers and had to develop bicultural skills. Their language experience resulted in an independent development of dialectical skills. Immersed in standard English, they learned the language of their elite peers while retaining the dialectical language of the home. On the other hand, Lisa Delpit rejects the idea of total immersion in standard English. She believes low-income minority students should be explicitly told the rules of conduct for the power elite. She also believes that learning standard English should be linked to the language of the home. She wants the students to be directly instructed in how to be bidialectical rather than, as is the case in the immersion model, students indirectly developing these skills. In contrast to the elite boarding school model, she believes her methods will reduce the sense of alienation from the student's family background.

In 2001, The No Child Left Behind Act dealt a severe blow to those advocating the protection of minority cultures and languages. First, it mandated that states use high-stakes standardized tests to measure educational outcomes. By their very definition and construction, high-stakes standardized tests given in elementary, middle, and high schools represent only a single culture. Given to all students, test questions could not be based on knowledge known only to students in a minority culture. Since teachers must teach to the test to ensure that their students are able to be promoted or graduated, teachers are forced to teach the culture embedded in the test items. In fact, the No Child Left Behind Act mandates that schools be ranked in quality according to the performance of their students on standardized tests.

Standardized tests create uniformity in the knowledge taught in public schools. In other words, these tests standardize knowledge. As a result, high-stakes tests created by state governments make a single culture the norm of schooling. The No Child Left Behind Act represents a victory for those advocating that schools teach a uniform American culture.

In addition, the No Child Left Behind Act undercuts attempts to preserve the usage of minority languages. The legislation requires that the name of the Office of Bilingual Education be changed to the Office of English Language Acquisition. Bilingual advocates wanted the schools to maintain minority languages as a means of maintaining minority cultures. The No Child Left Behind Act mandated that minority languages would be used as a vehicle for learning

TABLE 10–2   Cultural Education for Economic Success

	Cultural Immersion in Elite Boarding Schools: The Power Elite	Lisa Delpit
Relationship to Traditional Culture	1. Alienation (including difficulty at marriage and maintaining relationships in former community) 2. Independent development of bicultural skills	1. Develop links to traditional culture. 2. Education in cultural background 3. Educate teachers in traditional culture 4. Rely on parents and community members for goals and methods of instruction

Cultural Education	1. Immersion
	2. Development of social and cultural capital
	  a. Ability to talk to anybody about anything
	  b. Access to influential people
	  c. Social connections of peer group—networking
	3. Understandidng white people
	4. Academic liberation from peer pressure
	5. Learning dress and manners
		1. Direct instruction
		2. "Issues of power are enacted in classrooms."
		3. "There are codes or rules for participating in power; that is, there is a 'culture of power.'"
		4. "The rules of the culture of power are a reflection of the rules of the culture of those who have power."
		5. "If you are not already a participant in the culture of power, being told explicitly the rules of that culture makes acquiring power easier."
		6. "Those with power are frequently least aware of—or least willing to acknowledge—its existence. Those with less power are often most aware of its existence."

Relationship to Traditional Language	1. Not used in education 2. Independent development of bidialectical skills	1. Use of home language in learning standard English 2. For non-English speakers—literacy in traditional language makes it easier to learn a new language
Language Education	1. Immersion	1. Must be taught codes used in mainstream American society 2. In bidialectical instruction a clear distinction is made in "village" English and standard English 3. Bilingual/dialectical

No Child Left Behind and English Acquisition

Grades: College

Objective:
To understand the debate about language instruction in the schools.

Lesson:

1. Create two teams—a pro and a con—to debate the English Acquisition section of the No Child Left Behind Act.
2. Conduct a debate followed by a class discussion.

Teachers: This lesson provides an opportunity for summarizing language issues in the schools.

Outcome: Students will consider language issues related to multicultural education and the potential impact of the No Child Left Behind legislation.

English. Consider the following quote from the legislation regarding the use in schools of Native American and Spanish languages:

> Programs authorized under this part [of the legislation] that serve Native American (including Native American Pacific Islander) children and children in the Commonwealth of Puerto Rico may include programs . . . designed for Native American children learning and studying Native American languages and children of limited Spanish proficiency, except that an outcome of programs serving such children *shall be increased English proficiency among such children* [my emphasis].[42]

As stated in the above quote the primary emphasis in the legislation is on the acquisition of English rather than support of minority languages and cultures. The No Child Left Behind Act clearly placed the federal government's support on the side of English acquisition as opposed to bilingual education. Rather than concluding the debate over language diversity, the No Child Left Behind Act opened a new era of debate over language rights in the school.

PERSONAL FRAMES OF REFERENCE

It is important to consider the psychological stress, cultural conflicts, and learning problems for children attending schools where the language used is different from the language used at home.

1. If you have experienced this situation: Did you encounter any psychological, cultural, or learning problems?
2. If you have not experienced this situation: What psychological, cultural, or learning problems do you think you might encounter?
3. In a broader perspective:
   a. Do you think English should be the official language of the United States?
   b. If you come from a non-English-speaking family: What do you think would be the effect on your family of making English the official language?
   c. If you come from an English-speaking family: Will making English the official language be advantageous to you?
   d. Have you ever experienced any problems in cross-cultural communications?

Notes

1. Vivian Toy, "Bilingual for Its Own Sake, an Alternative School Bucks the Tide," *The New York Times on the Web,* www.nytimes.com 14 October 1998, p. 2.
2. Ibid.
3. Ibid., p. 3.
4. Leah Hager Cohen, *Train Go Sorry: Inside A Deaf World* (New York: Houghton Mifflin Company, 1994), p. 31.
5. Ibid., p. 116.

6. Ibid., p. 55.
7. Ibid., p. 118.
8. Ibid., p. 136.
9. As quoted by Timothy Reagan, "Nineteenth-Century Conceptions of Deafness: Implications for Contemporary Educational Practice," *Educational Theory* 39, no. 1(Winter 1989), p. 41.
10. Ibid., p. 44.
11. David Firestone, "Deaf Students Protest New School Head," *The New York Times*, 27 April 1994, p. B3.
12. Richard Barnet and John Cavanagh, *Global Dreams: Imperial Corporations and the New World Order* (New York: Simon & Schuster, 1994), p. 170.
13. Ibid., p. 172.
14. Ibid., p. 191.
15. William Gudykunst and Tsukasas Nishida, *Bridging Japanese/North American Differences* (Thousand Oaks, CA.: Sage Publications, 1994).
16. Ibid., pp. 41–2.
17. Ibid., p. 43.
18. "Anti-immigrant mood denounced in English-only measure," *Compuserve, Executive News Service, United Press,* 29 March 1994, #1245.
19. Quoted in Lawrence Cremin, *American Education: The Colonial Experience 1607–1783* (New York: Harper and Row, 1970), p. 261.
20. Quoted in Joel Spring, *Deculturalization and the Struggle for Equality: A Brief History of the Education of Dominated Cultures in the United States* (Burr Ridge, IL: McGraw-Hill, 2004), p. 27.
21. Gilbert Gonzalez, *Chicano Education in the Era of Segregation* (Philadelphia: The Balch Institute Press, 1990), p. 22.
22. Spring, pp. 34–41.
23. Ibid., pp. 93–98.
24. Ibid., p. 90.
25. Joel Spring, *Conflict of Interests: The Politics of American Education* (White Plains, NY: Longman, Inc. 1993), p. 41.
26. Rosalie Pedalino Porter, *Forked Tongue: The Politics of Bilingual Education* (New York: Basic Books, 1990), p. 188.
27. See Joel Spring, *The American School 1642–1993* (New York: McGraw-Hill, 1994), pp. 370–383.
28. Reporter's Notebook, "Two-Way Bilingual-Education Programs Show Promise, New Study Suggests," *Education Week* 23 March 1994, p. 6.
29. See Jim Cummins, "Empowering Minority Students: A Framework for Intervention," *Harvard Educational Review,* no. 1 (1986), pp. 18–35 and *The Empowerment of Minority Students* (Los Angeles: California Association for Bilingual Education, 1989).
30. Priscilla Ahlgren, "La Escuela Fratney," *Teaching Tolerance* (Fall 1993), p. 29.
31. As quoted by Jim Cummins, "Empowering Minority Students: A Framework for Intervention," in *Beyond Silenced Voices: Class, Race, and Gender in United States Schools,* eds. Lois Weis and Michelle Fine (Albany: State University of New York Press, 1993), p. 115.
32. Flora Ida Ortiz, "Hispanic-American Children's Experiences in Classrooms: A Comparison between Hispanic and Non-Hispanic Children," in *Class, Race, & Gender in American Education,* ed. Lois Weis (Albany: State University of New York Press, 1988), p. 69.

33. Ibid., p. 72.
34. Henry T. Trueba, Li Rong Lilly Cheng, and Kenji Ima, *Myth or Reality: Adaptive Strategies of Asian Americans in California* (Washington, DC: The Falmer Press, 1993), pp. 62–64.
35. Ibid., p. 66.
36. Ibid., p. 71.
37. Ibid., p. 63.
38. Ibid., p. 65.
39. Ibid., p. 69.
40. This interview with Naomi Silverman, acquisitions editor for education and English as a second language college textbooks, was conducted on 8 May 1994.
41. Malcolm W. Browne, "G.I. Settles in Vietnam, at Peace with Old Foes," *The New York Times,* 16 May 1994, p. A4.
42. Public Law 107–110, 107th Congress, 8 January 2002 [H.R. 1]. *No Child Left Behind Act of 2001* (Washington, DC: U.S. Printing Office, 2002). Federal legislation contains the English Acquisition, Language Enhancement, and Academic Achievement Act which overturns the 1968 Bilingual Education Act.

CHAPTER 11

Teaching Ethnocentrism

There are two seemingly contradictory trends in the development of world cultures. On the one hand, global media and international corporations are creating a world culture, while, on the other hand, there are attempts to restore previously dominated cultures. These two trends are occurring in the United States. There is a growing homogeneity of American culture, while, at the same time, there is a revival of previously dominated cultures.

Almost anyplace in the United States, strangers can relate to each other through discussions of television programs and brand names of manufactured products and clothing. Concurrently, with the growing uniformity of U.S. culture is the collapse of colonial domination over Native Americans, Puerto Ricans, Mexican Americans, and African Americans. This has resulted in attempts to restore these previously dominated cultures. In reaction to the restoration of dominated cultures, some groups are calling for cultural homogeneity through the continued imposition of European American culture.

This chapter will discuss the pedagogical goals and methods of several models of ethnocentric education. The first includes models for the education of indigenous peoples. Another example is Afrocentric education, which is designed to maintain and restore a dominated culture. And, finally, E. D. Hirsch's Core Knowledge curriculum is designed to create cultural homogeneity by teaching all students dominant European American cultural values.

MODELS OF INDIGENOUS EDUCATION: EDUCATING FOR THE CHILD, FAMILY, AND COMMUNITY

In 1997, fourteen representatives of indigenous peoples from around the world, including Maori, Okanagan, Blackfeet, native Hawaiian, Australian Aborigine, Cochiti Pueblo, Oneida, Cherokee, Ojibwa, and Athabaskan, met in Santa Fe, New Mexico. The goal was to understand the needs of indigenous children, to develop instructional methods and a knowledge base for indigenous peoples, and to balance native values with demands of the modern global economy. The result of the conference was 12 instructional models reflecting the culture and perspective of particular native peoples.[1]

The 12 models are loosely connected by the following themes:

- Achieving multilingualism. This includes a maintenance of native languages and a resistance to language imperialism, particularly the domination of English.
- Maintaining a native understanding of history and culture.
- Creating curricula that reflect self-determination, cultural esteem, and personal vision.
- Linking native and non-native worlds by learning how to cross the borders between the two.
- Developing native ways of knowing in the modern global world or, in other words, learning to think globally while relating the global to native culture.

Multilingualism is essential for preserving native cultures and crossing the borders between the native and global worlds. The native languages are endangered by government attempts at eradication and by pressure to learn other languages, particularly English, to participate in the global economic system. Native children are inundated by the language of mass media and consumption. Preservation of native languages is essential to the preservation of indigenous cultures. Native languages provide access to traditional history, heroes, customs, and beliefs. Without preservation of traditional languages, native cultures become lifeless forms. On the other hand, realism dictates the learning of English or other languages needed for participation in the world's economy. Therefore, multilingualism is a key part of indigenous education programs.

Linked to the preservation of native languages are native ways of knowing about history and culture. Running through the 12 proposed models of learning is a profound spiritualism that links the individual to the family, community, and nature. These spiritual linkages are rooted in traditional cultures and provide different ways of interpreting world events. By valuing these spiritual linkages, native cultures provide an alternative view to a global economy which rips up the earth to develop factories and harness natural resources and spreads mass-consumer culture. Native cultures provide a challenge to economic concepts of human happiness. Does the present course of economic growth and mass consumerism really contribute to human happiness? Or are the important sources of human happiness found in the family, community, and nature?

Consequently, the 12 models stress the importance of maintaining native language, culture, history, and values to temper the future course of civilization. In the proposed curricula, native cultures are not considered static but are treated as evolving cultures in the context of real world events. The curricula recognize that native cultures must adapt and change, while at the same time emphasizing the important contribution they can make to other cultures. Therefore, the curricula are designed to develop self-esteem and create a personal vision based on traditional knowledge.

The importance of multilingualism, native ways of knowing, linking native culture to the global economy, and the relationship of human happiness to the family, community, and nature can be found in the following models. Space does not allow me to do justice to these models by providing a full description. However, the following does indicate the direction of ethnocentric forms of education among indigenous peoples. I would like to extend my thanks to Maenette Kape'ahiokalani Padeken Ah Nee-Benham and Joanne Cooper for their book *In Our Mother's Voice: Educational Models for Native Communities* which is the source of the following models.[2]

CHILD CENTERED (MAORI)

In this model, children are considered gifts provided by nature. Children are at the center of learning. Surrounding the child are the intellect, the spirit, and the body. Encompassing these are the physical elements which include the earth, the female element (representing life and learning), and the sky, weather, and winds. The sky, weather, and winds represent the changing nature of education. At the bottom are the sea or waves symbolizing the philosophy and ideals of indigenous culture crashing against global cultural values.

The child learns in this model how to link the past with the present and to integrate an evolving native culture with the current world of business and technology. Through this form of learning, the child learns to manifest native aspirations in the global economy.

Central to the actualization of this model is the family. Education is a nurturing relationship based on the needs of the child. The nurturing family leads the child to an understanding of the relationship of the intellect, spirit, and body to the physical elements. After understanding these relationships, the child is prepared for balancing the ideals of native culture with the demands of economic development.

HOLISTIC EDUCATION (OKANAGAN)

In this model, the self is nested in the family, community, and land. One concern is the destruction of family and community by government policies that forced indigenous children to attend residential schools. At residential schools, they were separated from family and community and subjected to a conscious attempt to destroy their languages and cultures. The stress on family and community is considered important to counter social dysfunctionalism, such as alcoholism and broken families, caused by the boarding school experience and government policies.

Consequently, emotional health is linked to establishing the relationship with the family, community, and land. Central to this education is the development of physical and emotional health for the self and family. The key is an emotional sense of self-worth and self-value. With a strong foundation in the self and family, it is possible to link the self to the community. It is the community that ties the individual to the land. A healthy self, including emotional health, contributes to a healthy family which, in turn, promotes a healthy community and a healthy use of land.

The development of the intellect is dependent on establishing a relationship between the self, family, community, and land. Operation of the intellect is linked to making choices and decisions. Healthy choices and decisions cannot be made, according to this model, if there is an unhealthy self, family, or community. Linking all of these is a spiritual tie manifested in ceremony and an understanding of the wholeness of nature. The self-spirit is linked to the spirit of plant and animal life and the beauty of mountains, oceans, lakes, rivers, forests, and plains.

THREE BASKETS OF KNOWLEDGE (MAORI)

In Maori legend, Tani, a child of the sky father and earth mother, ascended through levels of heaven to attain knowledge and wisdom and returned with three baskets of knowledge. The first basket contained peace, goodness, and love. The second contained prayers and rituals. And the third contained knowledge of arts to promote the welfare of people, such as weaving and war.

These three baskets of knowledge are nested in Maori language, which, in the current model, is provided to preschool infants. They are immersed in Maori language. Within the linguistic structure of Maori language, 5- to 11-year-old students learn native customs and values. Through these customs and values, they dip into the basket of knowledge and wisdom and the basket of peace, goodness, and love. At the same time, they learn from the basket of arts which prepares them to function in the modern world.

STIMULATING AND LANGUAGE-BASED EDUCATION (NATIVE HAWAIIAN)

In this model, immersion in native language, in this case Hawaiian, is essential for the development of self-esteem. This model assumes that language is the key to one's identity and the essence of one's sense of self. Language becomes the means for learning native traditions and history. For Hawaiian youth, alienation from native culture results in a decline in self-esteem and a loss of self-identity. This causes social dysfunctionalism. Creating a Hawaiian language immersion program, it is believed, will result in youth feeling good about themselves. The grounding in native culture will make it possible to function with a high level of self-esteem in the non-native world.

In this model, elders are held in high regard as sources of wisdom and tradition. Elders must assume the responsibility for the teaching of language and traditions. In turn, children must learn to respect the wisdom of their elders. Through immersion in native language and learning from elders, native youth will become functional in their own communities and in the non-native world.

LINKING NATIVE PEOPLE TO THE SPIRITUALITY OF ALL LIFE (COCHITI PUEBLO)

This philosophy of education recognizes the spirituality of all life, including plants and animals. Oral tradition provides an understanding of this spirituality. In this oral tradition, words become very powerful. Words link the individual to the world. Therefore, education must encourage people to speak and to sing. Speaking and singing become the means of accessing the deep spirituality that binds all living things.

In the middle of this model is the storyteller who represents the educator. The storyteller is either a mother or a grandmother who engages in education and nurturing. The storyteller's role is to teach language and tradition. With the storyteller is corn that symbolizes what is required to sustain human life. The interrelatedness of life is characterized by animals, birds, and plants arranged to represent the four seasons and directions. Ceremonies renew the spiritual life of the people. The storyteller explains the meaning of ceremonies to children. Ceremonies serve to unite the community, and they maintain a relationship to all people.

Similar to the other indigenous education models, language instruction is central. Young children are immersed in Cochiti language. In classrooms, students are reminded of the power of the English language and, consequently, the importance of only speaking Cochiti. One goal of this model is to change the learning environment from the standard Western classroom to a traditional Cochiti learning environment, such as a ceremonial house or outdoor setting.

The more general goals of this model are the following:

1. Networking with indigenous people around the globe.
2. Supporting efforts to strengthen community.
3. Supporting native language, traditions, and values.
4. Validating tribal pride and using tribal names.
5. Using traditional methods of instruction.
6. Maintaining self-determination of indigenous peoples.

In summary, it is important to emphasize that these models of learning are considered a means of improving the conditions of the world. They are more than an attempt to build self-esteem through recapturing native traditions. They stand as a real alternative to a world in spiritual decay from a consumer-oriented culture and to environmental destruction caused by economic development.

ASANTE: CLASSICAL AFRICA

Molefi Kete Asante publishes textbooks for grades 6 through adult under the Asante Imprint with The Peoples Publishing Group, Inc.[3] In scholarly circles, Asante, who is professor and chairperson of the Department of African American Studies at Temple University, is known for his widely read book, *Afrocen-*

tricity.[4] Asante's textbooks include histories of Africa and African Americans and studies and readers on African American culture and literature. Asante's primary educational concern, as I will demonstrate in my discussion of his teaching methods, is teaching African American students to see the world from the perspective of African cultures.

In contrast to Asante, Jawanza Kunjufu is primarily concerned with saving African American boys from what he considers the destructive effects of European American–oriented public schools. He has published a variety of studies about the educational problems facing African American boys and teenagers, a curriculum for elementary school grades, and textbooks on African American history for elementary and high school grades.[5]

For the purpose of understanding Asante's approach to Afrocentric teaching, I will analyze the teaching method incorporated into his textbook *Classical Africa.*[6] A key element in Asante's pedagogy, and in the meaning he gives to the term *Afrocentricity,* is the concept of African centeredness. Within the context of cultural frames of reference, African centeredness means seeing the world through the lens of African traditions. Of course, one can argue that African traditions encompass a wide variety of cultures existing on the African continent. Asante, as he demonstrates in his textbook, recognizes this wide variety of cultures. He argues that African cultures are quite different from the European cultures that make up the European American tradition in the United States. Africa, like Europe, does represent different cultures. The person coming from the geographical area called Europe does have a cultural frame of reference that is different from that of a person coming from the geographical area of Africa.

The problem for African Americans, something Asante attempts to correct with his pedagogy, is that the European American cultural frame of reference imposed on enslaved Africans was psychologically destructive. Asante writes, "The person's [African American's] images, symbols, lifestyles, and manners are contradictory and thereby destructive to personal and collective growth and development."[7] Changing the cultural frame of reference of African Americans by teaching them to be Afrocentric, Asante argues, will result in a new consciousness. On the title page of the textbook *Classical Africa,* Asante conveys this concept of Afrocentricity with the inscription "Each centered person becomes an owner not a renter of knowledge. Center yourself."[8]

AFROCENTRIC PEDAGOGY

Asante's pedagogical method for achieving Afrocentricity involves six elements. First is giving the students a sense of ownership of the knowledge being acquired by placing the students in the middle of the text. What this means in practice is helping the students to understand the relevance to themselves of what they are learning. Second is presenting people of African descent as major actors in history as opposed to being on the margins of history. Third is identifying with an icon information that is the result of recent research on Africa. Fourth is the use of holistic learning methods that will extend students' knowledge to intellectual and emotional levels. An icon of four African people is used to identify passages in the text requiring holistic learning. Fifth is the use of scholars and educators to ensure, according to Asante, that the textbooks are accurate. And sixth, the use of questions and activities, which Asante calls "Personal Witnessing," is to help students reflect on what they have learned and to share their personal learning with the rest of the class.[9]

Also, in an effort to move from a Eurocentric to an Afrocentric perspective, the textbook uses certain conventions that are, according to Asante, compatible with an Afrocentric philosophy. Oral history is treated as being equal to written history. Asante uses the spellings for ancient gods and other names that can be transliterated from hieroglyphic writing. And he uses the African names rather than the Greek or Roman names for ancient countries and cities.[10]

To achieve the goals of student ownership and centeredness, each unit of the text begins with an exercise titled "Center Yourself." For example, the "Center Yourself" exercise at the beginning of Unit 1 on the early civilizations of Africa asks the student: "What traits, qualities, or characteristics of contemporary Africans would you compare with the ancient civilizations along the Nile River?"[11] Obviously, this question is designed to help the student think about the relationship of the past to the present. In addition, it serves as one step in learning to think from the perspective of African history.

Chapter 1 discusses three classical periods of African civilization or what Asante calls Classical Seasons. To help students think in non-Eurocentric terms, the dates for these periods are given in conventions that Asante claims reflect an Afrocentric philosophy. Therefore, Asante uses B.C.E. (Before the Common Era) instead of B.C. and C.E. (Common Era) instead of A.D. The First Classical Season extends from 60,000 B.C.E. to C.E. 525, the Second Classical Season from C.E. 525 to C.E. 641, and the Third Classical Season from C.E. 641 to C.E 1600.

At the end of each chapter is a set of questions titled "Centering Your Thinking." For instance, at the end of Chapter 1 "Centering Your Thinking" contains three questions. The first two questions ask the student about the dates and changes between the classical seasons. The last question reflects the attempt to help students gain an Afrocentric perspective: "Explain how the changes you described made the rest of the world aware of the knowledge, contributions, and ideas of Africa."

THE QUESTION OF KEMET

Chapter 5 of *Classical Africa* represents one of the core ideas and most controversial aspects of the Afrocentric movement. The chapter is one of the central pieces in demonstrating to African American students their relationship to ancient African history. It is also important in linking ancient Egypt to African history and in linking the contributions of Africa to the development of European civilization. The chapter is titled "Kemet, The Black Land" and it deals with the skin color of ancient Egypt. In this chapter, Asante presents a series of photographs of contemporary Egyptians with black skin color. The purpose of the pictures is to show the resemblance between contemporary black Egyptians, or Nubian Egyptians, and African Americans. Two of the pictures of Nubian Egyptians have captions indicating their resemblance to African Americans. Another picture depicts an African American woman standing with a young Nubian Egyptian girl and next to this picture is a photograph of an African American boy. All of the faces and skin colors in these pictures are very similar. The final picture shows Molefi Asante standing between a black-skinned Egyptian and a light-skinned Egyptian. The caption asks the student: "Can you tell which is Dr. Asante?"

Some Afrocentric curricula have been criticized for their treatment of the skin color of Egyptians. Asante's handling of the issue avoids the pitfalls of these other Afrocentric materials. For instance, one widely criticized Afrocentric curriculum is the African American Baseline Essays prepared by the Portland, Oregon, public schools. These essays translated Kemet to mean "Land of the Blacks" implying that Egypt was the land of black people. In an essay in the *American Educator* criticizing the Portland curriculum, Erich Martel writes that Kemet means "'the black land,' and refers to the black alluvial soil deposited by the Nile's yearly flooding."[12] In the same issue of the *American Educator*, Frank Yurco, an Egyptologist, writes, "Afrocentric claims that the Egyptians were described as black by other ancient people are misrepresentations. . . . Herodotus and his contemporaries distinguished the Egyptians from . . . Nubian neighbors to the south . . . [they] were the blackest in complexion, and had the wooliest hair, according to the classical sources."[13] Yurco argues that ancient Egypt was a multicolored society with skin colors ranging from light to dark.

In contrast to the Portland curriculum, Asante does translate Kemet to mean "Black land." Asante also clearly distinguishes Nubians from other Egyptians with lighter skin color. In the same chapter, he states, "The term Nubian has come to mean those Egyptians who have black skin. Of course, there is also a large Arab population in Egypt today with lighter skin tones."[14]

Given the similarities in skin tones and facial features, the photographs in Asante's textbook would probably help the African American student relate to the population of contemporary and ancient Egypt. In one of the "Center Your Thinking" questions in this chapter, students are forced to think about their relationship to ancient and modern Egypt and to understand different cultural frames of reference. This question is an important example of how Asante intends for students to think in an Afrocentric manner. The question is this: "In Egypt today, the people in Upper Egypt (the south) often refer to African Americans as Nubian Americans. Explain what *Nubian American* means to Egyptians today."[15]

THE CONTRIBUTION OF EGYPT TO THE DEVELOPMENT OF SCIENCE AND MATHEMATICS

After establishing that the population of ancient Egypt included large numbers of black-skinned people, Asante's textbook stresses the contribution of Egypt to the development of science and mathematics. The establishment of this relationship is very important for the Afrocentric argument. Traditionally, European-centered historians stressed the importance of ancient Greece for the development of mathematics and science. What was not stressed by these European-centered scholars was the importance of ancient Egypt in these areas of study. If one stresses the importance of Egypt, then the center of attention shifts from Greece to Egypt and, of course, to Africa.

Within the framework of the pedagogy of Afrocentricity, if African American students are made aware of the contribution of classical Africa to the development of world science and mathematics, then they will feel more positively about themselves and their heritage. Africans as founders of modern science is a far different image from the Africa portrayed in Tarzan movies and books. This approach is reflected in the "Center Yourself" exercise at the beginning of Unit 2. At the beginning of the exercise, the student is informed that science is important for the development of the modern world and that in classical Africa there were many scientific discoveries. The student is then asked: "What ancient African discoveries about human life, the earth, the rivers, the sun, birds, and animals would amaze you?"[16]

In the unit chapter "Early African Science and Art," the student is informed of ancient African development of geometry to map boundaries of land, the development of astronomy and a calendar based on the rotation of the earth, the creation of the first paper or papyrus, the architectural achievements of the pyramids, the stunning development of techniques of art represented in sculptures and wall paintings, and the extensive development of literature, including the Egyptian *Book of the Dead*. In the chapter's "Center Your Thinking" exercise, the student is asked about how ancient Africans left the world with important legacies in mathematics, science, architecture, art, and literature.[17]

Again, Asante's presentation of the intellectual contributions of ancient Africa avoids the criticisms made of other Afrocentric materials. Asante never claims a direct connection between the development of mathematics and science in ancient Egypt and its development in ancient Greece. All Asante does is claim that ancient Egypt made important advances that contributed to the world development in these fields. Certainly, it is not possible to deny this assertion. Critics of the Portland Baseline curriculum are concerned about claims that intellectual developments in Ancient Greece were a result of the influence of Ancient Egypt. Again, it is important to stress that Asante never makes this claim. Afrocentric critic Erich Martel writes, "While Egypt (and Mesopotamia via the Phoenicians) did make important contributions to ancient Greece, indigenous Greek achievements were central to that process."[18] Egyptologist Frank Yurco recognizes the important contributions of Egypt, but stresses the contributions of other societies (Asante never claims that other cultures did not make contributions). In placing the achievements of Egypt in the context of other cultures, Yurco writes, "Western civilization owes a considerable cultural debt jointly to Egypt in Africa and to Mesopotamia, and indirectly to the wider world. . . . This is the true legacy of the ancient civilizations, and not the monocultural and African-centered view that the Afrocentrists present."[19]

Personally, I wonder why critics such as Martel and Yurco express so much concern about the emphasis on Egypt as a source of the development of mathematics and science. They do not deny the importance of ancient Egypt's contributions. What they seem to resist, and, of course, this is the major concern of the Afrocentrists, is the shifting of attention from ancient Greece to ancient Egypt or, in other words, from Europe to Africa. Is this resistance a product of racism or Eurocentrism? Is it a product of a true concern about scholarship? Whatever the reason, this resistance highlights the ideological struggle over the content of the Afrocentric curriculum.

HOLISTIC LEARNING

Each unit in *Classical Africa* concludes with a summary, identifying with the icon of four African people the holistic learning goals of the chapter. For instance, Unit 5 concentrates on Ghana as the first major kingdom to develop in West Africa from 300 B.C.E. to C.E. 1200. In the unit summary, two items of holistic learning are identified. One deals with the relationship between economic practices, the sense of well-being of a country's population, and the peace of the country. The discussion of economics introduces the student to the concept of inflation. For instance, the population of Ghana, which was known as the Kingdom of Gold, used gold dust as a currency. The king retained all gold nuggets and gold reserves. By controlling the circulation of gold, the king was able to maintain, according to Asante, a stable economic system. The stability of the economic system resulted in the stability of the political and social systems. As an example of holistic learning, students are introduced to the history of Ghana and economic, social, and political ideas.

The second example of holistic learning introduces students to the relationship among religious concepts, national culture, and the family structure. In Ghana, there was no central religious leader or religious book. Each family had a member who was in charge of religion. This person would relate to the family an oral history of religion and national beliefs. As a result, the family was the central unit of religion and the nation. The student learns the history of religion in Ghana and the role of religion in the family and culture.

PERSONAL WITNESSING

Personal Witnessing exercises are also placed at the end of each unit. There are two parts to these exercises. One part is "Reflection," where students are asked reflective questions about the material discussed in the unit. The second part, "Testimony," has students sharing their knowledge with the rest of the class. The "Reflection" exercise for the unit on Ghana tells students that most religions have a basic set of beliefs and then asks the students to think about what they believe. The students are then asked to list the basic beliefs that guide their lives. The students are asked: "Should anyone be forced to accept the beliefs of another? How can you share your beliefs with others without being forceful?" These particular questions are related to the invasion of Ghana in C.E. 1055 by the Islamic Almoravids, who forced Ghana to convert to Islam.

In the "Testimony" exercise, students are asked to write a poem or rap or create a performance illustrating how the individual student thinks "the Almoravids felt about capturing the wealth of Ghana." In this exercise, the student is asked to relate to the feelings of historical subjects. This, of course, is an attempt to make history personal.

In conclusion, Asante's *Classical Africa* is one model of an Afrocentric pedagogy that stresses the centering of history in Africa, the changing of cultural frames of reference, the personal ownership of knowledge, holistic learning, and personal reflection. Kunjufu, as I will discuss in the next section, has a different set of concerns and methods.

THE CONSPIRACY TO DESTROY BLACK BOYS

While Jawanza Kunjufu shares Asante's concern with raising black consciousness, he is primarily concerned about saving the African American male from a destructive life of alcohol, drugs, and crime. From Kunjufu's perspective, the destruction of many African American males is a result of the tension between racism and the masculine image within the African American community. Contributing to the destruction of males is a passive group of conspirators consisting "of parents, educators, and white liberals who deny being racists, but through their silence allow institutional racism to continue."[20] His educational materials and recommendations are designed to provide what he considers to be a positive self-identity for African American males.

Kunjufu discusses racism in a global context. Historically, whites, he argues, created power systems to control the behavior of nonwhites. Currently, these forms of racism exist in institutional relationships. For instance, he gives the example of an African American male and a European American male, both with identical college degrees and grade point averages, applying for the same job. During his interview with a European American employer, the African American is told either that the job is filled or that he is inappropriate for the job. Interviewed next, the European American gets the job. The silent racial conspiracy in this situation, according to Kunjufu, is that the European American candidate for the job did not deny the benefit of his racial position and he did not make the hiring decision. In other words, the European American candidate was not actively racist but passively accepted the benefits of a racist system.[21]

Kunjufu argues that the institutional racism that permeates the public school system in the United States results in the academic destruction of black boys. He calls this process the "fourth grade failure syndrome." Citing statistics on reading progress, Kunjufu contends that black boys enter the primary grades full of enthusiasm for learning. During the primary grades this enthusiasm is nurtured, but after the third grade the achievement rates of black boys begin a downward spiral. Based on a study using the Iowa Reading Test scores, he cites examples of African American boys who are in the 90th percentile in reading in the third grade and by the seventh grade have declined to the 30th to 50th percentile range.[22]

Kunjufu identifies a variety of factors causing this decline in reading scores. One is the labeling process in schools, which sorts students into different ability groups and into special education classes. He states that a disproportionately large number of black male students are classified for special education classes. In addition, IQ and other tests used for classification purposes are culturally biased against black children.[23]

Besides lacking male role models, African American children encounter teachers and administrators who do not care. In the upper elementary grades, Kunjufu argues, teachers and administrators believe that their primary goal for African American males is to maintain order and not to teach. Little effort is expended in countering truancy and keeping black children in school. A caption to a picture accompanying a 1994 article on the Proviso school system in Illinois captures the attitudes of school officials criticized by Kunjufu. The picture shows a graying white male social studies teacher looking into a hallway full of African American students. After indicating that the teacher believes that black students are the cause of the school system's "decline," the caption quotes the teacher, " 'I have run into a lot of problems now that I have a lot of black kids,' he says. 'They won't shut up.' " The caption continues, "Some days he can barely face the class and relies on videos . . . to do the teaching for him."[24]

Of particular concern to Kunjufu is the lack of black male role models in elementary schools and in the family. The majority of African American boys, according to Kunjufu, live in single-parent families with women as the heads of the households. Also, he cites figures showing that, of the 17 percent of elementary school teachers who are male, only 1.2 percent are African American.[25]

Without positive male role models, according to Kunjufu, African American boys adopt an image of masculinity that is self-destructive. Kunjufu quotes a poem by Michael Brown, "Image of Man," that defines masculinity in terms of the following behavior for some, but not all, men in the African American community:

1. Inflict pain on others.
2. Impregnate, but not marry, many women.
3. Drink and consume large amounts of alcohol and drugs.
4. Remain unreformed by jail experience.
5. Wear flashy clothes and drive sporty cars.

Kunjufu adds to the traits described in this poem, "Men do not cry, ignore health symptoms, must bring home the 'bacon,' and do not display affection to anyone, especially their sons."[26]

The consequence of this macho image, Kunjufu argues, is a process of dehumanization. One major factor in this dehumanization is the difficulty black men face in "bringing home the bacon." Because of racism in the labor market, black men have a difficult time living up to their macho image. Compounding this situation is the image that men do not express their emotions. Arguing that psychologists believe that an expression of emotions helps stop suicidal tendencies, Kunjufu writes of the plight of the black male, "Men returning home from work, or never going, sitting in rocking chairs with a beer all evening, never fully sharing with their spouse or children how they feel. Men have be-come slaves to 'bringing home the bacon' and letting mama bring home the emotion."[27]

In summary, Kunjufu's approach to an Afrocentric education involves a concern with developing black consciousness and providing a positive role model for black boys. I will first describe his pedagogical methods for raising the consciousness of African American boys, and then I will discuss his pro-posed methods for providing these children with positive male role models.

LESSONS FROM HISTORY: A CELEBRATION IN BLACKNESS

Jawanza Kunjufu has written two textbooks titled *Lessons from History: A Cele-bration in Blackness*.[28] One text is an elementary edition and the other is a junior and senior high school edition. Unlike Asante's *Classical Africa*, Kunjufu's texts focus on the historical experience of African Americans. Both texts have the same chapter titles and chapter content, with the elementary text being a sim-plified copy of the junior and senior high school book. Each chapter includes a set of questions and exercises.

One of Kunjufu's goals is to create an Afrocentric perspective regarding U.S. history that emphasizes African American resistance to slavery and op-pression and the domination of the African American mind by European Amer-icans. Consequently, the book begins with a discussion of Africa as the begin-ning of civilization and, in the second chapter, with the European invasion of Africa and the capture and transportation of slaves to the Americas. Similar to Asante, Kunjufu wants African American students to understand the connec-tion among themselves, their African heritage, and the process of enslavement.

One example of the effort to establish this personal relationship with his-tory is an exercise at the end of Chapter 2 which asks the student to do the fol-lowing: "Write a paper to your ancestors who did not commit suicide during the Middle Passage and thank them for the opportunity you have to live."[29] The exercise refers to the large number of slaves who, while being transported to the Americas, chose suicide over slavery. In addition, the exercise establishes in the student's mind a powerful image of resistance to slavery.

Another exercise asks students to write a play about "seasoning." For Kun-jufu, the concept of seasoning is important for explaining the methods by which African Americans are kept subordinate to European Americans. Kun-jufu identifies four aspects of the process of seasoning. One is making the slave obedient by instilling fear of the owner through threats of death and torture for disobedience. The second is to make the slave loyal to the master. The third is to make the slave believe in the superiority of the white race over the black race. And the last is to make slaves hate Africa and lose pride in their heritage.[30]

This playwriting exercise reflects the emphasis throughout the book on methods of domination. Of particular importance are the methods used by Eu-ropean Americans to dominate the thinking of African Americans. For instance, in discussing the conflicting views of Booker T. Washington and W.E.B. DuBois regarding the best strategy for the advancement of the rights of African Americans in the late nineteenth and twentieth centuries, Kunjufu informs the student in Chapter 3, "White people and the media choose our leaders, provide more favorable information about those leaders with whom Whites are more comfortable, and then we make ill-informed decisions about messengers rather than critically looking at the messages."[31]

The first three chapters of the book focus on the issues of domination and resistance. From this perspective, the African American experience in the United States is primarily centered on issues of enslavement and liberation. At all times, Kunjufu teaches the student about the historic resistance of African Americans to oppression.

Kunjufu continues the emphasis on African and African American resistance in Chapter 4, titled "We Call Them Brave." In this chapter, Kunjufu helps the student to relate to historic African and African American freedom fighters ranging from Pharaoh Ramses II to the Tuskegee Airmen during World War II. Chapter 4 concludes with Kunjufu's interpretation of the African American perspective in recent history. It would be very hard to find this perspective included, or even discussed, in most textbooks written for U.S. public schools. In the concluding paragraph, Kunjufu argues that many African Americans choose military service because of the problems of unemployment. He describes the Vietnam War as being fought as part of the U.S. government's obsession with carving up the world for economic exploitation. The war was not, he states, for the purpose of providing democracy for South Vietnam. He suggests that the next war will be against people of color.

In language that challenges the European American perspective on U.S. history and politics, Kunjufu warns African American readers that there is a good possibility the next war "will take place in Africa or the Caribbean. Remember, the Japanese were placed in concentration camps during World War II."[32] The chapter ends with questions that force the reader to think of world problems from an Afrocentric perspective: "Will you fight against your own people? Will you kill your brother and sisters because you need a job?"[33]

The last chapter of the book, "Lessons from History," presents particular historical problems faced by Africans and African Americans and lessons to be drawn from these problems. For instance, the first historical problem is titled "Loyalty," and it discusses how some slaves betrayed their fellow slaves during slave rebellions and how some Africans trusted white slave traders. The lesson to be learned from these historical events, Kunjufu writes, is "Never trust people outside your race and be careful of those within."[34] This lesson on loyalty provides Kunjufu with the opportunity to state clearly what he means by an Afrocentric perspective. In the context of African Americans being loyal to other African Americans, Kunjufu states, "There are three criteria of Blackness: color, consciousness, and culture. To be Black or African means to look Black, think Black, and act Black."[35]

The remainder of the "Lessons of History" deals with the historical problems of Africans being taught a sense of inferiority regarding the cultures of

Africa and black skin color, the failure of African Americans to concentrate on economic issues, and the focusing by Europeans and European Americans on the development of military weapons and the building of colonial empires. The chapter also lists the historical strengths of African Americans and the lessons to be learned from those strengths. The strengths include a belief in education and the value of the family, bravery, ability in sports and music, a religious orientation, and a continued resistance to oppression.

Through the teaching of history, Kunjufu wants to raise African American consciousness by making the student aware of the methods of domination employed against Africans and African Americans. One important aspect of this domination is instilling a sense of inferiority. Overcoming this sense of inferiority and understanding its sources is important for the academic achievement of African American students. Besides attempting to strip away the crippling effects of an inferiority complex, Kunjufu attempts to build the spirit of African American students by teaching them about the bravery of Africans and the historical struggles of Africans against oppression. Finally, Kunjufu attempts to build a sense of loyalty in the black community.

THE RITES OF PASSAGE PROGRAM

Throughout his writings, Kunjufu emphasizes the importance of the family and religion to the African American community and to the salvation of African American boys. His textbooks represent one attempt to convey the importance of the family to students and to build positive male identities. His Rites of Passage Program provides black boys with positive male role models. He believes that the creation of stable black families depends on changing the image of black males.

To achieve this objective, Kunjufu proposes the creation of organizations similar to Big Brothers or the Boy Scouts. In these organizations, black men would meet weekly with black boys to study black history, learn skills, and take field trips. Kunjufu argues that there would be two distinct differences between these organizations and the Boy Scouts. One difference, Kunjufu writes, is that the Rites of Passage Program would "equip African-American boys ideologically with the tools to understand why Africans are oppressed and specifically African-American boys."[36] The second difference is that boys will be taught how "to remove the injustices of racism, capitalism, sexism, and to fuel liberation and the maximization of human potential."[37]

In addition to the Rites of Passage Program, Kunjufu recommends that parents monitor their children's classrooms, provide positive male role models, reduce the time children are on the streets and watching television, provide constructive activities, work with a church, and provide children with proper nutrition. For educators, he recommends more exposure of children to male role models, an emphasis on academic over athletic achievements, and greater teacher competency. The combination of teaching Afrocentric history, the Rites of Passage Program, the vigilance of parents, and changes in the educational system will result, Kunjufu believes, in a victory over oppression.

WHAT EVERY CHILD NEEDS TO KNOW

Since the 1987 publication of *Cultural Literacy: What Every American Needs to Know,* E. D. Hirsch has organized the Core Knowledge Foundation and published a series of elementary school textbooks called "The Core Knowledge Series."[38] The title of each textbook claims to present what every child should know. For instance, the textbook I will discuss is titled *What Your 2nd Grader Needs to Know: Fundamentals of a Good Second-Grade Education.*[39]

Hirsch rejects multicultural education and those forms of ethnocentric education based on the cultures of dominated groups. He believes that society should be united around a body of core knowledge found in what he calls "standard" U.S. society. He uses the term *cultural literacy* to indicate the acquisition of core knowledge. The sharing by all students of a common body of core knowledge, he argues, will increase equality of opportunity for all groups, including the children of the poor. Hirsch claims that poverty is perpetuated by the lack of cultural literacy. If the poor become culturally literate, he argues, they will be able to climb out of their state of poverty. From his perspective, Afrocentric programs provide only the cultural background to function in a narrow part of society. In contrast, cultural literacy based on the core knowledge of U.S. society would provide the African American child with the cultural background needed for participation in the U.S. economy.[40]

One of the important questions in Hirsch's proposal is this: What is the core knowledge of U.S. society? For his 1987 publication, *Cultural Literacy,* Hirsch teamed up with two of his colleagues at the University of Virginia, historian Joseph Kett and scientist James Trefil, to produce a list of 5,000 names, phrases, dates, and concepts that represented the core knowledge of U.S. society. The three consulted magazines, reference books, dictionaries, general books, and textbooks to create lists for their particular fields. They would meet to criticize each other's lists. After merging their individual lists into one, they submitted it to "more than a hundred consultants outside the academic world."[41] In addition, they began working on definitions of the items on the list. Hirsch writes that the definitions "consist of the associations that each item tends to call forth in the minds of *literate persons* [my emphasis]."[42] The work on definitions, Hirsch claims, will "reproduce the shared cultural schemata that underlie *literate communications* [my emphasis] of the present day."[43] Therefore, in Hirsch's early work, the core body of knowledge is that body of knowledge held by literate people in the United States.

For his later textbook series, Hirsch conducted research through his Core Knowledge Foundation. This research consisted of examining reports of state departments of education and professional educational groups for recommended outcomes for elementary and secondary education. Also examined were the knowledge and skills required by the educational systems of France, Japan, Sweden, and Germany. The foundation also formed a multicultural advisory group to determine a core knowledge of diverse cultural traditions.[44]

The results of this research were sent to 150 teachers, scholars, and scientists who were asked to create a master list of the core knowledge that children

What Did Columbus's Voyage Mean for Africa, Asia, Europe, and the Americas?

Grades: Middle School through College

Objective:
To understand differing cultural perspectives regarding the content of instruction.

Lesson:

1. Divide the class into four groups.
2. Assign each group a particular cultural perspective of the world's regions including Europe, the Americas, Africa, and Asia.
3. Have each group prepare a lesson to be taught to the rest of the class about the arrival of Christopher Columbus in the Americas from their particular cultural perspective.
4. Have each group teach their prepared lesson to the rest of the class.
5. In a general class discussion, list on the board the major differences among the lessons as a result of a particular cultural perspective.

Teachers: The most challenging part of this assignment will be the cultural perspective of African Americans and Asian Americans. Remember that Columbus's arrival in the Americas had important consequences for Asia and Africa.

Outcome: Students will gain an understanding of teaching from different cultural perspectives.

should have by the sixth grade. Other groups of educators were asked to determine the grade-by-grade sequence for learning this master list. And finally, the results of this process were tested at the Three Oaks Elementary School in Lee County, Florida.[45]

What is this finally arrived at core knowledge? In Hirsch's words, "Core knowledge is, first of all, a body of widely used knowledge taken for granted by *competent writers and speakers* [my emphasis] in the United States."[46] Therefore, I would conclude, based on Hirsch's references to "literate persons," "literate communications," and "competent writers and speakers," that core knowledge is that knowledge held by the dominant intellectual elite in the United States. It is not the knowledge held by the average Navajo in New Mexico or the Sioux in South Dakota. It is not the knowledge held by the average African American or Puerto Rican.

TEACHING CORE KNOWLEDGE

Hirsch explicitly tells parents and teachers that an important goal of the core knowledge curriculum is teaching "standard culture" to children from dominated and immigrant cultures. In the introduction to the "Sayings and Phrases" section of the Language Arts part of his second-grade textbook he states, "The category of sayings in the core knowledge sequence has been the most singled out for gratitude by teachers who work with children from home cultures that are different from the standard culture of literate American English."[47]

The section on "Sayings and Phrases" highlights Hirsch's technique for teaching children "literate American English." Popular phrases are presented, followed by an explanation and a short story illustrating the meaning of the phrase. The following phrases taught in the book indicate the extent to which Hirsch's core knowledge is centered in dominant European or English American culture: Better late than never; better safe than sorry; a dog is a man's best friend; where there's a will there's a way; easier said than done; get a taste of your own medicine; turn over a new leaf.[48]

Hirsch believes that the teaching of core knowledge is also a means for teaching common cultural values. Therefore, he selected stories for his language arts section that would instill ethical values through literature. He identifies these ethical values as honesty, courage, diligence, patience, tolerance, and civility.[49]

Multiculturalism is introduced to the student through the selection of stories from different cultures that exemplify the cultural values he wants taught. In other words, he only wants to teach the values of other cultures that are the same as those of the "standard culture" in the United States. For instance, he selects an Asian story because it teaches loyalty and a Native American story because it teaches kindness.[50]

Hirsch also believes that the teaching of fine arts will be a vehicle for instilling morality. He writes, "The development of artistic sensibilities can enhance the development of their [the students'] moral sensibilities."[51] The first section on fine arts is devoted to music. Reflecting a European American–

centered approach, he recommends that students listen to Prokofiev's *Peter and the Wolf*. Following this recommendation are descriptions of musical instruments which are all of European origin except for a Sioux Indian flute. The only photograph in the section is of a symphony orchestra.[52] In contrast to the Afrocentric focus on Egypt, the photographs in Hirsch's architecture section are of Greek temples. There is one drawing of a Buddhist temple.[53]

The Eurocentric nature of Hirsch's core knowledge is most clearly seen in his section on world civilization. Again, in contrast to the Afrocentric approach, there is no discussion of Egypt. The major focus is on Greece. Under the subtitle "Ancient Peoples of the Mediterranean," his second-grade textbook devotes approximately 1 page to Babylon, 1 page to the Persians, and 16 pages to the Greeks. His two references to the Egyptians are the following: "Writing developed in this area [Mesopotamia], as it did in ancient Egypt."[54] "But Babylon, along with Egypt, was conquered by fierce invaders who came from the North."[55] There is no mention of Egyptian accomplishments in developing paper, writing, literature, science, mathematics, or architecture. In fact, Egyptian accomplishments in the development of geometry are not even suggested in the following passage: "By asking questions the Greeks developed geometry and added new ideas to mathematics."[56] The 16 pages devoted to Greece on politics, sports, plays, literature, science, mathematics, and philosophy clearly convey the impression that it was the birthplace of modern civilization. One section is titled "Athens: Freedom's Birthplace."[57]

The section on world civilization concludes with three pages devoted to India, one and one-half pages devoted to China, and a half-page devoted to Vietnam. The Eurocentric perspective is most evident in this distribution of pages. Certainly, from a global perspective, the geographic size, history, and population of India and China would suggest more attention and pages than the small country of Greece. There is not one sentence devoted to Africa.

Hirsch believes that the teaching of American history should begin in early grades so that children from "less advantaged homes" will be able to compete with children from "advantaged homes." Hirsch argues that "knowledge of American history and society is gained through the pores by children from advantaged families." In his textbook, American civilization is treated primarily as European American civilization. There is no discussion of Native American cultures. Native Americans are only discussed in reference to their defeat by the U.S. government and their participation in Wild West shows. There is no discussion of African American culture. African Americans are discussed in reference to the underground railroad and the civil rights movement. Mexican Americans are discussed in reference to their defeat in the Mexican–American War. There is no discussion of Asian Americans.[58]

In summary, Hirsch's core knowledge curriculum teaches a form of ethnocentric education centered in the European American experience. He believes that the inculcation of this culture will benefit the children of dominated cultures by providing them with the same cultural background as those children from advantaged families. In contrast to an Afrocentric education, he offers a European American–centered education.

CONCLUSION

For business leaders of the United States, Europe, and Japan, the growth of a global market promises great economic benefits. From a European American–centered perspective, E. D. Hirsch believes that the teaching of core knowledge is important for a sense of world cultural unity. In the introduction to the world civilization section of his second-grade textbook, he explains to parents and teachers, "The new global economy has created a new cosmopolitanism which makes it desirable that children in all countries, and especially in our own culturally diverse one, should share a basic knowledge of world history."[59] Of course, he presents a core knowledge of world history, the arts, and literature that is centered on the culture and values of European traditions. His global marketplace would be dominated by these traditions.

In contrast to the global dreams of profit of the business leaders of the United States, Europe, and Japan, many people, particularly people of color, experience the global marketplace as another form of exploitation. Food, cars, clothes, manufactured goods, and electronic equipment are sold within a global marketplace from which many people are excluded. For instance, while large international conglomerates are buying food in a world market and selling it in supermarkets in prosperous countries, 75 percent of the world's population purchases dwindling food supplies in open-air markets. Local farmers in Africa and in Central and South America are being pushed off their lands so that international food corporations can grow specialty foods for prosperous nations. As local farmers lose their lands, the availability of food for local populations declines. Even in the United States, people of color face problems of nutrition because of the unequal distribution of food products. In reference to the depressed African American sections of New York and Chicago, Richard Barnet and John Cavanagh write, "Supermarket chains have abandoned many of these neighborhoods to local grocery stores and bodegas. The produce is old and wilted, and the prices are significantly higher than in better-off neighborhoods."[60]

Consequently, Afrocentric advocates like Asante and Kunjufu see little benefit in cultural unity in a world marketplace. The type of core knowledge advocated by E. D. Hirsch does little, at least from their perspective, to help Africans and African Americans. In fact, they believe that ending the domination of European American–centered thought is essential for the economic and social progress of Africans and African Americans. The creation of racial pride and unity through an Afrocentric education, they argue, will be an important way of resisting further exploitation and oppression.

PERSONAL FRAMES OF REFERENCE

The present cultural wars represented by the clash of Afrocentric and Eurocentric educations are part of a world economic struggle. The following questions are for the future of the global market and global culture:

1. What do you think will be the place of Africa in the new economic order and world culture?
2. Do you think people of color will be the exploited workers in the new world order?
3. Do you think the new world culture will be Eurocentric?
4. Do you think Afrocentric schools will improve the social and economic conditions of African Americans?
5. Do you think an educational program based on cultural literacy would improve your social and economic condition?
6. What do you think should be the cultural perspective of the curriculum of U.S. public schools?

Notes

1. Maenette Kape'ahiokalani Padeken Ah Nee-Benham and Joanne Cooper, *In Our Mother's Voice: Educational Models for Native Communities* (Mahwah, NJ: Lawrence Erlbaum, Inc., 2000).
2. Ibid.
3. For a catalogue write to this address:
   The Peoples Publishing Group, Inc.
   P. O. Box 70
   Rochelle Park, NJ 07662.
4. Molefi Kete Asante, *Afrocentricity* (Trenton, NJ: African World Press, 1989).
5. For a catalogue of Kunjufu's books and curriculum materials write to this address:
   African American Images
   1909 West 95th Street
   Chicago, IL 60643.
6. Molefi Kete Asante, *Classical Africa* (Maywood, NJ: The Peoples Publishing Group, 1994).
7. Asante, *Afrocentricity*, p. 1.
8. Asante, *Classical Africa*, p. i.
9. Ibid., pp. vi–1.
10. Ibid., p. ii.
11. Ibid., p. 7.
12. Erich Martel, " . . . And How Not to: A Critique of the Portland Baseline Essays," *American Educator* (Spring 1994), p. 34.
13. Frank J. Yurco, "How to Teach Ancient History: A Multicultural Model," *American Educator* (Spring 1994), p. 36.
14. Asante, *Classical Africa*, p. 24.
15. Ibid., p. 25.
16. Ibid., p. 33.
17. Ibid., pp. 39–45.
18. Martel, "A Critique," p. 34.
19. Yurco, "Ancient History," p. 37.
20. Jawanza Kunjufu, *Countering the Conspiracy to Destroy Black Boys* (Chicago: African American Images, 1985), p. 1.
21. Ibid., p. 3.
22. Ibid., p. 7.

23. Ibid., p. 10.

24. H. G. Bissinger, "'We're All Racist Now,'" *The New York Times Magazine*, 29 May 1994, p. 28.

25. Kunjufu, *The Conspiracy*, p. 11.

26. Ibid., pp. 16–17.

27. Ibid., p. 24.

28. Jawanza Kunjufu, *Lessons from History: A Celebration in Blackness, Elementary Edition* (Chicago: African American Images, 1987) and *Lessons from History: A Celebration in Blackness, Jr.–Sr. High Edition* (Chicago: African American Images, 1987).

29. Kunjufu, *Lessons from History, Jr.–Sr. High Edition*, p. 32.

30. Ibid., p. 19.

31. Ibid., p. 37.

32. Ibid., p. 64.

33. Ibid.

34. Ibid., p. 99.

35. Ibid.

36. Kunjufu, *The Conspiracy*, p. 33.

37. Ibid.

38. E. D. Hirsch, Jr., *Cultural Literacy: What Every American Needs to Know* (New York: Vintage Books, 1987). To become part of the Core Knowledge Network write to this address:
Core Knowledge Foundation
2012-B Morton Drive
Charlottesville, VA 22901.

39. E. D. Hirsch, Jr., ed., *What Your 2nd Grader Needs to Know: Fundamentals of a Good Second-Grade Education* (New York: Dell), 1993.

40. See Hirsch, *Cultural Literacy*.

41. Ibid., p. 135.

42. Ibid.

43. Ibid., pp. 135–36.

44. Hirsch, *What Your 2nd Grader Needs to Know*, p. 5.

45. Ibid., pp. 5–6.

46. Ibid., p. 2.

47. Ibid., p. 74.

48. Ibid., pp. 75–81.

49. Ibid., p. 16.

50. Ibid.

51. Ibid., p. 154.

52. Ibid., pp. 155–59.

53. Ibid., pp. 174–76.

54. Ibid., p. 101.

55. Ibid., p. 102.

56. Ibid., p. 112.

57. Ibid., p. 106.

58. Ibid., pp. 128–52.

59. Ibid., p. 98.

60. Richard Barnet and John Cavanagh, *Global Dreams: Imperial Corporations and the New World Order* (New York: Simon & Schuster, 1994), p. 243.

Conclusion: Cultural Tolerance, Social Empowerment, and the Intersection of Cultures in the Global Workforce and Classroom

There are two models for teaching cultural tolerance and social empowerment. One model is exemplified by the Arab World and Islamic Resources and School Services' publication *The Arabs: Activities for the Elementary School Level—The Things That Make for Peace: Empowering Children to Value Themselves and Others*.[1] The emphasis in this model is on teaching cultural tolerance and global peace. An example of the second model can be found in a model lesson written by Christine Sleeter and Carl Grant to exemplify "Education That Is Multicultural and Social Reconstructionist."[2] *Social reconstructionism* in this model refers to the empowerment of students to struggle for social and political justice. In concluding this chapter and book, I will discuss multicultural education in the context of the global workforce.

NATIONALISM, INTERNATIONALISM, AND SOCIAL EMPOWERMENT

The two instructional models I will be discussing highlight some of the tensions in multicultural education. Education for cultural tolerance is often in conflict with nationalist forms of education. This conflict represents the tension between nationalism and internationalism. I have discussed the European Union's efforts at creating Euronationalism and the movement in the United States to teach multicultural education from the perspective that "standard" American culture is superior to other cultures. These educational efforts are designed to promote an allegiance to a particular national culture and government. Ethnocentric education is a form of nationalism designed to win the allegiance of students to a particular culture. In conflict with these nationalist endeavors is the internationalism of world business. Leaping across national and cultural boundaries, international business is interested in promoting cultural tolerance in the workplace and marketplace.

The second model highlights the tension between the economic interests of international business and struggles for political and economic equality. International corporations are interested in multicultural education as a means of maintaining harmonious relations in a multicultural workforce and increasing profits by marketing products in a variety of cultures. Multicultural education for social empowerment can sometimes be in conflict with the profit motive of international business by educating people to struggle for a more even distribution of the world's wealth. On the other hand, international business and advocates of multicultural education for social empowerment can sometimes agree, since it does not threaten profits, on the goals of building cultural tolerance and ending racism and sexism. For instance, many international business leaders might agree with the objectives of cultural tolerance and peace in the following discussion of elementary school activities focused on Arab cultures.

CULTURAL TOLERANCE AND PEACE

This model for teaching tolerance focuses on Arab culture. In part, this particular instructional model is designed to make visible a culture that is often invisible in U.S. society. In *Affirming Diversity,* Sonia Nieto refers to Arabs as the "invisible minority" because her review of research literature uncovered no ethnographic studies of Arab children. In addition, she found that many Arab families assimilated into U.S. culture by anglicizing their surnames. Despite this apparent assimilation of many Arabs, there do exist religious and other organizations that help to maintain Arab languages and customs.[3] One of these organizations, Arab World and Islamic Resources and School Services, has been actively engaged in publishing educational materials designed to reduce anti-Arab feelings resulting from conflicts in the Middle East and terrorist activities in the United States.[4]

The educational goals of *The Arabs: Activities for the Elementary School Level* are teaching tolerance, building self-esteem, and teaching peaceful resolution of conflict. The concern with peace education is placed in the context of the Gulf War. The authors write, "We have been confronted with a Gulf War that has reinforced for our children their own violent behavior and as the violence in television programming continues and escalates we witness the creation of new war toys."[5]

The Arab community again felt criticized after the destruction of the World Trade Center on September 11, 2001. Educational resources began to flow to schools from the Arab World and Islamic Resources and School Services (AWAIR). School lessons on Arab Americans and Islam can be found at the organization's website: http://www.awaironline.org. The organization describes as its goals:

1. Recognizing that no work is of greater importance than the preparation of our young people for their roles as thoughtful and informed citizens of the twenty-first century, and recognizing too that U.S. involvement with the Arab World and with the wider world of Islam is certain to remain close for many years, AWAIR's goal is to increase awareness and understanding of this world region and this world faith through educational outreach at the precollegiate level.
2. At the same time, recognizing that equipping students at all levels to function and contribute within our own diverse society presents a challenge to democracy, AWAIR seeks to increase the larger society's understanding of Arab Americans and of American Muslims as contributors to this society and as citizens with their own unique roles to play as part of a pluralistic America. In this regard, AWAIR shares with critical pedagogists the goal of encouraging voices of students and adults to be nurtured and heard.[6]

The methodology for teaching cultural tolerance and peace education is the examination of similarities between the world's peoples and the teaching of conflict resolution skills. To teach similarities among cultural groups, the curriculum is divided into separate concepts and subject matter under the general heading "People: Alike and Different." The emphasis is on demonstrating Arab activities to non-Arab children. For instance, under the concept "All people need to eat," an "Art Experience" is proposed that involves making a collage of Arab foods; a "Math or Science Experience" involves making a meal of food from Arab lands; and a "Language Experience" involves the study of Arab words for food. Other classroom activities proposed under this concept include making and baking Lahem Ajeen [meat pastries], creating a classroom supermarket of Arab foods, and having students use their imaginations to display "How Arabs Recycle: Corn." The other concepts that are developed using similar Arab-oriented activities are "All people need shelter," "All people need language," "All people need to love & be loved," "All people need art," and "All people need to play."[7]

In addition to the activities designed to teach similarities among the needs of the world's peoples, there are 25 proposed activities designed to build tolerance of Arab culture. For instance, there are four Arab language activities in which students learn Arabic greetings, names, and nursery rhymes. Other activities involve food, housing, dancing, art, folktales, and games. One activity engages children in the building of mud brick houses that are typical of rural villages in the Arab world. In another series of activities, children color pictures that represent Arab folktales. In another activity, students are taught to play the Egyptian game of Seega.

What appears to be lacking in these cultural activities is any suggestion of significant cultural differences between the Arab world and European American culture. As I suggested regarding the clash of Native American and English cultures, there do exist important differences among cultures. For instance, there is no suggestion in the activities of the potential clash in values between Christianity and Moslem religions. There is no discussion of the potential clash between Arab and European American views regarding the role of women in society.

In other words, *The Arabs: Activities for the Elementary School Level* is based on the premise that cultural toleration can be achieved by introducing children to the foods, language, arts, and housing of the world's cultures. The building of cultural toleration, it is assumed, will contribute to world peace. Interestingly, the inherent problem with this approach is voiced in an Afterword to the activities. The Afterword is titled "Johnny, Please Don't Hit" and it is written by Diedra Imara who is a teacher at The Child Unique, Montessori School in Alameda, California, and it deals with some of the problems in peace education.[8]

The Afterword deals with the teaching of conflict resolution skills in the context of the Gulf War. The conflict resolution skills to be taught in this instructional model begin with the teacher listening and observing to determine whether to intervene in a problem situation. If the teacher perceives any unsafe or destructive behavior, then, it is suggested, he or she should intervene immediately. Second, the teacher should provide an opportunity for students to cool off before dealing with the situation. Third, the teacher should have the children restate the problem and explain how they feel. Fourth, the children should be asked if they can think of any choices for what should happen next. And, fifth, the teacher and students should develop a "mutually agreeable solution."[9]

What Diedra Imara discovered with the outbreak of the Gulf War was that building cultural toleration and conflict resolution was not necessarily an answer to real world conflicts. After the Gulf War erupted, she wrote, "I felt like a fool and a liar. I felt undermined by the powers that be. How can I continue to tell the children to 'use their words' and not handle a problem by hitting. . . ." Influenced by television, she found her students coming to school declaring, "We're beating those bad guys!" She discovered friction between her fellow teachers and a general agreement to avoid conflict by not discussing the war. "What did it all mean? Staff to staff, staff to parents, parents to child, staff to children. Where," she asked, "did PEACE education enter?" She found her answer in a world gripped by media stereotypes of savages and barbarians.[10]

Despite her realization that real peace might involve more than cultural toleration and conflict resolution, her final answer was that peace education can and must be taught. "Against all odds," she concludes, "Johnny, please don't hit. . . ."[11] Therefore, from the perspective of these elementary school exercises on Arab culture, peace can be attained by teaching how people are similar; teaching cultural tolerance by introducing students to the foods, language, art, and games of other cultures; and by following the principles of conflict resolution.

MULTICULTURAL EDUCATION FOR SOCIAL EMPOWERMENT AND SOCIAL RECONSTRUCTION

The social empowerment model of instruction is supposed to prepare students to "reconstruct" their political, economic, and social worlds. The term *social reconstruction* originated in the 1930s when, faced with the economic collapse of

the depression, a group of progressive educators believed the only hope for society was educating future citizens to organize a new economic and political
system.[12] Therefore, social reconstruction means literally the preparation of students to reconstruct society. Christine Sleeter and Carl Grant include under the
concept of multicultural education that is social reconstructionist, working for
the interests of oppressed people, social empowerment, developing cooperation and positive self-concepts, and ending racism and sexism.[13] In other
words, multicultural education for social empowerment that is social reconstructionist includes most of the educational goals discussed in the previous
chapters on teaching about racism, sexism, ethnocentric education for dominated groups, and bilingual education. What is added is educating students to
struggle for social empowerment. Multicultural education for social empowerment and reconstruction includes, besides Sleeter and Grant, a number of pio-
neer educators in the field such as Lois Weis, Sonia Nieto, and James Banks.

The pedagogical example that I will use of multicultural education for social empowerment and social reconstruction is Sleeter and Grant's "Putting It
Into Action."[14] This example describes three teachers planning a holistic learning exercise designed to teach students to struggle for social empowerment.
The holistic learning aspect of the exercise involves the teachers planning lessons around a common theme. That theme, besides preparing students for active political and social involvement, becomes a vehicle for teaching U.S. history, general science, and English.

The three teachers team up to present an integrated lesson. The U.S. history
teacher, Liz Harvey, is described as a veteran of peace marches and civil rights
demonstrations of the sixties. The general science teacher, Erick Cosby, is a Vietnam veteran. And the English teacher, Ross Wisser, is described as a sports en-
thusiast.

The three ninth-grade classes are composed of students reflecting a multicultural background. Liz Harvey's class is typical of these three classes. It is
composed of 13 European Americans, 8 African Americans, 3 Mexican Americans, 2 Puerto Ricans, 1 Guatemalan, and 1 Native American. These 28 students
are described as coming from families with incomes below the poverty line. Ten
of the students are reading on or above the ninth-grade level while the other 18
are reading below grade level.

The holistic lesson is planned so that topics are covered from all three
classes. In this example, Liz Harvey is teaching about city government and
local agencies, Erick Cosby is teaching about health, and Ross Wisser is teaching composition. The theme that is decided upon involves the recently announced closing of the local county hospital. The announcement generated a
great deal of local controversy about whether the hospital should be renovated
and how other hospitals in the area would be able to pick up its services.

From the standpoint of Liz Harvey's U.S. history class, an investigation of the
issues involved in the closing of the county hospital would teach students about
the operation of the local government and the way laws are passed. It could also
serve as an introduction to the racial politics of the community. During Erick
Cosby's class, students could investigate the health issues involved in the closing

of the hospital including the role of science and doctors in the decision-making process. And during Ross Wisser's class, students could interview neighborhood people, publish a newspaper on the issue, and write letters to the local newspaper.

In choosing the issue of the closing of the county hospital, the three teachers, according to Sleeter and Grant, are reflecting their beliefs that instructional activities should reflect the students' lives outside school and their economic backgrounds. In addition, the teachers believe that if the students are going to succeed in life they must learn how to negotiate and change the existing political, social, and economic structure of society.

Besides reflecting a holistic approach to learning, the Sleeter and Grant example exemplifies some of the fundamental aspects of the pedagogical principles of Paulo Freire. As I discussed, with regard to teaching about sexism through consciousness raising, one of the important principles is relating the subject matter to the personal lives of the students. This relationship should involve some problem involving issues of social empowerment. In this example, the families of the students, because they are below the poverty line, depend on the county hospital for medical services. The closing of the hospital has a direct impact on the students and their families. In Freire's language, the announcement of the closing of the county hospital is a generative theme that can evoke a whole range of social issues and lead to some form of social action.

Another important principle of Freire's method is that the choice of a generative theme is a product of dialogue between the teachers. In this case, the three teachers worked together to develop a generative theme that would touch the lives of the students and had the potential for generating a larger dialogue about social empowerment issues.

The last important pedagogical principle is that the teachers engage in a dialogue with the students about the generative theme. Teachers should adopt the attitude that they do not know the answers to the problems raised by the generative theme and that any solutions will emerge from the dialogue between the teachers and the students. In this example, the teachers bring their three classes together to discuss the generative theme of the closing of the county hospital. Out of the dialogue with the students will emerge plans for dealing with the generative theme.

Reflecting the emphasis on cooperative learning, which is an important aspect of teaching for social empowerment, it is assumed by the teachers that the students will work in groups. And reflecting the multicultural emphasis, the teachers plan that each group will be integrated according to race, gender, class, and students with disabilities. The social empowerment and social reconstructionist goals of the example are contained in the concluding statements of Liz Harvey and Erick Cosby.

> Liz Harvey: I believe it is important that we guide the class in a way that students learn how the system works and how they can make it work for them.
> Erick Cosby: Anywhere you go in this world, there are people making decisions that will affect your life. You need to know and understand this fact and learn to become a part of the process. Otherwise, those decision makers will make many of your life decisions for you.[15]

In summary, education for social empowerment and social reconstruction includes most of the instructional goals discussed in the chapters on racism, sexism, bilingualism, and cultural tolerance. It diverges from the goals of ethnocentric education by emphasizing instruction about cultural diversity and building tolerance of other cultures. On the other hand, multicultural education for social empowerment and social reconstruction includes the concern of ethnocentric education for the social and economic injustices experienced by members of dominated cultures. And, in the framework of Paulo Freire's pedagogy, education for social empowerment and social reconstruction is designed to liberate all people, including members of the dominant economic and cultural group, from the grip of racism, sexism, and economic and political oppression.

The inherent problems of multicultural education for social empowerment and social reconstruction are in the areas of cultural tolerance and the politics of public schools. It might not be possible or desirable to create tolerance among differing cultures. Cultural relativity assumes that all cultural values are of equal worth. Is this true? Multicultural education for social empowerment and social reconstruction also assumes that public schools can be centers for teaching students to bring about radical social change. But, as I have argued in another book, public schools are inherently conservative.[16] It is hard to imagine any government in the world maintaining public schools that would educate students to reconstruct society. If this were to occur, then it would most likely be an accident of the public school system rather than a planned goal. For those interested in multicultural education for social empowerment and social reconstruction the questions are these: How do we politically organize a public school system so that it can educate students for radical social change? Is it possible?

MULTICULTURALISM
AND THE GLOBAL WORKFORCE

The evaluation of all forms of multicultural education, including the tolerance and social empowerment models, must be made in the context of the global economy. As I have discussed throughout this book, one of the major contributors to the growth of multicultural education is the global workforce. Workers migrate throughout the world in search of the highest wages, while international corporations shift their industrial sites in search of the lowest wages. Workers in the United States are now part of a global workforce. Consequently, since the 1970s, there has been a steady decline in real wages as corporations move their plants abroad and immigrants entering the United States accept jobs at lower wages. Since 1973, real wages have declined by about 9 percent in the United States.[17]

In addition, corporations are able to cut costs by hiring part-time workers who are not given the benefits of pension plans and health insurance. Between 1980 and 1987, half of all new jobs were for part-time workers.[18] In a newspaper article that expresses concern that U.S. high school graduates can no longer look forward to manufacturing jobs paying more than $12 per hour, Chuck W.

Thomson, vice president of personnel for Federal Express, told a reporter, "We try to be very up-front about it. We tell them [high school graduates] they should take this job with the understanding that it will be part-time indefinitely."[19] In the same article, Jack Overbrook, the head of personnel for Kroger supermarkets, said that they offer high school graduates entry level jobs for $4.50 an hour with promotion to a full-time job and a wage of $7 to $8 an hour in 3 or 4 years.[20]

While the growth of a global workforce is resulting in a worldwide leveling of wages, which for U.S. citizens means a lowering of wages, there still continue patterns of racial and sexual discrimination. For instance, about four-fifths of the economic activity on earth takes place in the two dozen richest nations—the countries of Western Europe, the United States, Canada, Japan, Australia, New Zealand, and South Africa. These are the countries with the highest concentration of the world's wealth and the highest wages. Except for Japan and South Africa, the majority of people in these countries are white or, in other words, of European descent. And in South Africa, the wealth is held by those of European ancestry.[21]

In contrast to these wealthier nations, 40 of the poorest nations are in Africa and Latin America. Most of these countries export one or more natural resources. They exist in a state of economic exploitation by the wealthier nations. Barnet and Cavanagh put these countries at the bottom of the global economic pyramid. The 47 poorest nations, which are almost all in Africa, are not even part of the global economic pyramid. In the words of Barnet and Cavanagh, "They are so poor that their economic connection with the rest of the world is pretty much limited to cashing relief checks and opening bags of food from government and private relief agencies . . . they remain locked into a cycle of poverty and dependency."[22]

Therefore, the global workplace and workforce is divided along racial lines with whites and Japanese at the top of the economic pyramid and people of color at the bottom. In addition, the global workforce is being divided by gender. In what Barnet and Cavanagh call the "feminization" of the global workforce, international corporations are seeking female employees for manufacturing jobs because they can pay them less money. A Malaysian investment brochure designed to lure U.S. industries promises, after a description of the efficiency of the "oriental" girl, that "female factory workers can be hired for approximately US $1.50 a day."[23] An ad from El Salvador promises U.S. companies female workers for 57 cents an hour who "are known for their industriousness, reliability, and quick learning."[24] In India, 5 million women spend their days making cigarettes at home. In the United States, the large numbers of women entering the workforce work harder and receive lower pay than men. On the average, women in the United States earn 69 percent of what men earn.[25]

Consider the global workforce from the perspective of a U.S. employer interested in keeping wages down and maximizing profits. First, the employer would be interested in increasing the immigration of foreign workers into the United States. By simply increasing the number of workers in the labor pool, the employer could probably pay lower wages and provide fewer benefits. In addition, since most of these immigrants come from countries with low wages, they will often accept lower salaries and benefits than native U.S. workers. In addition, the employer might be interested in reducing costs by hiring only part-time workers who would not be given benefit packages. And, since women earn less than men, it would be cheaper to hire only women. And, if employers feel that they are paying too much in wages and benefits in the United States, they can move their companies to another nation where they can employ women of color and provide no benefits.

Now consider the impact of this global workforce on classrooms in the United States. Obviously, as I have discussed throughout this book, the global workforce is filling classrooms with students representing a variety of cultures and languages. In addition, it is resulting in U.S. schools functioning as welfare agencies and as surrogate parents. As real wages decline, more family members must enter the workforce to keep family income above the poverty line. This means that for most families both the mother and father must work. Many children go home to empty houses. In addition, with the rise of part-time work and the decline of employer benefits, many families must increasingly rely on welfare agencies for medical, dental, and other services. Even some working parents now live below the poverty line.

Therefore, one of the major effects of the global workforce is a call for the establishment of closer linkages between schools and social services. Illustrating this concern is the publication of the 1994 yearbook of the Politics of Education Association titled *The Politics of Linking Schools and Social Services*. In recognition of the new economic conditions in the United States, the editors, Louise Adler and Sid Gardner, argue for a new organization structure to U.S. education that will link "schools and social services . . . once provided by separate organizations."[26] Thus, the global workforce produces the multicultural classroom and contributes to making the school a welfare institution.

Therefore, the global workforce is not only changing the composition of U.S. classrooms, but it is also expanding the social role of public schools. In addition, the problems facing the global workforce highlight the concerns of multicultural educators with issues of cultural domination, exploitation of people of color, sexism, and growing economic inequalities. Can education for cultural tolerance and social empowerment overcome these problems? Is multicultural education the solution for the growing inequalities in the global economy?

CONCLUSION: THE INTERSECTION OF CULTURES IN THE CLASSROOM

The debate about multicultural education will continue as societies adjust to a global economy and workforce. The spread of a world culture will probably continue to be resisted by dominated cultural groups. The debate includes advocates of multicultural education for social empowerment, ethnocentric education for dominated groups, and ethnocentric education for dominant groups.

Each set of advocates envisions a different future for the global economy. Advocates of multicultural education for social empowerment envision a future of political and economic equality where differing social groups live in tolerance of each other. Advocates of ethnocentric education for dominated groups envision a future where people of color are able to overthrow the domination of European cultural traditions and end economic oppression. They envision a future where people of color achieve equality of political, economic, and cultural power. And advocates of ethnocentric education for dominant cultures envision the continuing importance of European and European American cultural traditions in the world economy. To understand this debate, the reader needs to appreciate the importance of cultural difference and the effect of cultural domination. In addition, any advocate of cultural tolerance must grapple with the effects of different cultural frames of reference.

As a summary of these issues, I will describe the intersection of cultures at Rachel L. Carson Intermediate School in the Flushing, Queens, section of New York City. The students at this school come from 60 countries with nearly half being born outside the United States. Immigrant students enter a different culture when they go through the school's doors. For many of them it is unusual not to bow to the teacher or stand when the teacher enters the room. Over 50 languages and dialects are spoken by the students. The school has adapted to these language problems by employing three English as a Second Language (ESL) teachers, a Korean and Chinese bilingual education teacher, and 10 paraprofessionals speaking languages ranging from Persian to Pashto.[27]

An example of gender relations in the intersection of immigrant and U.S. cultures is the friendship of a 16-year-old Indian girl, Nitu Singh, and a 15-year-old Indian boy, Jatinder Singh. In the culture of India, it would not have been proper for a boy and girl of this age to be close friends. But the immigrant experience, language problems, and the culture of the U.S. schools brought them together. Nitu Singh was in her second year of the ESL program when Jatinder Singh, knowing no English, entered the country. Since they shared the same native language of Punjabi, Nitu became his guide through the culture of the school. Nitu had to demonstrate how to use the combination lock on Jatinder's locker 15 times before he could do it. She introduced him to the mysteries of the school cafeteria and acted as a guide in learning English.

The cultural transformations taking place in the school are exemplified by a Muslim student from Iran, Salima Nabizada. Muslim religious practices require that girls keep their heads covered. For her first 6 months at school, Salima frequently had her headscarf ripped off by other students. She told a school counselor, "I would feel like everybody was looking at me. I wore it, and they took it off. And so I went home and told my mother I don't want to wear it anymore. I can't. It's so hard."[28] She now wears a T-shirt, jeans, and a black hair band.

The desire to fit in causes many of the children to adapt quickly to U.S. culture. Lia Hou, 14, complained that when she first arrived from Taiwan, "I felt excluded from the group because you look different, because you don't dress the way they do. I wanted to be part of them." When 15-year-old Eli Pantazis left her small Greek village in Albania she did not speak English and had never heard of Michael Jackson. There was no telephone in her village and the women did not wear makeup until marriage. Now Eli uses a plum-colored lipstick and is a fan of Michael Jackson's sister, Janet. While she claims not to remember a word of Albanian, she still speaks Greek.

Both Lia Hou and Eli Pantazis play an important function in their families' adaptation to U.S. society. Their education in U.S. schools has taught them the valuable tool of English. They both function as translators for their families. They help their families deal with banks, credit card companies, utilities, and other contacts requiring a use of English.

Will a global culture emerge from the type of multicultural schools represented by the Rachel L. Carson Intermediate School? Will this global culture be dominated by U.S. popular culture? Will it be a hybrid of all the world's cultures? Writer Dan Hofstadter thinks that fashion trends indicate that a blend of cultural styles are composing the new world culture. He writes, after attending the 1994 spring fashion week in Paris, "Everybody's wearing somebody else's national hat. The French call it *metissage,* or cultural miscegenation, and it's been going on for about the last 5,000 seasons, or at least since the ancient Egyptians took to wearing Greek sandals."[29] But, from Hofstadter's perspective, there is something different about the current cultural miscegenation. In his words, the difference is "the delight in raiding across class, ethnic, age and gender lines, the coolness of being confused of being weird, of being all-turned-around."[30] Is this the world culture of the future?

As exemplified by the intersection of cultures at the Rachel L. Carson Intermediate School, teachers in U.S. schools today must understand the differing cultural frames of reference brought to class by their students. In addition, they need to understand how different cultures intersect with the culture of U.S. public schools. Since racism and sexism persist in the global economy, educators need to avoid racist and sexist behavior and to know how to teach antiracist and antisexist attitudes. With the global workforce comes the language diversity of the modern classroom. Teachers need to understand the problems of cross-cultural communications and the language barriers that can exist in the classroom. And, as people of color continue to be exploited in the global economy, teachers need to appreciate Afrocentric education and the arguments for cultural literacy.

PERSONAL FRAMES OF REFERENCE

Your vision of the future of education is directly related to your vision of the world's future.

1. What do you think should be the organization of the global economy?
2. What do you think should be the role of schools in the global economy?
3. What do you think is the best form of multicultural education?
4. How would you adapt your teaching methods for the cultural and language diversity represented at the Rachel L. Carson Intermediate School?

Notes

1. Audrey Shabbas, Carol El-Shaieb, and Ahlam An-Nabulsi, *The Arabs: Activities for the Elementary School Level—The Things That Make for Peace: Empowering Children to Value Themselves and Others* (Berkeley: Arab World and Islamic Resources and School Services, 1991).
2. Christine Sleeter and Carl A. Grant, *Making Choices for Multicultural Education: Five Approaches to Race, Class, and Gender* (New York: Macmillan Publishing Company, 1994). The case study is titled "Putting It Into Action" on pages 232–34.
3. Sonia Nieto, *Affirming Diversity: The Sociopolitical Context of Multicultural Education* (White Plains: Longman Inc., 1992), pp. 133–40.
4. For a catalogue of publications write to:
    Arab World and Islamic Resources and School Services
    1400 Shattuck Ave., Suite 9
    Berkeley, CA 94709.
5. Shabbas et al., p. 1.
6. "About Us," http://www.awaironline.org/aboutus.htm.
7. Ibid., pp. 6–7.
8. Diedra Imara, "Johnny, Please Don't Hit" in Shabbas et al., pp. 55–56.
9. Shabbas et al., p. 5.
10. Imara, pp. 56–57.
11. Ibid., p. 56.
12. Joel Spring, *The American School 1642–1993* (New York: McGraw-Hill, 1994), pp. 294–96.
13. Sleeter and Grant, p. 231.
14. Ibid., pp. 232–234.
15. Ibid., p. 234.
16. Joel Spring, *Conflict of Interests: The Politics of American Education,* 4th ed. (White Plains: Longman Inc., 2002).
17. Richard J. Barnet and John Cavanagh, *Global Dreams: Imperial Corporations and the New World Order* (New York: Simon and Schuster, 1994), p. 293.
18. Ibid., p. 293.
19. Peter T. Kilborn, "For High School Graduates, A Job Market of Dead Ends," *The New York Times,* 30 May 1994, pp. 1–23.
20. Ibid., p. 23.
21. Barnet and Cavanagh, p. 284.
22. Ibid., p. 287.
23. Ibid., p. 325.
24. Ibid., p. 325.
25. Ibid., p. 293.
26. Louise Adler and Sid Garner, "Introduction and Overview," *The Politics of Linking Schools and Social Services,* ed. Louise Adler and Sid Garner (Washington, DC: Falmer Press, 1994), p. 2.
27. Charisse Jones, "Melting Pot Still Bubbles at I.S. 237," *The New York Times,* 12 June 1994, pp. 41, 48.
28. Ibid., p. 48.
29. Dan Hofstadter, "The Lonely Crowd," *The New York Times Magazine,* 12 June 1994, p. 66.
30. Ibid.

Index

"A Better Chance" (ABC) program, 22–24, 26

A Darker Shade of Crimson: Odyssey of a Harvard Chicano (Navarette), 111

Ability grouping, 145, 148

Absenteeism, 149

Academic competition, 158

Adler, Louise, 254

Adonnino Committee, 92–93

Adult-training programs, 215

Advani, Balu, 66

Affirmative action, 112

Affirming Diversity: The Sociopolitical Context of Multicultural Education (Nieto), 57, 109, 247

African Americans
 "acting white," 149, 152, 158
 bicultural frame of reference, 111
 bidialecticalism, 47
 Black consciousness, 234, 236, 238
 cultural frames of reference, 114
 double consciousness and, 44
 educational efforts, 46–47
 educational history of, 132
 encounter stage, 116–117
 oral tradition of, 45
 positive role models, 235–236
 pre-encounter stage, 115
 resistance and, 149, 151
 rites of passage program, 238

African Americans *(Cont.):*
 slavery and, 8, 44
 textbooks and, 125–126

African cultures, 40–48

Afrocentric education, 48, 50, 124, 229–230
 Classical Africa, 229–230, 233–234, 236
 conspiracy to destroy black boys, 234–236
 contribution of Egypt, 231–232
 holistic learning, 233
 Kemet question, 230–231
 personal witnessing, 233–234

Afrocentricity, 229

Afrocentricity (Asante), 229

Alford, Thomas, 156

Ali Mohamed, Abdulhakim, 77

Alienation, 156–158

All-girls schools, 194, 196

American Association of University Women, 196

American (U.S.) culture
 American Empire (lesson), 60
 black mobility and assimilation, 21–24
 characteristics of, 13
 consumer icons of, 10
 cross-cultural marriages, 11
 cultural freedom and, 11–13
 culture of economic success, 20–21

American Association of University
Women *(Cont.):*
culture of fear, 4, 13
defining of, 14–20
dominant culture, 21
economic success and, 17, 20–21
general culture of, 5–7, 34
historical conflicts of, 8–9, 13
language and culture in,
207–209
lesson for, 18
major contradiction of, 10–11
as melting pot, 17
multicultural education and, 14,
34–35
as multicultural society, 11
multiculturalism and, 13–14
personal freedom, 11
popular culture, 107
white Anglo-Saxon values,
28–29
American English, 96
American Indian Movement, 13
American Sign Language (ASL),
203–205
Americanization programs, 17
An UnAmerican Childhood
(Kimmage), 64–66
Anderson, James, 46
*Anti-Bias Curriculum: Tools for
Empowering Young Children,*
177–178
Antibias curriculum, 177–179
Antischool attitudes, 149
Apaches, 113–114
Apoliona, H., 54
Arab Americans, 246–247
Arab World and Islamic Resources
and School Services (AWAIR),
246–248
*Arabs: Activities for the Elementary
School Level–The Things that Make
for Peace: Empowering Children to
Value Themselves and Others*
(Shabbas, El-Shaieb, and
An-Nabulsi), 246–247, 249

Ariane program, 93
Asante, Molefi Kete, 48–49, 118,
228–234, 236, 243
Asian Americans
academic achievement, 155
Confucian values of, 154–155
dominated and immigrant
cultures, 154–156
family values, 155
language issues among, 214–215
male roles, 136–137
as "model" minority, 116
power elite and, 26
stereotyping of, 116
textbooks, 128
Asian Indian immigrants, 81, 84
Asian Pacific immigrants, 81
educational attainment of, 81
English proficiency, 84
occupational attainment of, 81
Association of Bilingual
Education, 210
Australian English, 96
Autonomy, 176
Aviles, Pedro, 207–208
Axtell, James, 30
Ayach, Souhair, 75

"Bad boy rule," 192
Baldwin, James, 47
Banks, James, 56–57, 250
Barnet, Richard, 243, 253
Bell, Alexander Graham, 204
Bell, Lee, 57
Belonging, 119
Beloved (Morrison), 46
Benham, Maenette K., 52, 54–55
Bessie, Delany, 133
Biculturalism, 22, 47, 50, 79–80,
108–114, 118
Bidialecticalism, 47
Big Brothers, 238
Bilingual education, 38, 58, 98, 203,
209–211
maintenance, 210

Bilingual education (Cont.):
  multicultural and language debate,
    217–221
  problems in, 213–214
  research and corporate support for,
    211–213
  transitional programs, 210
  two-way bilingual education, 210
Bilingual Education Act of 1968, 209
Black consciousness, 234, 236, 238
Black Culture and Black Consciousness:
    Afro-American Folk Thought from
    Slavery to Freedom (Levine), 45
Black militants, 118
Black mobility
  biculturalism and, 23
  dominant culture and, 21–24
  prep school education, 23
  skin color and, 22
Black power movement, 126
Black rage, 173
Black in the White Establishment?: A
    Study of Race and Class in
    American ad Diversity in the
    Power Elite (Zweigenhaft and
    Domhoff), 20
Boarding schools, 131, 138, 157, 218
Boorstin, Daniel, 126
Bourdieu, Pierre, 23
Bourgeois Blues (Lamar), 140
Bowling for Columbine, 4
Boy Scouts, 238
Bridging Japanese/North American
    Differences (Gudykunst and
    Nishida), 206
British English, 96
Brown decision, 197
Brown, Dee, 49
Brown, Kevin, 39
Brown, Maccene, 23
Brown, Michael, 235
Brunt, Lloyd Van, 173–174
Burchfield, Robert, 96
Bury My Heart at Wounded Knee: An
    Indian History of the American
    West (Brown), 49

Calvinism, 31
Cambodian immigrants, 73–75
Capitalism, 144
Cassadore, Elenore, 128, 131
Cassasquillo, Angela, 159
Catovic, Abir, 77
Cavanagh, John, 243, 253
Central American immigrants, 154
Cha Shou C., 71–74
Chang-Lin Tien, 26
Chavez, Gene T., 210
Cheng, Li Rong Lilly, 214–215
Cherokee language, 38–40
Cherokee Phoenix, 38
Child centered (Maori) model, 226
Children; see also Immigrant children
  antibias curriculum, 177–179
  indigenous education models,
    224–226
China Boy (Lee), 136–137
Chinese immigrants, 80–81
Choctaws, 30–31
Cicero, 167
Citadel, 197
Citizenship, 171
Civil rights groups, 125–126
Civil rights movement, 17, 21–22,
    29, 131
Clan system, 31
Clark, Edward, 190
Classical Africa (Asante), 229–230,
    233–234, 236
Classroom
  glass ceiling and, 191–194
  intersection of cultures in, 254–256
  sex bias in, 192–193
  single-sex classrooms, 194–197
Cleveland, Grover, 53
Clinton, Bill, 26, 74
Cochiti Pueblo education model, 228
Cohen, Leah, 203
Cold War, 4
Coleman, Michael, 157
Coleman, William T., Jr., 22
Cologne conference, 93–94
COMENIUS plan, 95

Common schools, 144
Communicating Effectively in Multicultural Contexts, 206
Communications, 203, 205–206
Competition, 160
Confederate flag, 9, 12
Confucian values, 154–155
Consciousness raising, 57, 197–198
Consumerism, 4, 8–11, 13, 17
Contact, in identity formation, 176
Cooper, Joanne, 226
Core knowledge, 241–243
Core Knowledge curriculum, 224
Core Knowledge Foundation, 239
Core values, 29
Corporate cooperation, 160
Corporate culture, 145, 215–217
Corporate efficiency, 145
Corporate model of schooling, 145
Corporate structure, 147
Counseling, 148
Countering the Conspiracy to Destroy Black Boys (Kunjufu), 136
Critical pedagogy, 57–58
Cross-cultural communications, 203, 205–206
Cross, William, 108, 111, 115–18
Crow Dog, Mary, 133, 136
Crystal, David, 95
Cultural capital, 23–24, 26
Cultural conflicts, 158–160
   competition vs. competition, 158–159
   individualism, 158–159
Cultural diversity, economic success vs., 26–27
Cultural domination
   African-European American cultures, 40–48
   voluntary immigration and, 39–40
Cultural frames of reference, 107–108, 114
   cultural perspective (lesson), 110
   folk history, 124, 128–132
   gender, 132–137
   monoculturalism and biculturalism, 109–114

Cultural frames of reference *(Cont.):*
   official history, 124–128
   social class, 137–140
Cultural freedom, 11–13
Cultural identity, 13, 58, 115
Cultural immersion, 218
Cultural literacy, 17, 27–28, 217, 239
   defined, 27
   multicultural education and language issues, 217
   poverty and, 28
Cultural Literacy: What Every American Needs to Know (Hirsch), 239
Cultural miscegenation *(metissage),* 256
Cultural perspectives, 107–108
Cultural power, 59–61
Cultural rights, 97
Cultural rights (lesson), 99
Cultural self-identification
   cultural flag (lesson), 15
   identifying the "other" (lesson), 16
Cultural tolerance, peace and, 247–249
Cultural unity, 26–27
Cultural values, 50
Culture; *see also* Intersection of cultures
   American; *see* American (U.S.) culture
   corporate culture, 145, 215–217
   defined, 3, 13
   dominant culture; *see* Dominant culture
   dominated; *see* Dominated cultures
   emotion and, 8–9
   general culture, 3
   global culture, 4
   identification of, 13
   language and power, 203–205
   melting pot, 17
   multicultural love, 10
   public schools, 144
   relationship to language, 203–205

Culture of economic success, 17; *see also* Power elite
Culture and Education Policy in Hawaii: The Silencing of Native Voices (Benham and Heck), 52, 55
Culture of fear, 4, 13
Culture of poverty, 14
Culture of power, 59
Cultures values, public schools, 144
Cummins, Jim, 213
Curricula
  antibias curriculum, 177–179
  Core Knowledge curriculum, 224

Davila, Burt, 73
Day, Jennifer, 19–20
Deaf culture, 203
Deaf pride and power movement, 203, 205
Declaration on European Identity, 92
Decline of the Californios: A Social History of the Spanish-Speaking California, The (Pitt), 132
Delany, Bessie, 114, 119
Delpit, Lisa, 59, 61, 218–219
Derman-Sparks, Louise, 178
Dhillon, Mandeep Singh, 66
Disintegration stage, 176
Disuniting of America, The (Schlesinger), 28
Diversity, 88; *see also* Language diversity
  multicultural education and language issues, 217
  public school diversity parade (lesson), 67–69
Dole, Sanford, 53
Domhoff, G. William, 20–24, 26, 138
Dominant culture
  American culture, 21, 35
  black mobility and, 21–24
  cultural literacy and, 27–28
  multicultural education and language issues, 217

Dominant culture *(Cont.):*
  teaching value of, 29–30, 35
  as white Anglo-Saxon values, 28–29
Dominated cultures, 17, 35, 38, 108
  access to power preparation, 59–60
  classroom instruction (lesson), 51
  defined, 39
  education based on, 50
  educational questions of, 39–40
  ethnocentric education, 48–49
  family multicultural tree (lesson), 41–43
  misinterpretation of cues, 113
  multicultural education and language issues, 217
  resistance of, 149–152
  textbook inclusion and, 126
  white trash as, 54–56
Douglas, Frederick, 176
Driscoll, Marie, 24
DuBois, W.E.B., 44–47, 176, 237
Dugger, Celia, 80
Duroselle, Baptiste, 93
Dustitiis, Bernard, 90

Economic individualism, 34
Economic success; *see also* Black mobility; Power elite
  American culture of, 20–21
  cultural diversity vs., 26–27
  culture of, 17
  education and, 19
  gender and, 19
  Hawaiian culture and, 52–54
  race and, 19–20
Educating New Americans: Immigrant Lives and Learning (Hones and Cha Shou), 71–72
Education; *see also* Public schools
  Afrocentric; *see* Afrocentric education
  bilingual; *see* Bilingual education
  dominated cultures debate, 50

Education *(Cont.)*:
  for economic success, 19
  European Union's policy, 3, 92–95
  holistic education, 226–227
  income and, 138
  indigenous education models,
    224–226
  inequality in, 148–149
  multicultural; *see* Multicultural
    education
  resistance to, 149–152, 160
Educational Rights Amendment,
  98–102
Edwards, John, 31
Egypt, 231–232
Elite boarding schools, 128, 218–219
Emigration; *see also* Immigrant
    cultures
  cultural divide of, 65
  psychological and social
    consequences of, 64–66
Emotions
  culture and, 8–9
  imagined memories and, 9
  lessons on emotions and
    history, 12
Empire (Hardt and Negri), 3
Empowerment
  defined, 56
  multicultural education and
    language
    issues, 217
  self-esteem and, 57
  social empowerment; *see* Social
    empowerment
  through multicultural education,
    56–59
Encounter stage, 116–117
English language, as imperialism,
  95–96
English Language, The (Burchfield), 96
English-only movement, 210
English proficiency, 84
English as a Second Language (ESL),
  73, 96, 210–11, 215
Enryo (reserve or restraint), 206

Epstein, Terrie, 126
Equality of opportunity, 144–145
ERASMUS plan, 95
Escuela Fratney, La, 180–181
Estrich, Susan, 196
Ethnic correctness, 118
Ethnic group, 114
Ethnic identity, 118–119, 211
  defined, 115
  development of, 114–119
  encounter stage, 116–117
  immersion-emersion stage, 117
  immersion stage, 117–118
  internalization stage, 118–119
  lesson plan for, 120
  pre-encounter stage, 115–116
Ethnic studies, 57
Ethnocentric education, 224–243;
    see also Afrocentric education
  Asante's *Classical Africa*, 228–233
  child centered (Maori), 226
  Columbus's voyage (lesson), 240
  cultural perspective of, 48
  defined, 48
  dominated cultures, 48–50
  holistic education (Okanagan),
    225–227, 233
  indigenous education models,
    224–226
  multicultural education and
    language issues, 217
  native people and spirituality
    of all life (Cochiti
    Pueblo), 228
  stimulating and language-
    based education (Native
    Hawaiian), 227
  three baskets of knowledge
    (Maori), 227
*Eurolit: The Study of Literature in
    Europe* (Cologne University), 93
Euronationalism, 92
Europe—A History of Its Peoples
    (Duroselle), 93
European American culture, 40
European Commission, 93

European Community, 93
European Economic Community, 92
European Educational Projects, 95
European Union (EU)
   COMENIUS plan, 95
   educational plans of, 3, 92–95
   ERASMUS plan, 95
   LINGUA program, 94
   multiple language policy, 94
   SOCRATES program, 95
   unity with diversity, 92–95
Europeanism, 3

Failing at Fairness: How America's
   Schools Cheat Girls (Sadker and
   Frazier), 191
Family multicultural tree (lesson),
   41–43
Faulkner, Shannon, 197
Faulkner, William, 9
Fedullo, M., 113, 128
Female domination, 189
Female emancipation, 189
Foggin, John, 216
Folk history, 124, 128–132
Forked Tongue: The Politics of Bilingual
   Education (Porter), 210
Foster, William, 23
Founding Fathers, 170–171
France, 88, 90
Franklin, Benjamin, 170, 207
Fratney Elementary School,
   180–181, 212
Frazier, Nancy, 191
Freedom, 11
Freire, Paulo, 57–58, 197–198
Friedan, Betty, 191
Frost, Robert, 126

Gallaudet, Edward Miner, 204
Gallaudet University, 205
Gangs, 73
Gardner, Sid, 254
Gates, Henry Louis, Jr., 22, 184

Gender, 123, 132–137;
   see also Women
  in advertising (lesson), 188
  Asian women, 135
  economic success and, 19
  family teaching on
    (lesson), 134
  immigrant families, 133
  male roles, 136
  women's rights and, 133
Gender discrimination, 187
General culture, 3
Genocide, 4, 29, 31–32, 125, 141
German-American Anti-Defamation
   League, 116
Girls' Clubs of America, 193
Givens, W. E., 53
Glass ceiling, 191–194, 199
Glass Ceiling Commission, 22
Glenn, Alan, 23
Global culture, 4
Global economy
  clothing labels and cheap labor
    (lesson), 89
  English language in, 96
  multiculturalism in, 88–102
  "new world teens," 3
  racism and, 182–184
  right to language and culture,
    96–98
Global workforce
  feminization of, 253
  multiculturalism and, 252–254
Globalization and Educational Rights
   (Spring), 98
Goizueta, Roberto, 26
Goldberg, Carol, 24
Goldstein, Laurie, 66, 70
Gonzalez, David, 79
Gonzalez, Gilbert, 209
Gonzalez, Jose, 210
Googer, Greg, 23
Gordon-Reed, Annette, 166
Gottlieb, Alma, 47
Grant, Carl, 56, 246, 250
Group identity, 123

Gudykunst, William, 206–207
Gun violence, 4

Hacker, Andrew, 167, 172–173, 192
Hardt, Michael, 3
Hawaiian culture
   Kamehameha Early Education
      Program (KEEP), 54
   Native ways and Western
      views, 66
   pidgin English, 52–53
   teaching of, 52–54
Hawkins, Joseph, 179–180
Heck, Ronald H., 52, 54–55
Heller, Carol, 180
Helms, Janet, 176
Hemings, Sally, 165–166
Hindu Heritage Summer
   Camp, 66
Hirsch, E. D., 27–29, 34, 217, 224,
   239, 241–243
History
   educational history, 131–132
   folk history, 124, 128–132
   official history, 124–128
   oral history, 123, 230
   resistance to public
      education, 151
Hmong immigrants, 71–74
Hofstadter, G., 256
Holistic education, 226–227, 233
Hones, David, 71–74
Honig, Bill, 29
How the Irish Became White
   (Ignatiev), 55
Hughes, Langston, 47
Hune, Shirley, 135
Hunger of Memory (Rodriquez), 158
"Hyphenated Americans," 135

Identity
   cultural identity, 13, 58, 115
   ethnic; see Ethnic identity
   formation of, 176

Identity (Cont.):
   group identity, 123
   individual identity, 123
   self-identity, 128
   white identity; see White racial
      identity development
Identity crisis, 112
Ignatiev, Noel, 55
Igoa, Christina, 84, 112–113
Illinois Math and Science
   Academy, 196
Ima, Kenji, 214–215
"Image of Man" (Brown), 235
Imagined memories, 9
Imara, Diedra, 249
Immersion-emersion, 117, 176
Immersion stage, 117–118
Immigrant children, 70–71
   biculturalism of, 112
   negative stereotyping of, 116
Immigrant cultures, 17, 64, 108
   Cambodian immigrants, 73–75
   challenges of, 66
   educational experience of,
      80–84
   educational program design
      (lesson), 85
   family multicultural tree (lesson),
      82–83
   gender roles, 133
   Hmong immigrants, 71–73
   language map (lesson), 78
   maintaining traditional
      language/cultures, 66
   Mexican immigrants, 77–79
   migratory causes (lesson), 76
   Muslim schools, 75–77
   summer camps for traditional
      language/cultures, 66, 70–71
   teacher guidelines, 84
   transnationalism and, 79–80
Immigration, 4
   psychological strain of, 113
Imperialism, 11, 170, 225
   English language as, 95–96
Imperium romanum, 167

In Our Mother's Voice: Educational Models for Native Communities (Kape'ahiokalani Padeken Ah Nee-Benham and Cooper), 226
Income
  education and, 138
  social class and, 137
Indian Citizenship Act, 170
Indian English, 96
Indian Peace Commission report, 207
Indigenous education models, 224–226
  Afrocentric pedagogy, 229–230
  Asante's classical Africa model, 228–229
  child centered (Maori) model, 226
  holistic education (Okanagan) model, 226–227
  multilinugalism of, 225
  native people and spirituality of life (Cochiti Pueblo), 228
  stimulating and language-based education (Native Hawaiian), 227
  three baskets of knowledge (Maori), 227
Individual economic achievement, 144, 147
Individual identity, 123
Individualism, 34, 144, 147, 158–160
Inequality, 144–149, 160
  in education, 148–149
Inner World of the Immigrant Child, The (Igoa), 84–86, 112
Institutional racism, 234
Internalization, 118–119
International Labour Organization's Convention No. 169, 98
Internationalism, 246–247
Intersection of cultures
  African and European American cultures, 40–48
  alienation, 156–158
  in the classroom, 254–256

Intersection of cultures *(Cont.):*
  concept of, 14
  cultural conflicts, 158–160
  cultural frames of reference and, 107–108
  dominated cultures and immigrant cultures, 108
  emotions and, 9
  Hawaiian culture and western views, 52–55
  Latinos/Latinas and school culture, 153–154
  Native American and English cultures, 30–34
  school culture and dominated/immigrant cultures, 144–151
Islamic schools, 75
Italian-American League to Combat Defamation, 116

Jackson, Andrew, 32
Jain, Anshu, 80
Japan, 9, 206–207
Jasmine (Mukherjee), 11, 117, 135
Jefferson, Thomas, 165–166
Jefferson and the New Nation (Peterson), 166
Jefferson the President, First Term, 1801–1805 (Malone), 166
Jeffries, Leonard, 34
Jensen, Arthur, 173
Jews, 24
Jim Crow laws, 133
Jordan, Winthrop, 126
Joy Luck Club, The (Tan), 135

Kachru, Braj B., 95–96
Kaestle, Carl, 144
Kamehameha Early Education Program (KEEP), 54
Kanner, Bernice, 10
Kape'ahiokalani Padeken Ah Nee-Benham, Maenette, 226

Keeping Track: How Schools Structure Inequality (Oakes), 148
Kemet, 230–231
Kennedy, John F., 126
Kett, Joseph, 27, 239
Khmer Rouge, 74
Kimmage, Ann, 64–66, 70, 73
King, Martin Luther, Jr., 116, 176
Kitchen God's Wife, The (Tan), 136
Koreans, 114, 155–156
Kotahwala, Shyama Devi, 80
Kotlowitz, Alex, 140
Kozol, Jonathan, 138, 140, 148
Kramer, Betty Jo, 152
Kunjufu, Jawanza, 49, 136, 149, 157, 229, 234–238, 243

Lakota Woman (Crow Dog), 133
Lamar, Jake, 140, 171
Language diversity, 202–221
    Asian Americans and, 214–215
    bilingual education, 209–213
    cross-cultural communications, 205–206
    cultural differences in, 207
    culture and power, 203–205
    Japan-U.S. communication, 206–207
    language of corporation, 215–217
    language, culture, and power, 203–205
    misinterpretations of messages, 205–206
    No Child Left Behind and English acquisition (lesson), 220
    problems in bilingual education programs, 213–214
    research and corporate support for, 211–213
    in United States, 207–209
Language segregation, 52
Latino Civic Rights Task Force, 207
Latinos/Latinas, 7–8
    eye contact, 113
    intersection of cultures, 153–154
    power elite and, 26

Lee, Eugene, 47
Lee, Gus, 136–137
Lee, Helen, 135
Lee Hsien Loong, 91–92
Lee, Larry, 202
Lee, Valerie, 196–197
Lee, Yongsook, 154–156
Lelloche, Pierre, 90
Lessons from History: A Celebration in Blackness (Kunjufu), 236–238
Levine, Lawrence, 45, 48
Lexington School for the Deaf, 203–204
Liberal educators, 59
Liberty, 11
Light of the Feather: Pathways Through Contemporary Indian Culture (Fedullo), 113
Lili'uokalani, Queen, 53
LINGUA program, 94
Linguistic rights, 97
Linguistic rights (lesson), 99
Literacy, 47; *see also* Cultural literacy
Literate communications, 239
Literate persons, 239
Liuzzo, Viola, 176
Locke, John, 189

Mabley, Moms, 48
McClure, David, 32
Macho image, 132, 136–137
Maintenance of culture, 71
Maintenance stage, 210–212
Malcolm X, 126
Mall culture, 13
Malone, Dumas, 166
Marginalization, 46
Martel, Erich, 231–232
"Masculine ethic," 199
Mateo, Fernando, 80
Mathematics instruction, racism and, 181–182
Media, 116
Melting pot, 17

Members of the Club (Driscoll and Goldberg), 24
Metissage (cultural miscegenation), 256
Metzger, Tom, 179
Mexican American Anti-defamation Committee, 116
Mexican Americans, 111–112
  educational history of, 131–132
  English language education, 208–209
  immersion stage, 117
  pre-encounter stage, 115
  resistance of, 153–154
Mexican immigrants, 77–79
Migration, 3, 8, 88
Migratory causes (lesson), 76
Mintz, Sidney, 45
Mitsubishi Corporation, 199
Monoculturalism, 108–14
Monroe, Sylvester, 23
Moore, Michael, 4
Morcillo, Fox, 167
Morgan, Thomas, 131
Morrison, Toni, 46–47
Moses, Elissa, 3, 10
Mother tongue, 97
Mukherjee, Bharati, 11, 117, 135
Multicultural education, 5–6, 8
  American culture and, 14, 34–35
  Ariane program, 93
  attitudes about institutions, 123
  challenges of, 14
  critical pedagogy and, 58
  for cultural power, 59–61
  empowerment through, 56–58
  European Union (EU), 92–95
  language issues and, 217–221
  power elite and, 27
  for social empowerment, 249–252
  social reconstruction, 249–252
  unity with diversity, 92–93
Multicultural immigrant, 79–80
Multiculturalism, 8–11, 118
  American culture and, 13–14
  challenge of, 3

Multiculturalism *(Cont.)*:
  core knowledge and, 241–243
  educational rights amendment proposal, 98–102
  English language as imperialism, 95–96
  European Union's educational plan, 92–94
  in France, 88, 90
  in global economy, 88–102
  global workforce and, 252–254
  language and cultural differences (lesson), 100–101
  right to language and culture, 96–98
  in Singapore, 90–92, 94
  unity with diversity, 92–95
  whiteness as excluded, 54–55
Multilingualism, 3, 91, 225–226
Mundi, Mandeep Singh, 70–71
Muslim immigrants, 75, 136
Muslim schools, 75–77
Myth or Reality: Adaptive Strategies of Asian Americans in California (Trueba, Cheng, and Ima), 214

National Association for the Education of Young Children, 177
National Association for Multicultural Education, 10
National Council of Teachers of Mathematics, 181
National Education Association, 187, 191
National Merit Scholarship, 196
National Organization for Women, 193
National Project on Asia in American Schools, 128
National unity, 28
National Women's History Project, 194
Nationalism, 246–247
Native American Languages Act of 1990, 209

Native Americans, 4–8, 13, 29
  alienation of, 156–157
  attitudes about school, 123
  child-rearing practices, 31
  "civilizing" of, 32
  clan system, 31
  concept of property, 30–31
  concept of work, 30
  educational history of, 131
  English culture conflict,
    30–34, 49
  eye contact, 113–114
  immersion stage, 118
  intersection of cultures, 30–34
  maintaining culture of, 27
  off-reservation boarding
    school, 131
  pre-encounter stage, 115
  resistance of, 152–153
  "Trail of Tears," 32
Native languages, 225–226
Native people and spirituality of life
    (Cochiti Pueblo), 228
Naturalization Act of 1790,
    170-171
Navarette, Ruben, Jr., 111-112, 117,
    128, 131, 157
Negative stereotypes, 115-118
Negri, Antonio, 3
"New world teens," 3
Newburger, Eric, 19-20
Newitz, Annalee, 54, 56
Nieto, Sonia, 57-58, 109, 159,
    247, 250
Nineteenth Amendment (1920), 190
Nippon Insurance Company, 199
Nishi, Setusko, 116
Nishida, Tsukasas, 206-207
No Child Left Behind Act (2001),
    219, 221
Norton, Mary, 187, 189

Oakes, Jeannie, 148
Office of English Language
    Acquisition, 219

Official history, 124-128
  defined, 124
  dominated groups, 125
  people's history vs. (lesson), 127
Ogbu, John, 149, 151-152, 157
"One drop" rule, 165
Oppressed cultures, 6
Oral history, 123, 230
Oral traditions, 45, 47
Oralism, 203-204
Ortiz, Flora Ida, 213-214
Overbrook, Jack, 253

Pagden, Anthony, 167
Peirce, Samuel R., 21-22
"Persona" dolls, 178
Personal freedom, 11
Personal Witnessing, 233-234
Peterson, Bob, 181
Peterson, Merrill D., 166
Phillips, Max, 88
Phillipson, Robert, 91
Pho, Sokunthy, 74
Pidgin English, 53
Pitt, Leonard, 132
Polish-American Guardian
    Society, 116
*Politics of Linking Schools and Social
    Services, The,* 254
Porter, Rosalie Pedalino, 210
Portland Baseline curriculum,
    231–232
Poverty, 28
Powell, Colin, 22
Power elite, 20–21, 183
  Asians, 26
  black mobility and, 21–24
  gays and lesbians, 26
  golf as social skill, 24
  Jews and, 24
  Latinos/Latinas, 26
  lesson plan for, 25
  multicultural education and, 27,
    50, 218
  skin color and, 22, 26

Power elite *(Cont.)*:
  teaching of culture of, 48
  "white trash," 26, 56
  women and, 24
Pratt, Richard, 31
Pre-encounter stage, 115–116
Prep school education, 23, 26
  "A Better Chance" (ABC) program,
    22–24, 26
Price, Richard, 45
Private schools, 138
Property accumulation, 144–145,
    147, 160
Protestant work ethic, 30, 34
Protestantism, 144
Pseudo-independence, 176
Public schools
  ability to compete, 145
  basic values of, 144, 147
  corporate model of, 145
  corporate values of, 147
  cultural values of, 144
  cultural values of (lesson),
    146, 150
  equality of opportunity, 147
  individual economic
    achievement, 147
  inequality and, 145, 147–148
  property and, 147
Puerto Ricans
  cultural frames of reference, 114
  educational history of, 131
  pre-encounter stage, 115
  resistance of, 153–154

Race
  concept of, 166–172
  culture and, 167
  economic success and, 19–20
  family teaching on (lesson),
    129–130
  skin color and, 171
  traditional European thought
    on, 167
Racial identity, 109

Racial segregation, 52, 131
Racial stereotypes, 181
Racism, 6, 11, 31–32, 40, 46–49, 135,
    140–141, 170, 172–174
  death penalty as racist law
    (lesson), 168–169
  global context of, 234
  global market and, 182–184
  institutional racism, 234
  Malcolm X (lesson), 175
  mathematics instruction and,
    181–182
  social class and, 183
  teaching about, 165–184
Rafael, Vicente, 167
Raffles, Thomas Stamford, 91
Raza, La, 117
REACH project, 197–199
Reagan, Michael, 88
Reagan, Timothy, 204
Reeb, James, 176
Reich, Robert, 138
Reiff, David, 88, 183
Reintegration, 176
Republican motherhood, 187–191
Republicanism, 144
Resistance, 149–152, 160
  African Americans, 237
  historical origins of, 151
  Latinos/Latinas, 153–154
  Native Americans,
    152–153, 157
  white guilt and, 174
Rhodes, Cecil, 40
Rites of Passage program, 238
Rodriquez, Richard, 158
Role models, 235

Sadker, David, 191–194
Sadker, Myra, 191–194
Sage Publications, 206
*Savage Inequalities: Children in
    America's Schools* (Kozol), 138
Savage inequalities, 148
Savagery concept, 32

Schlesinger, Arthur, Jr., 28–29, 35, 125, 144, 170
Scholastic Aptitude Test (SAT), 193–194
School activities, 148
School uniforms, 73
Schools That Work (Wood), 180
Schwerner, Michael, 176
Segregation, 46, 151
Sekaquaptewa, Helen, 157
Selby, Cecily Cannan, 24
Self-esteem, 57, 192, 194, 227
Self-hatred, 115, 117
Self-identity, 128
Sequoyah, 38–40
Sethi, Vinit, 80
Sex in Education (Clark), 190
Sexism, 173, 187–199
    classroom sex bias, 192
    Freire's consciousness raising, 197–198
    glass ceiling of classroom, 191–194
    in other cultures, 199
    republican motherhood, 187–191
    single-sex schools and classrooms, 194–197
Sexism in School and Society (Sadker and Frazier), 191
Sheridan, Philip, 49
Shockley, William, 173
Shuang Wen Academy, 202
Signing, 204
Sikh summer camps, 66, 70
Silverman, Naomi, 215–217
Simon, Fermin, 79
Simon, Pedro, 79
Singapore, 90–92, 94
Singh, Inder Paul, 70
Single-sex schools, 194–197
Skrzycki, Cindy, 191
Skutnabb-Kangas, Tove, 97–98
Slavery, 4, 8–9, 11, 29, 40, 44
Sleeter, Christine, 56, 246, 250
Smith, Robert C., 79–80
Smith, William, 207
Sobol, Thomas, 28–29, 126

Social class, 56, 124, 137–140
    family influences on (lesson), 139
    inequality and schooling, 148–149
    mean household income, 137
    public education and, 144
    racism and, 183
Social contract, 189
Social empowerment, 57, 246–247, 249–252
    consciousness raising, 57
    ethnic studies and, 57
    multiculturalism for, 58
Social justice, 58–59
Social reconstructionism, 246, 249–252
SOCRATES program, 95
Some Thoughts Concerning Education and An Essay Concerning Human Understanding (Locke), 189
Sontag, Deborah, 79–80
Soul of Black Folks, The (DuBois), 44
Southern Poverty Law Center, 179–180
Spaulding, Asa T., 21–22
Spring, Joel, 98
Standardized tests, 145, 187, 219
Stereotypes, 115–116, 141
Stimulating and language-based education (Native Hawaiian), 227
Suarez-Orozco, Marcelo, 153–154
Submersion programs, 210
Summer camps, cultural, 66, 70–71
Symbolic-analytic services, 138

Takaki, Ronald, 31
Talayesva, Don, 157
Tan, Amy, 135–136
Tannenbaum, Frank, 125
Tardiness, 149
Tate, William, 181–182
Tatum, Beverly, 176
Taylor, Hobart, Jr., 22
Teacher expectations, 148
Teaching Tolerance Project, 179–180

"Textbook Town," 125
Textbooks, 125, 193
   African Americans and, 125–126
   Asian Americans, 128
   civil rights groups and, 125–126
   inclusion issues of, 126
Theroux, Paul, 107
Thomson, Chuck W., 252–253
Three baskets of knowledge
   (Maori), 227
Title IX, 191
*To Be Popular or Smart: The Black Peer
   Group* (Kunjufu), 157
Torres, Ana, 72
Tosawi (Comanche), 49
Tracking, 145, 148
Transition, 71
Transitional bilingual education
   programs, 210
Transnationalism, 79–80
Treaty on European Union (Maastricht
   Treaty), 92–93
Treaty of Guadalupe Hidalgo, 208
Treaty of Rome, 92–93
Trefil, James, 27, 239
Troy Female Seminary, 189
Trueba, Henry, 214–215
Turan, Saffiya, 75
*Two Nations: Black and White, Separate,
   Hostile, Unequal* (Hacker), 167
Two-way bilingual education,
   210–213

United Nations' 1991 Declaration on
   the Rights of Persons Belonging
   to National or Ethnic, Religious
   and Linguistic Minorities, 98
United Nations Draft Declaration
   of Indigenous Peoples Rights,
   96–97
United States
   culture of; *see* American (U.S.) culture
   culture of fear, 4
   Educational Rights Amendment
     proposal, 98–102

United States *(Cont.)*:
   general culture of, 4–5
   language and culture in, 207–209
*United States v. Bhagat Singh
   Thind*, 171
Unity with diversity, 92–94
Universal Covenant of Linguistic
   Human Rights, 97–98
"Unspeakable Rituals" (Theroux), 107
Ute Indians, 152

Vandalism, 149
Veil, Simone, 136
Villagomez, Fabiola, 79
Voluntary immigration
   cultural domination and, 39–40
   family multicultural tree (lesson),
     41–43

Wa (group harmony), 206
Washington, Booker T., 173, 237
Wayles, John, 165
Wayles, Martha, 165
Weinberg, Meyer, 71, 73, 81, 84
Weis, Lois, 151, 250
Westerinen, Dorothy Jefferson, 165–166
Wharton, Clifton, Jr., 22
*What Your 2nd Grader Needs to Know:
   Fundamentals of a Good Second-
   Grade Education*, 239
White Anglo-Saxon Protestant
   tradition, 17, 28–29, 115, 125, 144,
   149, 159, 170
White culture, 40
White guilt, teaching about, 174
White identity, 176
"White love," 167, 170
White racial identity development, 176
   autonomy, 176
   contact stage, 176
   disintegration stage, 176
   immersion/emersion, 176
   pseudo-independence, 176
   reintegration, 176

White Trash: Race and Class in America
    (Wray and Newitz), 54
"White trash," 5–6, 174, 183
  as dominated culture, 54–56
  power elite and, 26
Willard, Emma, 189–190
Wilson, August, 47
Wollstonecraft, Mary, 189, 191
Women
  classroom sex bias, 192–193
  culture of success for, 24
  educational opportunities of, 190
  glass ceiling of classroom, 191–194
  republican motherhood, 187–191
  right's of, 133
  social and economic roles
    (lesson), 195
  textbook representations, 193

Wood, George, 180–181
*Work of Nations: Preparing Ourselves
  for 21st-Century Capitalism, The*
  (Reich), 138
World Economic Forum, 90
Wray, Matt, 54, 56
Wright, Richard, 47

Yarborough, Ralph, 209
"Yellow peril," 183
Young, Shirley, 26
Youth gangs, 73
Yurco, Frank, 231–232

Zweigenhaft, Richard, 20–24, 26